Social Psychology

FOR

DUMMIES

A Wiley Brand

Social Psychology

FOR

DUMMIES®

A Wiley Brand

by Daniel Richardson, PhD

Social Psychology For Dummies®

Published by: **John Wiley & Sons, Ltd.,** The Atrium, Southern Gate, Chichester, www.wiley.com

This edition first published 2014

© 2014 John Wiley & Sons, Ltd, Chichester, West Sussex.

Registered office

John Wiley & Sons Ltd, The Atrium, Southern Gate, Chichester, West Sussex, PO19 8SQ, United Kingdom

For details of our global editorial offices, for customer services and for information about how to apply for permission to reuse the copyright material in this book please see our website at www.wiley.com.

The right of the author to be identified as the author of this work has been asserted in accordance with the Copyright, Designs and Patents Act 1988

For general information on our other products and services, please contact our Customer Care Department within the U.S. at 877-762-2974, outside the U.S. at (001) 317-572-3993, or fax 317-572-4002. For technical support, please visit www.wiley.com/techsupport.

For technical support, please visit www.wiley.com/techsupport.

ISBN 978-1-118-77054-2 (pbk) ISBN 978-1-118-77053-5 (ebk)
ISBN 978-1-118-77051-1 (ebk)

Printed in Great Britain by TJ International, Padstow, Cornwall.

10 9 8 7 6 5 4 3 2 1

Contents at a Glance

Table of Contents

Introduction

● ●

*T*he world is not short of advice. Self-help books, sermons, parents and celebrities regularly dispense advice on every aspect of your social life. If you want to know how to win friends and influence people, how to capture hearts and changes minds, how to believe in yourself or doubt other people, then someone will tell you five easy steps. But social psychology, and this book, offers you something better than advice. It can give you insight.

Social Psychology for Dummies uses the tools of science to understand why people behave as they do. Why they are attracted to some people, but not others? Why they are not convinced by an elegant political argument, but are persuaded by a celebrity endorsement. Where does prejudice comes from, and how does it influence our thoughts and actions? In this book, you will see how experimental methods can be used to reveal the inner workings of all of these psychological phenomena. And yes, there is a bit of advice too.

About This Book

Social Psychology for Dummies covers the full range of topics and phenomena that you would discuss in a typical university psychology course. However, it has been written with as little of the jargon and off putting technical terms as possible. There are no pre-requisites for this book. You will be able to understand it with no exposure to psychology or scientific study before. A healthy curiosity about people is all that you need bring, and the book will provide you with an overview of one of the most exciting and dynamic areas of social science.

Social psychology is about the huge scope of human behaviour, but it is also about *your* behaviour. Wherever possible in this book, I've given you little exercises to try that are modelled on real psychology experiments. If you try them yourself you will be able to *experience* the social phenomena that you are learning about.

And one more thing: the Internet has forever changed the world of science and education. There are remarkable resources on-line for learning about social psychology, such as lecture courses, experiments you can participate in, and high quality blogs written by the scientists themselves as they carry out their research. But as with every aspect of the internet, the trick is knowing where the good stuff is and avoiding the rest. We provide you with an in depth list of the best resources to explore online.

Foolish Assumptions

In writing this book, I've made a few assumptions about you. Don't think too badly of me. In particular, I've assumed that you:

- ✔ Are either a college student studying psychology who wants an accessible guide to social psychology as an adjunct to your course reading, or a general reader who's simply keen to know more about this fascinating area.

- ✔ Have a basic grasp of psychology in general, but are by no means a subject expert.

- ✔ Know that there's quite a lot of psychological research behind all this but don't necessarily want to plough through all of it.

- ✔ Will be highly selective about which parts of the book you read.

Icons Used in This Book

Icons are handy little graphic images that point out particularly important information about social psychology. Throughout this book, you find the following icons, conveniently located along the left margins:

When you see this icon, you can expect to be surprised: It covers a range of widely-held beliefs and widely-believed stories, and hold them up to interrogation. Things aren't always what they seem . . .

Remember what follows this icon, as it is vital that you grasp these points to make sense of the rest of the chapter.

This icon directs you towards more detailed, technical information about the concept or experiments we are discussion. They provide nourishment for your inner science nerd.

It's all very well reading about other people's thoughts and behaviour, but these little exercises allow to directly experience psychological phenomena for your self. If you see this icon, then get ready to put your own brain under the microscope!

Useful little wrinkles that help you gain understanding and insight.

Beyond the Book

In addition to the material in the print or e-book you're reading right now, this product also comes with some access-anywhere goodies on the web. Check out the free Cheat Sheet at www.dummies.com/cheatsheet/socialpsychology, and for a run down on the historical development of the subject and some other worthwhile articles on social psychology, check out www.dummies.com/extras/socialpsychology.

Where to Go from Here

If you are new to the science of psychology, then you may want to start at the beginning of this book and work your way through to the end. Social psychology covers a bewildering array of topics, methods and ways of understanding human behaviour. Simply turn the page and you're on your way! If you have already taken some psychology classes, or are taking one right now, you can turn to a particular topic to address a specific need or question you have. Use the table of contents and index to help you navigate. Regardless of how you find your way around this book, we're sure you'll enjoy the journey.

Part I
Getting Started with Social Psychology

For Dummies can help you get started with lots of subjects. Visit www.dummies.com to learn more and do more with *For Dummies*.

In this part . . .

✔ Find out about the basics of social psychology – understand identity, motivation and the power of social forces.

✔ Come to grips with the range of disciplines that comprise social psychology, and discover how to get the right answers to the right questions.

✔ Understand experiments, operationalisation and the importance of drawing sound conclusions from results.

Chapter 1

Introducing the Science of Social Psychology

In This Chapter

▶ Mapping out the territory of social psychology

▶ Understanding the people around you

▶ Exploring relationships, families, groups and cultures

Social psychology is a fascinating science. It investigates feelings, thoughts, cultures and the ways that people relate to one another. Before social science, these aspects of human life were discussed only in the context of art, religion and philosophy. But now, humans can generate scientific knowledge about their social selves.

In this chapter, I define the scope of social psychology, the sorts of behaviour, actions and thought processes that it tries to understand, and the tools that it uses. In its quest, social psychology has gobbled up ideas and techniques from the neighbouring sciences such as cognitive psychology, neuroscience and evolutionary biology. Although they have shifted during social psychology's short history, its goals have remained constant: To understand people and their relationships to each other.

Looking Down the Social Psychologists' Microscope

What is the focus of social psychology? Is it thoughts in the mind, people in society or cultures across the world? It is all of these levels together. Imagine a giant microscope looking not at cells or creatures, but people. At the start of this book, I train this microscope on the smallest building blocks of social psychology – the thoughts and attitudes that exist inside people's heads and govern their behaviour. Then I zoom out to look first at the beliefs people have about other people, and then the ways that they exert power and influence over each other. In the final part of the book I zoom out again, and look at how people interact and relate, forming friendships, families and cultures.

So if it's not a scale on a microscope, what defines the science of social psychology? The boundaries are continually shifting, as they are in many active and developing sciences. But if you want a short, concise definition of the scope of social psychology, you can do no better that the definition Gordon Allport gave in 1954. He said that social psychology is:

> *The scientific investigation of how the thoughts, feelings, and behaviour of individuals are influenced by the actual, imagined or implied presence of others.*

I'd like to highlight two aspects of this definition:

- ✔ What distinguishes social psychology from the rest of the field is the focus on cause and the effects of the 'presence of others'.
- ✔ These other people do not have to be physically present. So you can be under the influences of social forces when you're in the middle of a party or all alone. For example, I discuss conformity, obedience, and persuasion and authority in Chapters 12, 13 and 14, respectively, the power of stereotypes in Chapter 10 and belonging to groups in Chapters 16 and 17.

To put it bluntly – if it is an aspect of human behaviour that involves more than one person, it is of some interest to social psychologists. Social psychologists want to understand whom you like and whom you love, why you seek to help some people and harm others, what you think of yourself and what you think of other people, and the connections you make between yourself and others. The next sections reveal in more depth the phenomena social psychologist study and the scientific tools that they employ.

Rummaging through the social psychologists' toolkit

Social psychology is an interdisciplinary science. When you socially interact with another person, you are using your visual system to recognise their emotions, your auditory system to process their speech and your memory systems to make sense of what they are saying and predict what they may say next. So to understand this social interaction, social psychologists can draw on the many fields of cognitive psychology and neuroscience.

What's more, during this social interaction, your behaviour is a precise and well-learnt ballet of co-ordinated actions – a polite incline of the head to show that you are listening, nodding and murmuring 'uh-huh' at precisely the right moments, and shifting your body posture to show that you accept what the other person says. All of these things you learnt as a child, and all of these things may be slightly different in different cultures. So to fully understand this social interaction, social psychologists may turn to developmental psychology, cross-cultural psychology or even sociology or anthropology.

In Chapter 2 I examine how social psychology connects to these closely related disciplines. Also, I look inside the social psychologists' tool kit to see how they developed their own tools such as surveys, interviews and field studies. But there is one tool that is so important to social psychology that it deserves a chapter of its own: the experiment.

Mastering the power of the experiment

Experiments are the most powerful tool that we have in social psychology, and indeed, in all of science. They allow us to make strong, lasting conclusions. With an experiment, we can distinguish between two things that happen to co-occur, and one thing that causes another. For example, rich people tend to be less kind drivers. They are more likely to cut you up on the road. Is this because if you are a selfish driver, then you are more self-interested throughout your life, and more likely to make money for yourself? Or does having money and owning an expensive car make you a meaner person? The surprising answer, as I discuss in Chapter 15, is that money and power can *cause* you to be less considerate towards others. It is only because of carefully designed experiments that we can make that bold claim.

Experiments get their power from careful design and analysis. In Chapter 3, I examine what makes a good experiment in social psychology, and what makes a bad one. As you will see, people who study chemistry and physics really have life easy. They are doing a simple science where you have to measure straightforward things like mass, heat and velocity. But in social psychology we have to measure things such as happiness, prejudice and a sense of belonging. There is no stereotype-o-meter for prejudice in the same way that there is a thermometer for heat. So, as I will show you, social psychologists have to be clever and creative in the ways that they do their science.

Digging for the foundations of social psychology

To understand the way that we do social psychology today, you have to understand the past. As much as social psychology studies phenomena such as conflict, aggression and prejudice, it is also the outcome of events in real life such as the Second World War and the Holocaust. Also, social psychology is a child of psychology itself. In the recent past, psychology conceived of people as very different things – as learning machines, as computers, as social beings and as sets of competing desires. The way that psychology has defined people has had profound consequences for the way that social psychology studies the interaction between people.

No couches here!

This sidebar is the only place in the whole book that I talk about Sigmund Freud. This may seem very strange to non-psychologists, who often assume that he is the dominant figure in psychology. Indeed, if you tell people that you are currently studying psychology, the first thing that they may say is, 'Oh don't analyse me!' (This will quickly become tiresome for you). In fact, Freud is a marginal figure, at best, in contemporary empirical psychology. His ideas had an enormous influence on popular culture and the novels and films at the time. And his ideas on therapy had a lasting influence on psychiatry, although few people follow his original theories now. The traces of his ideas that remain in psychology are often unhelpful. For example, some parenting books tell parents not to hug their young babies too much during the first months of life. The reason for this advice can be traced to Freud's belief that unconditional love from a mother could produce an over-dependent child that never frees itself from the mother's influence. Now we know (from doing the hard work of studies and experiments) that this is nonsense, and parental affection has no such negative effects on an infant. Similarly, there is simply no evidence for most of Freud's specific theories about unconscious drives and the causal influences a parent's actions have upon a child.

In short, Freud was an exceptional thinker but a poor research scientist. He only ever had a small number of patients that he used to generate his ideas, and he never sought to measure their success systematically. There is even evidence to suggest that the small number of his patients he did treat never improved, or even got worse, but Freud continued to push his theories regardless. So, if someone assumes that you are learning how to perform Freudian analysis on them, feel free to tell them it's mostly nonsense. Or tell them to call their mother.

On the other hand, one can say that social psychology is one of the youngest sciences that there is. The sort of social understanding that our species has been doing for thousands of years is nothing like a proper *science*. It is not knowledge that has been built up from a systematic method of experimentation and hypothesis testing. Since its inception around 500 years ago, the scientific method has been applied to understanding every facet of the world around us. But it was long after we studied stars, planets, oceans, animals, cells, molecules and atoms that we turned the microscope upon ourselves and our own behaviour. In this sense, social psychology is indeed one of the youngest of the sciences.

Understanding What People Think and What Makes Them Act

If you are a zoologist and want to understand the social behaviour of ants, you are going to spend a long time on your knees with a magnifying glass, and you're probably going to get bitten. Social psychologists have a luxury that zoologists do not: we can just ask people what they think and the reasons for their behaviour. We can directly measure people's attitudes. And we rarely get bitten.

As I show you in Part II, social psychologists have developed many sophisticated tools to measure, survey and record people's attitudes towards a whole range of things: people of other races, prayer, ice cream flavours and taxation. But they quickly discovered a big problem. What people say about their attitudes doesn't always – in fact rarely does – tell you what they are actually going to do at all. So the zoologists may have the last laugh after all.

Asking people what they think

Do you think that our society should spend more money helping people who are poor? That seems like a pretty straightforward question. I imagine that you have some opinions and could give me a one-word answer or an hour-long argument. In both cases, you would be reporting what social psychologists call your *explicit attitude*: the opinions and beliefs that you can state out loud.

But here's the problem. In Chapter 4, I show you the remarkable number of factors that can change the answer you give to that question. Were you asked by an attractive young person? Did they introduce themselves as being from a homeless charity or the TaxPayers' Alliance? Before asking the question, did they talk to you about your latest tax return, or about a time that you yourself felt the effects of poverty? What were the exact words they used – did they say spending more money on 'poor people' or on 'the welfare state'?

Social psychologists have found time and time again that they can easily influence the explicit attitudes that people report. People may say they have one attitude, but then behave in a completely opposite manner. This leads to a number of practical and scientific questions: how do you measure what people *really* think? Do they even have lasting, stable attitudes that cause them to behave one way or another?

Measuring what people really think

Social psychologists now have the scientific tools to look under the surface of your everyday attitudes. If I ask you, 'Do you think that men and women are equally capable in the workplace' you would probably say yes. In other words, your explicit attitude would be that men and women are equal.

But imagine that I flashed up a picture of a person and you had to press one button to identify them as male, and another as female. I would predict that you would be very slightly slower to press the female button if she was shown wearing a business suit or a fire-fighters outfit than if she was shown in the home or the kitchen. The difference in your button press may be imperceptible to you, a matter of a few milliseconds, but social psychologists have computers that can measure and add up such differences.

Even though most people report explicit attitudes that treat people the same regardless of sex, race or nationality, in experiments like this their millisecond reactions to words or pictures are different depending on if they refer to men or women, Black faces or White faces, and Christian names or Muslim names. These differences are called *implicit attitudes*. In Chapter 5, I show you how they are measured and how they can be used to predict people's behaviour. I address the sometimes uncomfortable question: do these implicit attitudes reflect what people *really* think?

Predicting people's behaviour

When was the last time someone asked you, 'Why did you do that?' Perhaps it was after you pointedly ignored a friend, were unexpectedly kind to a stranger or punched a sibling. The person asking you wanted to know about your attitudes, I imagine, because they assumed that your behaviour was caused by your attitudes. You were angry with the friend, you were attracted to the stranger or mildly irritated with the sibling. This seems like a reasonable, common-sense assumption, but social psychology has discovered remarkable evidence that the assumption has things completely the wrong way round. Often, our behaviours cause our attitudes.

In Chapter 6 you will meet cognitive dissonance, one of the most powerful, elegant, and counter-intuitive theories in social psychology. Do you think that you'd be happier with this book if you got it at half the price? If your partner treats you poorly, do you think you'd love them more or less? These seem like obvious questions, but cognitive dissonance makes a series of remarkable predictions that are borne out by careful experimentation.

Who Am I, Who Are You and Why Did They Do That?

Like a collector looking at a butterfly pinned to a board, so far we've focused on the individual outside of its natural habitat. We've explored the attitudes and beliefs that exist inside individuals' heads, and how this might determine their behaviour. But people, like butterflies, live in a social context in which they interact with each other and the world around them. In Part III of the book I start to explore how people generate beliefs about themselves and the people around them, and how they understand each other's social behaviour.

As you may have guessed, the opinions people have about others are not always completely fair, objective and rational. In this part of the book we explore how you make judgments about other people, and how stereotypes and prejudice can build up about certain groups and types of people. But first, there is one person who is on the receiving end of more of your prejudice and biased thinking than any other: yourself.

Constructing your sense of self

My favourite recurring scene in the science fiction show *Dr Who* is when he regenerates from an old body to the new. The new actor playing the Doctor would leap up from behind the console of the TARDIS, stare wildly at his hands and run to a mirror. He would then try and figure out who he was, what he was like and whether he liked his new taste in clothes.

Though you aren't a Time Lord (probably) you too have to go through a process of self-discovery and identity formation. This takes more than the five minutes that the Doctor has before the Daleks attack again. In Chapter 7, I explore this process. It begins in childhood, takes a left turn in adolescence and continues into adulthood. You are not just figuring out who you are, but also, importantly, how you fit into the social world. The conclusion that most of us reach during this process is that, actually, I'm a pretty good person.

Loving yourself

You are awesome. You are better than average at most things, you are more moral, more correct in your opinions and you make the right choices. At least, that is what you tend to believe. The problem is, that's what everyone else believes too. And though everyone can't all be better than average, that is what, on average, everyone believes.

No matter how self-deprecating or modest you may seem on the surface, you maintain a pretty good opinion of yourself. In Chapter 8, I look at the evidence that you, like everyone else, have a robust set of self-serving biases. You tend to believe that your successes are due to your personal qualities, but your failures are due to your bad luck. Whereas other people have prejudices and subjective opinions, your own views are more like objective facts.

Although you may think I'm making you out to be a horrible egotist, you are perfectly normal and healthy. Indeed, these self-serving biases appear to be a vital part of your psychological 'immune system' that, more or less, keeps you happy and sane no matter what you experience.

Explaining the actions of others

We don't spend our entire lives thinking about ourselves, however. Pick up a gossip magazine, turn on the TV or eavesdrop on a conversation and the chances are you'll hear people trying to figure out other people. Why did your boss snub you in the hallway? Why did one blond, beautiful celebrity dump another beautiful blond celebrity? Why did the waitress give you that funny look?

If you have the misfortune not to have read this book already – and probably even if you have – then you are likely to reach systematically incorrect explanations for the behaviour of other people. As I demonstrate in Chapter 9, in everyday life, you, like everyone else, tend to explain other people's behaviour in terms of their personalities. The boss who snubbed you is rude, the celebrity is in love, and the waitress is a snob.

You tend to leap to these conclusions about personality and overlook explanations in terms of the situation. You don't consider that the boss was just thinking about something else, that the waitress thought she recognised you, and that the blond celebrity has a film coming out and her PR team just need her to be in the magazines. Later, in Part IV of this book, I try and convince you just how powerful these situational factors are in determining behaviour. But in Chapter 9, I explain how this bias towards personality explanations – called the *fundamental attribution error* – dominates your thinking about other people.

Judging and labelling others

The detective Sherlock Holmes was famous for his ability to deduce remarkable things from people at only a glance. He would infer that a visitor to 221b Baker Street, for example, was a schoolmaster from the countryside who suspected his wife of having an affair from the mud on his shoes, a dusting of chalk on his sleeve and the lack of starch in his collar, suggesting a Victorian wife that no longer cared for him.

You may not have the eye for detail and the deductive powers of Sherlock Holmes, but that doesn't stop you leaping to generalisations and unfounded conclusions whenever you meet other people.

You are hardwired to categorise and label other people. I explain in Chapter 10 how this process of impression formation, judgment making, and generalisation can be a very useful way to understand and predict the people around you. But it can also easily lead to bias and prejudice, as you make conclusions based on your own assumptions rather than the people you see in front of you. I examine how this process of stereotyping occurs and how it can be avoided.

Measuring the Power of Social Forces

You may think of yourself as an independent person who stands up for their own opinions, even if you are a bit headstrong sometimes. No matter how independent you *think* you are, I would bet that much of your life and your decisions are under the thumb of social forces.

Walk out onto the street or into a room filled with people about your own age. Are they wearing the same sorts of clothes as you, some of the same labels? Look on your music player or your bookshelf – how many of those authors or musicians did you discover entirely yourself, and how many have your friends heard and read? In fact, I might argue that even your very conception of yourself as an independent, unique person is something that you have picked up from those around you, or that it's an idea that has been marketed to you by the fashion industry so that (ironically) they can sell unique you the same clothes that everyone else is buying.

I explore in Part IV of this book all the ways that the world and the people around you can influence your actions, from the way that your job changes who you are, to why you obey your boss or your teachers. I explore the reasons why you feel an urge to mimic and follow your friends and peers, and why salespeople and advertisers have such an easy time persuading you to buy things.

Controlled by the situation

Have you ever had to wear a uniform? The white and black of a waiter, the fatigues of a soldier, or just the same business outfit that everyone else wears at the office. Does wearing that uniform change who you are and how you act?

I tell you the story of one of the most famous studies in social psychology, the Stanford prison experiment, in Chapter 11. It was a stark demonstration that as much as your attitudes, beliefs and intentions, the situation that you are placed in – the restaurant, the army unit or the office – can determine your behaviour. In the case of the Stanford prison experiment, a group of regular, happy young men turned into broken, spiritless prisoners or oppressive, sadistic guards, depending on which identity they were assigned by the researcher. The experiment's conclusions reverberate through society today.

Obeying authority

Mr Tanner was the name of the worst teacher at my school. He had a boil on his neck like a half-buried snooker ball and a sadistic streak as thick and ugly as his ginger wig. He taught PE, mostly by yelling. Once he told a boy to run over to the side of the field, and the poor boy ran straight through a thorn bush rather than go round it so he didn't get shouted at.

We obeyed Mr Tanner out of terror. But most obedience in our society does not come from fear. Rationally we know that the consequences of disobedience are small. It would be easy to violate parking laws or tax regulations, or to shoplift and get away with it. But the moment someone in authority – a policeman, a teacher or even a scientist – asks us to do something, we are compelled by a force to obey.

I explore the power of authority in Chapter 12. You, like many people, may feel that obedience to authority is something that other people do, conjuring up images of jackbooted Nazis saluting their leaders. Our culture, you would think, prizes rebels and challenges authority. But some very compelling experiments proved that you don't need threats and fear of Mr Tanner to make people obey. You just need a white coat, a calm voice and authority, and you can make nice people commit the most evil acts.

Being one of the crowd

Being a sheep is not much fun. You exist to be shaved or slaughtered, and all for the benefit of people who use your name as an insult. Who would be a sheep? Well, it may not be much of a consolation, but those people wearing jumpers, eating lamb and taking the name of sheep in vain – they are sheep too. For as much as people need warmth from wool and nourishment from meat, they have a basic human need to belong with others, to act and feel the same, too.

I explore the urge to conform in Chapter 13. Sometimes we follow the actions of others because we are clueless. The first time you got on a bus or paid at a self-service checkout, you probably looked at the person in front of you to see how it was done. More often, though, we follow the actions of others just because it feels right. Or perhaps, as I shall discuss, because not following others, being left out of the group, feels so bad. The only thing worse than being a sheep, is a lonely sheep.

Persuading and convincing

Perhaps you are flicking through this book in the shop, deciding whether to buy it. Or perhaps, given my comments on obedience, whether to steal it. Let me say a few things.

Firstly, you clearly have a good eye for books. You appreciate a quality, well-written book. If you are thinking about buying this book – and it's entirely your choice, of course – then you may want to do it sooner rather than later. It's already sold out in many markets, as many, many students and interested readers have already bought copies. In fact, since this copy is half price, you may need to act fast. But I tell you what – don't decide to buy it now. Finish reading a couple more pages of this chapter first, and then make your decision. Would that be okay? After all, I did write it just for you!

I reveal the Jedi mind tricks that I (or advertisers before me) employed to compel you to buy this book in Chapter 14. I explain the techniques of labelling, low-balls, foot-in-the-door, reciprocity and others. You can use these mind powers yourself, or armed with the knowledge, resist persuasion attempts upon you. But you have to buy the book.

Living the Social Life

I've shown you how the attitudes inside your head relate to the actions you take, how these lead to thoughts about the people around you, and how those people can influence and determine your actions. In Part V, the final part of the book, I discuss how all those ideas and forces come together when you interact with other people, generating friendships and families, in groups and out-groups, and cultures and conflicts.

Liking, loving and respecting

The groups of people that define your life – friends, families and colleagues – are bound together by social forces. Some of these people you like. Some of them you love. And there are a few whose authority you respect. Thankfully, for people who have to write soap operas at any rate, you don't always respect the ones you love, like the ones you respect or even like the ones you love.

I map out these competing and intertwining forces in Chapter 15. If you've ever wanted to know why some people are attractive and some not, why you fall in love with one type of person and not another, or what happens to you if you gain power and money, this is a good place to start.

Thinking and deciding

The man who designed the Mini did not have a high opinion of camels: 'A camel is a horse designed by committee,' he said sniffily. Though I think he is a little unfair on the camel, he makes a good point about the problems with group decision-making. No matter how smart the individual people in a group may be, together in a committee they are capable of spectacularly bad decisions.

I explain the dangers and failures of *group think* in Chapter 16. One particularly disastrous meeting in the 1960s between President Kennedy and his top advisors led to a series of decisions that came frighteningly close to starting a nuclear war. Following this, social psychologists saw the urgency in studying exactly why and what goes wrong when people gather together to make decisions.

Despite these pitfalls, we are remarkably successful social creatures, however. When he was able to avoid nuclear war, the same president inspired a nation to co-operate on a vast scale and send men to the moon with a tenth of the technology that is in your mobile phone. In the rest of the chapter I explore when and how people do co-operate and help each other.

Living in different cultures

And so, in Chapter 17, our social psychologists microscope pulls back to the widest field of view – a culture. As I show you, there are many differences in how people across the world think of themselves, their society and their place within it. These are not just abstract, theoretical differences in philosophical outlook. They translate to measurable shifts in behaviour, differences in how people literally move their eyes across a scene, interpret what they see and remember their world.

The discovery of widespread cultural differences also leads me to re-examine a scientific assumption that has supported many of the experiments than run throughout this book: that people are pretty much the same the world over, and so it is justifiable to perform experiments on (mostly) rich white American psychology students, and assume that our conclusions hold for the rest of the world's population. That is an assumption that social psychologists have lazily made for many years, and we are only just figuring out its consequences.

Looking Back Up the Microscope

I began this chapter by asking you to imagine a giant microscope zooming in on the subject of its science. But in one crucial way, a social psychologist looking down a microscope is very different from a biologist looking down a microscope. Don't forget while you're reading about all these theories and experiments that when you are looking down the social psychology microscope you are not just peering at organisms, or people, you are looking at yourself, too.

Chapter 2

Exploring the Territory of Social Psychology

*W*hen you think of a scientist, you probably think of a single person: A lone genius, working in a laboratory full of bubbling test tubes or scrawling illegibly on a blackboard. But modern science is really a team effort. Social psychologists, like all scientists, work with many other people, sharing ideas and methods and data. They also collaborate with colleagues in very different disciples, from neuroscience to sociology to evolutionary biology. So rather than solitary geniuses, perhaps you should think of social scientists more like a team of superheroes, each with their own specialty and superpower (although now I'm picturing many of my colleagues wearing Lycra jumpsuits . . .).

In this chapter, I introduce you to the many specialties and disciplines that make up modern social psychology. I discuss the disciplines of personality and cognitive psychology, sociology and ethnography, and the exciting new research in social neuroscience that's invigorating the science with a new source of data. I reveal how ideas from evolutionary biology are being used to understand puzzling findings and generate novel hypotheses.

But what is a team of social science superheroes without a mission? In this chapter I show you how the different disciplines of social psychology can bring their insights and expertise to tackle one question in particular. Of course, science can investigate all sorts of issues, but in this chapter I investigate why homicide rates are so high among males in the southern United States. Or to put it more directly, why do cowboys get into fights? Exploring this question shows that social questions can be approached from many different angles and demonstrates how the various disciplines of social psychology can be used to test ideas using a range of ingenious methods.

Looking at the Disciplines that Comprise Social Psychology

In this section I provide an overview of social psychology as it's practised in the real world today. The advantage of being a relatively young discipline is that social psychology is open to new perspectives. It has rapidly incorporated findings in personality and cognitive psychology, and it eagerly applies the tools of modern neuroscience and biology to understand social phenomena.

Surveying the surveys of personality psychology

Personality psychology is sometimes called the psychology of individual differences. Its goal is to measure and quantify the ways in which we differ from one another. *Personality* is a familiar term in everyday talk. In psychology, your personality is the pattern of behaviour, beliefs and emotions that makes you different from other people. Your personality is something that is stable over time and across different situations. In other words, if you are very angry one day because of an unfair parking ticket, we wouldn't term that as part of your personality, because it would be limited to that day and that experience.

The principle tools of personality psychology are questionnaires and surveys. Researchers ask participants to answer a large number of questions about their behaviour, habits, likes and dislikes. Then the researchers perform statistical analyses on the answers (called factor analysis) to see if there are consistent patterns. For example, a researcher may find that if people said that they had a large number of friends, then they also said that they enjoyed parties and that they didn't like being alone. A different group of people may answer consistently in the opposite manner that they have fewer friends, don't like parties and enjoy being by themselves. Statistics can identify these patterns, and then classify people along a scale. In this case, researchers have named the scale introversion-extraversion. If researchers know where someone is on that scale – the extraversion score – then they can predict how the person will answer all those questions, and also predict how she might behave across a large number of situations.

Personality psychologists debate the exact number, but it looks like about five different scales are needed to capture the main differences that we see between people. These are called the Big Five personality traits. They are openness, conscientiousness, extraversion, agreeableness and neuroticism (often remembered by the acronym OCEAN). The claim is that most of the differences between people can be expressed by those five traits. In other words, if we know where you lie along those scales, we know most of what there is to know about your personality.

The interaction between personality and social psychology is interesting. In a sense, they are at odds with one another. Personality psychology asks how the characteristics of different individuals determine their behaviour, regardless of the situations they happen to be in. Social psychology asks how different social situations can determine behaviour, regardless of the differences that exist between people.

This is a useful tension between the two fields. For example, following the Second World War, people wanted to understand how regular German people could have supported what the Nazis did. A personality hypothesis was that German people were more responsive to authority, and so more likely to obey orders. In contrast, Stanley Milgram hypothesised that there was no difference between German and American people, for example, and that both might act to obey horrific orders if the *situation* compelled them to do so. We'll see how he tested this hypothesis in Chapter 12.

Entering the laboratory of cognitive psychology

Cognitive psychology is the study of mental processes and functions. Cognitive psychologists investigate what things people remember and what things they forget; how we can focus our attention on some things in the world and ignore others; how we learn and use language; and how all of these allow us to take action and make decisions.

You can read about the rich interaction between social and cognitive psychology in Chapter 4. In many chapters throughout this book you see how a social process can be broken down into a series of cognitive processes. For example, imagine deciding whether to trust someone you have just met. This is a social judgment, and may be influenced by social representations such as stereotypes. But it is determined by cognitive processes such as how you perceive the person you've met, how you allocate your visual attention to them, what memory representations you activate of other people, how you apply this past knowledge to categorising this person, and how you weigh that information when making your decisions.

Using a stopwatch to understand the mind

To understand these cognitive processes, psychologists use reaction-time studies. They're still the most used tool in a cognitive laboratory, and increasingly, in social psychology too. The logic behind reaction-time studies is quite elegant. It was first used in the laboratory by a Dutch ophthalmologist called Franciscus Donders at the end of the nineteenth century, though. As you recall, psychological science is all about turning mental concepts into things you can count, and Donders figured out a way to do this using what he called *mental chronometry*.

Donders gave his participants a very simple task called a *choice* reaction-time experiment. A light flashed on a screen and they had to press one button if it was green and a different one if it was red. Nowadays we'd measure your reaction time in this task with computers, but Donders had wonderful brass clockwork devices for his measurements. The participants did this task many times, and worked out how long on average it took participants to identify the colour. Donders realised that this reaction time includes many things: the time it takes for the eyes to process the signal, for the brain to process the colour, for the participant to make

a decision, for the brain to send a signal to the hand and for the muscles to twitch. But Donders was only interested in one element of this – the decision time.

His clever solution was to give his participants a second task. In this *simple* reaction-time study, the light was just one colour and the subjects pressed one button. In both experiments, the participants had to perceive a picture and make a button press, but only in the first one did they also have to make a choice. So Donders *subtracted* the time for the second, simple reaction-time experiment from the first, choice reaction-time experiment. The difference between these two corresponds to the decision time alone. With this simple but magical method, Donders measured mental functions, and began scientific psychology.

This method continues to be used in cognitive and social psychology today. The basic logic remains that differences in reaction time correspond to differences in mental processing. In Chapter 5 you will see examples of reaction times being used to probe the implicit attitudes that people won't admit to out loud.

I don't want you to think that social psychology is basically cognitive psychology that happens to be applied to social things. To be honest, I used to be a cognitive psychologist myself and held pretty much that opinion. But some experimental findings changed my mind and emphasised the importance of social forces.

For example, consider the sort of simple choice reaction-time experiments that Donders studied a hundred years ago (see the nearby sidebar 'Using ta stopwatch to understand the mind'). In the past few years, Natalie Sebanz and Guenther Knoblich have found that if two people performing such a task sit next to each other, then they are immediately influenced by each other's tasks and instructions. In other words, when you add in another person to the experiment, even the first and simplest experiments in cognitive psychology show that *social* influences have an immediate and powerful effect.

Playing with the gadgets of neuroscience

Neuroscience is the study of the brain. If cognitive psychologists are interested in the software of the mind, then neuroscientists are interested in the hardware: the blood and the guts and the biological mechanisms that allow you to think. They study the anatomy and structure of the brain and how it works in action. They want to know where language is processed in the brain, what happens to the visual information sent from the eyes and where memories are formed, stored and lost.

Previously, our knowledge came mostly from picking through the brains of patients who had died or inserting probes into the brains of animals and measuring the behaviour of individual neurons. But now we have various technologies that allow us to record brain activity in the whole brain of an awake, living person.

The past 30 years have seen this technology make its way into the hands of social scientists, who often refer to themselves as social neuroscientists. Their brain imaging technique that you will read most about is fMRI, which stands for functional magnetic resonance imagining. It is much like the MRI machine in hospitals (or every episode of *House*). The patient lies on a table and is slowly moved into a small white tunnel or ring. This scanner produces a strong magnetic field that interacts with various atoms in the body in different ways. By measuring this interaction, the scanner can build up a three-dimensional image of the insides of the body, distinguishing bone and different types of soft tissue. Check out the sidebar 'Looking inside the brain' for details.

Techniques such as fMRI give indirect measures of brain activity while a participant is watching a computer screen and making simple hand actions. Other techniques, such as ERP recordings, measure brain activity from scalp electrodes, and diffusion tensor imaging can map the connections between brain areas. These techniques all differ in exactly what they tell you about the brain, how accurate they are about the timing of events and the size of the regions that they can discriminate.

Using these techniques to study social interaction directly is very hard. But using clever experimental designs, researchers can get around these limitations. For example, Chris Frith and colleagues placed their participants in an fMRI scanner and asked them to play the children's game paper-scissors-stone. On the count of three they made their hand shapes, and then saw on screen what their opponents had chosen and who had won.

Looking inside the brain

An MRI scanner can do more than take photographs like an X-ray machine. It can look at changes that take place over time. When used on the brain, an MRI scanner is able to detect changes in blood flow (blood-oxygen-level dependent or BOLD contrast). Neurons in the brain require energy that they get from blood, so blood flow is an indirect way for us to measure neuronal activity.

The *f* bit of fMRI refers to the *function* that the brain is carrying out. So while participants are in the scanner, researchers can show pictures of faces, for example. The changes in blood flow that occur while they look at those images can tell us what parts of the brain have the function of understanding faces.

Well, not quite. Remember that the fMRI is looking at the activity of the whole brain. And while the participants are in the scanner, they are doing more than just looking at faces. They are also processing patches of two-dimensional colour, remembering the images, thinking about the instructions the researcher told them, feeling bored, trying not to move too much, hoping that the experiment will be over soon, and planning what to have for dinner that night. All of these thoughts are mental activity that is happening in the brain and changing the flow of blood.

To figure out which bits of brain activity correspond to which bits of mental function, researchers can use a form of the technique that Donders invented a hundred years ago: subtraction. For example, researchers interested in emotion perception will show the participants pictures of happy faces, but also show them something else, like pictures of neutral faces with no expression. They then subtract the brain activity during the happy face viewing from the brain activity during neutral face viewing. What's left over, the researchers hope, is the brain activity that is specifically related to looking at emotion, not looking at images in general, or faces in general, or being in the scanner in general. With this technique, researchers can try and *localise* mental function to precise regions of the brain.

The key to doing a good social neuroscience experiment is choosing the right control condition. And particularly in social psychology, that can be a tricky decision. In the example here, the control condition was a neutral face with no expression. But does such a thing exist? Isn't a face with 'no expression' a face that actually looks sort of bored and resentful? In social neuroscience it's vital to understand exactly how stimuli are seen and interpreted by the people in the scanner if we want to understand exactly what their brains are doing.

Here's the clever bit of the experiment: they were told that either their opponent was another participant in the experiment or that they were playing against a computer choosing at random. So in both of these conditions, the participant has to choose a hand shape, follow a strategy and try and win. But in the case where they think that they are playing against a real person, they are also predicting the behaviour of another person: they were doing social cognition. If we look at the differences between brain activation in

---

Science fiction and science fact

There are many extravagant claims made about neuroscience. Several companies are marketing fMRI machines that detect if someone is lying, they say. There have been claims that brain imaging could detect if a prisoner was likely to commit a crime again. Following September 11, several companies were marketing fMRI machines that could be placed in airports to identify terrorists. There is no indication right now that brain imaging can (or should) carry out any of these functions, and good reasons to think that they never could. Indeed, some neuroscientists argue that many of the basic assumptions we've been making about brain imaging need to be re-thought. All of this makes modern neuroscience a very exciting field, but a healthy dose of scepticism is often required.

---

these two cases, subtracting one from the other, we are left with the brain activation that specifically corresponds to thinking about another person's behaviour.

Understanding where in the brain something happens can give us valuable insights that we cannot always discover by looking at behaviour alone. For example, when some participants look at particular faces, researchers have found activation in the amygdala. The exact function of this brain area is hotly debated, but it seems to be related to uncertainty and fear. And this activation is highest when one group, such as White Americans, look at the faces of an out-group, like Black Americans.

In another application of neuroscience to social psychology, researchers asked participants to consider moral and political questions, like should gay couples be allowed to adopt. In some participants, considering these questions activated brain areas relating to disgust, but in others it did not. If we just look at their behaviour, we would only know the outcome of the decision, but neuroscience can help reveal the thoughts and motivations that produced it.

Engaging with sociology

Sociology is the study of human social behaviour, societal structures and interpersonal interactions. In many ways then, it seems very similar to social psychology. There is certainly a lot of overlap between the disciplines. The key difference is in the scale of analysis. Sociologists tend to focus on groups of people, such as the upper middle class, elderly people, Catholics or unemployed teenagers. They survey and study these groups of people and then try to understand how they interact with each other. Social psychologists always focus on the *individual*, however. Since all groups of people are made up of individuals, there is a useful and productive interaction between sociologists and social psychologists.

For example, a few years ago in London there were riots throughout the city. I could hear them from my front room, in fact. Afterwards, a large team of sociologists tried to understand why they took place by interviewing the people involved. In part the riots were a reaction against the police who, days before, had shot an unarmed man who they thought was carrying a gun. Another issue was the tension between an increasingly materialistic culture that values owning the latest gadget and most expensive shoes, and the relative poverty and unemployment of large numbers of young people in the capital. Another motivation was simply boredom and the thrill of adventure.

While sociologists were able to identify these recurring themes amongst groups and subgroups of rioters, social psychologists can investigate how they play out in the minds of individuals. They can run experiments on people to see if violence is intrinsically rewarding, and for whom. They can investigate if people see police officers as part of their community or as an out-group to be mistrusted, and what factors produce this 'them and us' thinking. And lastly, they can look at the decision-making of the police officers themselves. What might have caused them to jump to the conclusion that their suspect was armed, since none of them had directly seen a gun?

Tracing the ideas of evolutionary biology

Evolutionary biology is the study of how organisms change over time as they adapt to their environment. Human beings are the outcome of millions of years of evolution. And, like ants, chimps and marmosets, a central part of your evolutionary story is how human beings adapted to live and co-operate with each other. When a social psychologists asks a question such as 'why do we mistrust strangers?' or 'why do we feel jealousy?', an evolutionary biologist might answer that people evolved to be that way. Evolutionary psychologists seek answers to your everyday behaviour in your evolutionary past.

Evolutionary psychology has a puzzling aspect though. The world you live in today is not the world in which your ancestors evolved. In many ways, you are just like the kakapo parrot – not really suited to the world you inhabit (see the sidebar 'What do the world's fattest parrot and your brain have in common?').

What do the world's fattest parrot and your brain have in common?

In New Zealand lives a parrot called the kakapo. It is fat and green and cannot fly. The male kakapo attracts a mate by building a bowl-like structure called a lek and making a loud bass rumble. This takes so much effort that it can only go through the mating process once every four years when one particular tree bears an energy-rich fruit that drops to the ground. Females find the bass sound hard to localise, and often never find a male. If two are able to breed, parenthood is often unrewarding. The kakapo builds a nest on the ground, which is easily raided by rats and ferrets. The rodents are able to find the kakapo because it emits a strong odour that is not unlike the smell of the inside of a violin case. The parrot's means of defence is to flatten itself on the ground and stay very still indeed. This rarely troubles the rodents. They eat many of the eggs that are produced every four years.

It won't surprise you to hear that the kakapo is on the verge of extinction. Thankfully, they still survive today thanks to a concerted effort by a large team of conservationists. But why does the kakapo exist at all? Whether you believe in evolution or intelligent design, the kakapo seems a spectacularly poor example of both.

The answer to this puzzle lies in the first thing that I told you about this bird. It lives in New Zealand. The islands had been geographically isolated for millions of years, producing unique biodiversity with very few mammals and many unique bird species. Then, with the arrival of the Maori in the thirteenth century and Europeans in the eighteenth century, rats, ferrets and other small land predators were introduced. For thousands of years, the kakapo's only threat had come from eagles. These predators hunted from above and were unable to see the green kakapo if they flattened themselves on the floor and stayed very still. Until human beings began denuding the islands of trees, the fruit-bearing plant that the kakapo favoured was common and bore fruit regularly. The large number of kakapo meant that a male and female would usually find each other, even if their calls were hard to place.

In short, the kakapo is a perfectly evolved creature for a specific environmental niche. It's just that the niche no longer exists. It evolved for a world that it lives in no longer. The provocative proposal of evolutionary psychology is that we are kakapo too. Evolutionary psychologists have studied human thinking and social interaction and claim that we have many biases and strange quirks. Like the kakapo, your brain is a productive of evolution that does not quite make sense in today's world.

The defining characteristics of the human species – farming, cities, writing – appeared only 5,000 to 10,000 years ago. This is remarkably recent in the scale of biological history. Some of the most pervasive features of our lives today – use of machines, electricity, computers – happened relatively mere moments ago, a couple of generations in some cases. Evolution doesn't require hundreds of generations to change a species; it can happen very fast. But many of the selection pressures that existed for hundreds of thousands of years, shaping our species, no longer exist for us today.

Some evolutionary psychologists claim that there are features of our cognition and behaviour that don't make sense in the context of our lives today. But they do make sense when we consider the adaptive pressures that shaped the course of our evolution. We like symmetrical faces, we are poor at reasoning with probability and we make irrational decisions repeatedly. In this way, we are frozen in defence against now-redundant dangers. We make decisions that only make sense in the context of our evolutionary history.

If you are lucky enough to have known them both, think of your two grannies. Now answer this question: which one loves you the most? It's a terrible thing to ask, and I'm sure you'd say at first that they both love you. But – if you had to pick one – which do you think loves you more?

When researchers asked this question, and whenever I ask it in lectures, the clear answer is always the same. One granny lived closer to them growing up, visited more times or gave better birthday presents. For the clear majority of people, this more loving granny was their mother's mother. Why do you think this might be?

Evolutionary psychologists have offered one answer to this strangely reliable fact about grannies. There's no easy way to break this to you, but it's all to do with your mother's infidelity. Or rather, the possibility of it. Your mother can be really quite certain that you are biologically related to her. Of course, there can be adoptions, egg donations, mistaken baby swaps at the hospital, but these cases apart, your mother can be sure that you are hers.

This is not true of your father, however. I don't want to cast aspersions on your family, but it is logically possible that the man who was at your birth and signed your birth certificate was not the person who had conceived you nine months previously. This is just an unavoidable feature of the way we mammals reproduce.

So now consider the perspective of your grandmothers. Assume that they are hardwired to maximise the success of their genetic material. Assume that they have limited resources that they can use to ensure the success of their genes. Your mother's mother is certain that half of her genes are in your mother, and that half of those are in you. Your father's mother does not have this certainty. So, if your grandmothers follow Darwinian logic, your father's mother is less likely to invest her resources in you. There's the chance that you carry none of her genetic material, and that investment would be lost. Even though today we have DNA testing that can remove such uncertainty, the evolutionary perspective is that favouring a daughter's daughter became hardwired in our species, and the behaviour persists today.

Of course, you may be able to think of alternative explanations why in general a mother's mother seems the more affectionate grandparent. But this example illustrates how evolutionary reasoning can be applied to human behaviour today.

Evolutionary psychologists try and identify these ancestral qualities of our behaviour and fit them into the framework of our long evolutionary past. Their ideas are often highly contentious to other psychologists. The chief criticism is that many of these theories are completely untestable. Since we cannot go back in time and observe or experiment on our ancestors, there is no way to falsify these ideas. We will come across these arguments many times during the course of this book.

Social Psychology in Action

By now you have an idea of the territory of modern social psychology and the disciplines that populate it. But remember that science is a tool for rooting out answers. So now let's put all those ideas and methods to use!

In this section, I illustrate how the ideas and methods of social psychology can be applied to one particular issue: the violent culture of the White male in the southern United States. This section reports the work of Dov Cohen and Richard Nisbett, who thoroughly researched this question. Of course, in social psychology one could ask many questions, and take many routes to the answers. But this case serves as a great example of the process social psychologists use and the way they can utilise all the tools at their disposal to hunt down the answers to their question.

Asking the right questions

Understanding the causes of violence is of obvious practical value, so how can social psychology help?

Asking the question is the first step in understanding. And it's the most important one. Asking the right question can unlock the phenomena you are trying to understand. Asking the wrong question can lead to fruitless years of frustration. Social psychology, like all science, follows a process of hypothesis testing that – hopefully – drives our understanding forward.

Here's a question to begin our enquiry: in the US, why is the homicide rate higher in the southern states than the northern states? If you rank all the states by the number of homicides per 100,000 of the population, the 2003 figures show that of the ten states at the bottom of that list, with the highest homicide rates, nine are in the South. Of the ten best states with the lowest homicide rates, none are in the South. Why does this difference exist?

At this point, a social scientist could put forward a number of hypotheses. A hypothesis is a guess, a possible explanation. A good hypothesis makes a clear statement about the causes of something, and so makes predictions about what will happen in the future. Scientists can then test these predictions with studies and experiments. If the predictions are wrong, then they can reject that hypothesis.

As I explore in Chapter 3, this is how scientists make progress, by rejecting possible hypotheses and narrowing down the ways that we can explain something. It sounds strange, but for this reason, a good hypothesis is one that we can clearly show is wrong. Indeed, having ideas that we can conclusively prove are wrong is the definition of scientific progress!

So let's generate some hypotheses about why there are more homicides in the southern states of the US.

- ✔ The southern states are hotter, on average, and an increase in heat leads to an increase in violence.
- ✔ The southern states have more poverty than the northern ones, and poverty leads to crime.
- ✔ There are differences in gun laws in the South that mean that violence and crime are more likely to end in homicide.

All these hypotheses are plausible. Studies have shown, for example, that violent crime increases whenever the temperature gets hotter. And poverty is indeed correlated with crime rates. But these hypotheses can't be the full story. There are hotter and poorer states outside of the South, for example, that don't have the same homicide rates. Other states in the US and other countries, like Canada, have similar gun laws as the South, but they don't have the high homicide rates.

Here's another hypothesis:

There is a cultural difference between the North and the South which produces more male violence.

This is the hypothesis that I'm going to explore in more detail. It is at just the right level of analysis for social psychology, as it focuses on the individual and their cultural mindset. The hypothesis immediately generates many questions that can be explored: what is the nature of the cultural difference between the North and the South? Where did it come from? What function does it serve? What are the psychological and behavioural differences that are produced by this cultural difference? You can use the many tools of social psychology to answer these questions.

Understanding the culture of cowboys

Anthropologists have described what they call a 'culture of honour' that exists in many places across the world. In these societies, what is most important is one's honour, or reputation. If that reputation is threated, by an actual or perceived slight or insult, then a man (typically) has to do whatever he can to punish the perpetrator and restore his honour. Often this means resorting to violence. You can find cultures of honour across the world, and even in Klingon society.

The idea of a culture of honour seems to capture some of the stereotypes people have about southern males in the United States. When people think about a cowboy they often picture a stereotype of a cowboy fighting to protect his honour in a gunfight at high noon or a brawl in a bar. In each case, violence can start from a small insult and escalate into something fatal. It is also evident in how people in the South see themselves. The phrase 'Don't Mess with Texas' began life as an anti-litter slogan placed along the Texas highways. But quickly, Texans seized upon it as a way to sum up their own attitude. Now you can find it printed on t-shirts, bumper stickers, holsters and even a nuclear submarine, in the crest of the *USS Texas*.

Finding the roots of the culture of honour

Sociology can play a vital role in framing questions for social psychology. As I discussed in the case of the London riots, sociologists were able to identify potential motives and beliefs in the minds of the rioters that generated hypotheses that social psychologists can test.

What can sociology tell us about the 'culture of honour', and how it ended up in the south of the US? The answer lies in the waves of immigration from Europe and the different types of immigrants.

- **Farmers:** One wave of immigration to America came from the south of England. These were the Pilgrims of American folklore, and were mostly farmers. They settled in what is now the north-east of America, and established farmlands.

- **Herders:** Another wave of immigration came from the north of England, Scotland and Ireland. These people were mostly herders. They moved into areas in the southern US and then pushed west across the country.

Why would these two different types of people develop different cultural practices?

When you own a field, you can feed a large number of people and stealing it is quite hard for someone. In other words, farming communities tend to be quite stable. They can provide food and wealth, but only with concerted effort over a long time. Successful farming communities can support a large number of people and are able to employ people to keep order in their societies. In the North, wealth doesn't tend to change hands very quickly because it takes a long time to accumulate land and for it to yield a profit.

The southern herders had a very different society. When you own a herd of animals, you have to look after them constantly. Someone can steal them all overnight. In other words, herding communities can be quite volatile. Wealth can change hands overnight and does not gradually accumulate. Herding societies are also quite thinly populated. Animal herds take up a lot of space, and they don't feed as many people as crops do. These sparsely populated, relatively poor societies couldn't afford to employ policemen or people to protect their wealth. Even if they did, they couldn't look after everyone's herd at once.

Sociologists argue that the only thing stopping people stealing from each other in the herder societies of the South was the culture of honour. Without effective law enforcement, the only thing to deter thieves is the threat of retaliation from the person they have wronged. If you have a reputation as someone who is not to be crossed, who hits back twice as hard, then people will be dissuade from stealing from you. But if you are someone who is easily pushed around, who doesn't stand up for themselves, then there is nothing to stop people stealing from you. In other words, your honour is the only protection that you have. So it makes sense that you have to defend your honour at all costs.

But we are talking about people hundreds of years ago, you might object. What evidence is there that these attitudes persist, let alone explain the homicide rate of the southern states today? Before we turn to psychology for an answer, we can make two more sociological observations:

- If you look at a map of the US coloured by those waves of immigration to the North and the South 200 years ago, it bears a striking similarity to the map of the votes for Republicans or Democrats in the last few elections. In other words, it seems possible that events from many generations ago still have some bearing on society today.

- We can peer a little more into those homicide statistics comparing the South and the North. Some homicides were carried out in the course of another crime. A robber shoots the bank clerk, for example. For these felony-related homicides, the South and the North are equal. There is no difference. But you can also count the non-felony-related homicides. In the South today, more than twice as many of these homicides exist that resulted from something like an argument in a bar.

So clearly, a difference between these two societies exists that needs explaining. But how do we prove that the culture of honour persists to this day, and how does it influence the behaviour of modern-day cowboys?

Finding answers with social psychology

Sociology, history and anthropology can all serve social psychology by identifying social phenomena. That's not all though. I've seen many conference talks in social psychology that have begun with something a researcher has noticed in an episode of *The Simpsons* or another TV show. One talk, for example, explored an issue raised in *Seinfeld* – why doesn't Elaine realise that she is a really bad dancer? This began an entire empirical project examining how part of people's incompetence is not recognising what competence looks like.

The other social sciences, art and media are a vital source of inspiration for hypotheses in social psychology. But all they can do is help us identify and ask interesting questions. To find the answers, to test those hypotheses, we need the tools of social psychology.

In seeking answers about violence in the south of the US, we've drawn on sociology to inform our concept of the culture of honour and historical context to give us an idea about the function of this behaviour. But so far, we have no direct psychological evidence. For example, the image of a 'cowboy' that I've described may not be an accurate description of what people are really like in the American South. Now I'll show you how social psychology can test our hypotheses on Americans today.

Survey data

As a first step in social psychology, surveys are often employed. A large number of people are surveyed and asked specific questions that explore the researchers' hypotheses. All that surveys can offer is correlational evidence, however. By that I mean that all they can show is that the answers people give to questions are connected in some way. As I will show, what we can conclude based on patterns of response in survey data is always limited.

The hypothesis being tested is that the culture of honour described by anthropologists and historians still exists today in the mind of the southern American male. Turning that idea into something that can be counted, researchers construct a survey study. In this example, researchers sent surveys to people in the south and north of the US. They asked them some simple questions about how they might behave. For example, they asked, 'Would you approve if a man punched an adult male stranger if that stranger was a drunkard who bumped into the man and his wife?' Significantly more people from the southern states approved of that action. Similarly, they were asked whether it was okay for a 10-year-old boy to fight back when someone stole his lunch money. So this gives us some reasons to think that our hypothesis might be true.

However, might there be other explanations for this pattern of survey responses? Other surveys have found that the more likely someone is to be involved in crime, the more likely they are to have just eaten an ice cream, and the less likely they are to own a pet. Does this mean that to reduce crime we should ban ice creams and give everyone a puppy?

No, there are other explanations for these patterns of survey data. As I mentioned already, when it gets hotter outside, people are more likely to commit violent crimes, and so are also more likely to consume ice creams. Also, richer families are more likely to own a pet (as keeping one is very expensive), and richer people are less likely to have family members involved in crime. In these cases, the puppies and the ice cream aren't directly related to crime, but are connected through the additional factors of the weather and wealth.

Other explanations may exist for our surveys of people in the North and the South too. Perhaps the South simply has more violent crime, and so people are more familiar with, and accepting of, violent behaviour. But it has nothing to do with the culture of honour. Not that we can prove with just a survey.

Field studies

In a field study, researchers observe something about behaviour as it naturally occurs 'in the wild'. They control some factors about the situation, so a field study is a bit like an experiment. But it is missing the key ingredient of random assignment – I'll get to that in the next section.

In one famous field study Philip Zimbardo (we'll meet him many times in this book) left a car parked by the side of the road with its hood up. In fact, he left two cars – one in Palo Alto, California and one in the Bronx, New York. Both were left within a block of famous universities, Stanford University and New York University respectively. The researchers then snuck across the road to observe what happened.

However, the researchers had barely set up their equipment in the Bronx before passers-by had helped themselves to the car battery, the contents of the glove compartment and the radiator. Forty-eight hours later, 23 acts of theft and vandalism had left the car on blocks, stripped and beaten.

The car in Palo Alto also drew the attention of the locals. After five days, a passer-by noticed that it was raining and lowered the hood to protect the car. Other than that helpful gesture, the car was untouched.

This field study clearly reveals that there were different attitudes to property and crime in Palo Alto and New York. In New York at the time, vandalism and crime were commonplace and visible everywhere. Palo Alto, in contrast, is almost oppressively clean and well behaved. When I lived there, I always felt embarrassed going out without freshly pressed clothes and a manicure.

But what can you conclude beyond the fact that there are differences between the two communities? From a field study, not that much. The differences could have been to do with wealth, the weather, local attitudes, the likelihood of police taking action or even the relative value of the cars.

Field studies have similarly been used to illuminate the difference between cultures in the north and south of the US. Researchers carried out a field study by sending letters to car dealerships in the North and South. The letters were asking for a job interview, and appeared to be genuine. There were two types of letter. In one, the applicant explained that he was having a hard time getting an interview because, 'I have been convicted of a felony, namely manslaughter.'

He goes on to explain that one night at a bar, a drunk boasted of sleeping with his fiancée, and then challenged him to a fight. Not wanting to back down, they went outside. The drunk jumped him from behind and, in defence, the man struck out with a pipe that he found on the ground, killing the man. As you can see, there are many details here that appeal to the culture of honour. The applicant was defending his reputation and his fiancée's good name. He was attacked unfairly and struck back in defence.

The second letter began the same way, 'I have been convicted of a felony'. But this time the crime was motor vehicle theft. The applicant explained that he'd been young and needed money to pay the bills, and so he'd decided to steal expensive cars. As you can see, this letter has commonalities with the first, but the crime is not connected to the culture of honour in anyway.

Would car dealerships in the North and South responds differently to these two job letters? The researchers *operationalised* these questions in two ways (that is, they took the initial concept and turned it into something they could measure).

> ✔ **First operationalisation:** They just counted the number of car dealerships who responded with an application form and an invitation to apply. For the motor theft letter, there was no difference between the North and the South in their responses. For the manslaughter letter, however, southern car dealerships were more likely to reply with an application form.

✔ **Second operationalisation:** The researchers counted the number of positive words in the dealerships' cover letters (we warmly encourage you to apply, many thanks for your letter, and so on). The northerners used more positive words in replying to the applicant who had confessed to stealing. For the southerners, however, they expressed equal or more warmth to the person who had killed a man than the person who had been convicted of theft.

This field study clearly shows that – in this sample of car dealers – there are different attitudes in the North and South towards crime that is committed in defence of one's honour. But how far can we generalise this result? Are there other explanations? Perhaps it's just the case that people in the South are more accustomed to cases of homicide because it's more common; this familiarity explains the difference with the North – it has nothing to do with a culture of honour, per se. To escape these circular arguments, we need stronger data, and so the researchers turned to laboratory experiments.

Experiments

Experiments are the most powerful tool that a social psychologist can use. A well-designed experiment, with clear and unambiguous data provides a solid building block of evidence. It may only be a small block, more like a Lego brick, but every well-designed experiment conclusively says *something*, and from these little blocks we build scientific knowledge.

Experiments are so important to social psychology that I've devoted the whole of Chapter 3 to explaining what makes a good one, what makes a bad one and how to design one yourself.

The key idea is that in an experiment, the researchers take control of the social situation – everything that the participants in the experiment see and hear. They create (at least two) different versions of an experiment that differ in one regard and one regard only. For example, in a simple experiment, participants might interact with a researcher who asks them their political opinions. The only different between two versions of the experiment is whether the researcher they interact with is male or female. The experimenter will then analyse some aspect of the participants' behaviour that they have carefully measured. For example, they may quantify if the participant gave more left- or right-wing answers. If there is a systematic difference between participants who interacted with a man or woman we can conclude – cautiously – that the sex of an interviewer can change the political beliefs a participant will publicly espouse.

Chapter 3 has many more examples of the experimental method at work. For now, let's see how they can help us test our hypotheses about the culture of honour. Researchers performed a series of experiments at a university in the middle of the US state of Illinois. This campus is unusual in having a roughly equal number of male students from the more rural area to the south, and the more urban areas to the north. In other words, they have both southern and northern participants and can randomly assign them to experimental conditions.

I particularly like these experiments for the range of creative ways that the researchers operationalised their ideas. Questionnaires, chemical swabs and mechanical measuring devices were all used to quantify the culture of honour.

I'd like you to imagine being a participant in one of these experiments. Like all their participants, you'd be a White American male from either the North or the South. You turn up to the laboratory and someone in a lab coat asks you to give a saliva sample. Then you're asked if you'd mind taking it to another lab down the corridor. You agree. On your way down the corridor you see a large, muscular guy. You think that he's another person doing the experiment, but actually he's acting out a role given to him by the researchers. In the insult condition he bumps into you, mutters 'asshole', then wanders off. In the control condition he walks silently by. You then give a second sample at the next laboratory.

As you can see, the insult condition is a clear case of your honour being under threat. So how would you react? And how could we measure the responses of participants to compare the southerners and the northerners?

First of all, the researchers simply asked the participants who were insulted about the incident. Northerners were more likely to say that they were amused by the whole thing. Southerners reported more anger than amusement. They also asked participants whether they thought others who saw the incident would see them as less masculine as a consequence. Southerners felt that their masculinity would decrease in the eyes of others if they'd been insulted, but there were no differences between the North and South in the control condition. These answers clearly fit the pattern of the culture of honour for the South. But are these southerners really angry? Maybe they are just giving the answer that they feel is correct, given their upbringing, but they don't really feel angry or less masculine.

Next, the researchers turned to more innovative operationalisations to explore this question. In one experiment, the participants had to walk back past the same muscular man who'd insulted them (or not) previously. The corridor was very narrow, especially given how wide the man was. Two people couldn't pass shoulder to shoulder. Someone had to back down and stand aside to let the other person pass. The muscular man was told to stand his ground and not to back down at all. In this situation, what would the participants do?

The researchers watched the participants walk towards the large man and measured how close they got to him before deciding to stand to the side and let him pass. In the control condition, where no one had been insulted, the southern males stood aside at a large distance. In a sense, they were more polite and accommodating to the other person. But in the insult condition they got much closer to the man, less than half the distance away, before they backed down. The northerners showed a much smaller difference between the two conditions.

In another version of the experiment, the participants came into the laboratory after being insulted (or not) and shook the researcher's hand. They were able to measure the strength of the participants' grips during their handshakes. Sure enough, if the southern subjects had just been insulted, they gave a much stronger handshake.

So here we have two aspects of behaviour – the strength of their handshakes and the distance between themselves and another male who won't stand out of the way. The participants were probably barely aware of how they were acting in this regard. Yet nevertheless, the southern males showed more aggressive and assertive behaviour in exactly the conditions where their honour had been insulted.

Finally, the researchers actually looked at the chemicals in those saliva samples. Remember that they got two, before and after the insult incident, so that they could measure changes in cortisol and testosterone. They have a complex function in the body, but very simply these hormones appear to be related to stress and aggression. The northerners showed little difference, regardless of what happened to them in the corridor. But the southerners had a marked increase in these hormone levels if they had just been insulted.

The experimental data tell a remarkably consistent story. From reported feelings of anger and masculinity, to subtle aspects of behaviour like handshakes and interpersonal distance, to the bodily production of behaviour-influencing hormones: southerners are affected when their honour is threatened. These are full experiments that use random assignments and have well-designed control conditions. So we know that it is not just that southerners always have firmer handshakes, or that everyone gets a testosterone spike when insulted. We can conclude that these changes occur specifically in southerners specifically when they are insulted.

That power and precision is what experimental social psychology can deliver at its best. In Chapter 3 I explore how social psychologists design and analyse experiments in order to probe the processes and mechanisms that lie behind our social lives.

Chapter 3

Kitting Out: The Tools of Social Psychology

*W*e use knowledge about other people every day. For example, when we guess why a parent seems angry today, when we predict how a friend will react to a surprise party or when we deduce why a person is running down the street. These beliefs are shaped by our experiences, stories, education, religious instruction and watching soap operas. But often, this everyday knowledge is quite different to scientific social psychology. In fact, I show you in this chapter that often, everyday 'common sense' is social psychology's greatest enemy.

How do social psychologists prove their claims? Like all professionals, social psychologists need a set of tools to carry out their job. The tool that they reach for most often is the experiment. Here I talk about the logic behind experiment design and how it gives scientists the ability to draw conclusions about the causal roots of human behaviour. To do so, I have to talk about something that can make people uncomfortable: statistics. If you are uneasy with maths and feel tempted to skip those sections, please stick it out. There are no intimidating formulae or equations in this chapter, I promise.

In this chapter, I show you *how* social psychologists combat the enemy glib common sense, and *why* the tools of experimental and statistical techniques are so important in building knowledge. I won't go into the nuts and bolts of how you perform statistical calculations, but I want to convey the remarkable connection social psychology can make between the ineffable qualities of human experience and the power of the scientific method. It makes social psychology much more interesting than talking about novels, and much harder to do than physics and chemistry. It may even encourage you to pick up a book on statistics.

Facing Social Psychology's Greatest Enemy: Common Sense

When you excitedly tell people about the findings of a carefully performed, ingenious experiment in social psychology, a very common response you will hear is, 'Well, that's just common sense, isn't it?' If you are a student, you'll hear this from friends who study other subjects and from your family at home. To them, after several years of hard study, you end up with a degree in basic common sense.

In this section, I pit social psychology knowledge against common sense knowledge. I show that things that seem obviously and boringly true to many people are shown to be simply false when scientists carry out careful experiments. Why is it then that people often want to stick with their common-sense beliefs and ignore the conclusions of social psychology? The answer to this is itself a fascinating bit of social psychology that I introduce here and discuss more in Part III of this book.

Social psychology in art and religion

The *Epic of Gilgamesh* is one of the oldest stories that our species has told that still survives to this day. It was created, we estimate, around 4,000 years ago. Versions were written down on palm-sized stone tablets a few hundred years later and rediscovered in the nineteenth century. It is the tale of a Gilgamesh, a king, of gods and monsters and the underworld. But it is not just a list of battles won and lost. It is a complex account of pride, jealously, love and friendship (it's also a cracking good read). Even our very earliest stories are psychologically rich. They contain knowledge about what motivates people, what they fear and how they love.

Scripture – the Vedas, the Bible, the Koran and the Torah – are similarly rich with social psychological insight. They contain parables about how people behave, what they believe and how they should act towards each other. In sermons, these stories are recounted to this day and applied to modern life. In many ways, this activity is a form of social psychology. For thousands of years, in a religious and artistic context, people have been making generalisations about human social behaviour and applying them to novel situations. But in one very important way, this knowledge is a long way short of science. These observations and generalisations are not distilled into theory, and they are not systematically tested. For that, we need the scientific method.

Challenging the notion of common sense

I once read a newspaper article in which the columnist was discussing a recent scientific paper. The researchers had found that when people experienced long periods of anxiousness, they tended to gain weight. The columnist was angry that money had been spent to prove this fact. It was obvious from everyday experience that we eat when we are sad or nervous. He summed up the research in a wonderfully pithy remark: 'This is just common sense expensively turned into science'. Common sense is social psychology's greatest enemy, blithely dismissing the results of scientific research.

Certainly, people have a rich sense of folk psychology, an understanding of others' minds and behaviour that they use every day. But thinking that this is the same as a *scientific* understanding of behaviour is a big mistake. But don't take my word for it: put your own common-sense knowledge to the test!

Read each of these statements and use your common sense (not an Internet search) to decide if it feels true or false.

1. To change the way people behave, you must first change their attitudes.

2. The more you're rewarded for an activity, the more you'll enjoy it.

3. When people decide things as a group, they usually make more moderate decisions than an individual deciding alone.

4. If they are alone, people are less likely to help someone on the street who may be in trouble.

5. On average, heterosexual men have more sexual partners than heterosexual women.

Now read on and see how many you got right. . . .

None of those statements was true. Even though each one seems to agree with most people's common sense, social psychology has solid evidence that every one is false.

You can read much more about the troublesome aspects of attitudes in Chapters 4 and 5, and more relating to statements 1 and 2 in Chapter 6. I discuss group thinking in Chapter 16.

Social psychology and society

Science seems ever more central to our lives and conversations. It is not just that science stories are headline news, like the discovery of the Higgs boson subatomic particle or the mapping of the human genome. The scientific perspective informs many stories and ideas in public discussions, and none more so than social psychology. When we talk about the best way to raise children, why some people commit horrible crimes (I discuss the idea of evil in Chapter 11), or even why a particular celebrity couple have broken up, a social scientist is often called upon.

As a scientist, this seems to me like a very positive step. It's not because I think that current scientific views are necessarily correct and should dominate the discussion. It's because increasingly people realise that what matters are not who holds the opinion and the volume with which they shout, but the *evidence* that supports an opinion. And scientists are the people who collect and analyse evidence. The increased attention to social science has a downside, however. It means that more and more, social psychology has to come face to face with its worst enemy: common sense.

I don't have evidence that proves that statement 5 is false. In fact, we don't even need evidence here. Logically, the statement must be untrue. Consider this: heterosexual sex, by definition, means sex between a man and a woman. So if we are counting sexual partners, every time heterosexual sex takes place, there is one more male sexual partner and one more female. If we want to find out how many sexual partners men and women each have on average, we divide the number of male and female sexual partners by the number of men and women. Well, we've seen there are an equal number of sexual partners of each sex, and there is an equal number of men and women. Therefore, they must have an equal number of sexual partners, on average. For much more on interpersonal relationships, check out Chapter 15, rather than relying on your common sense.

Accepting that common sense can be nonsense

If you found out that your own common sense wasn't as good as you thought, then you can cheer yourself up by trying this experiment on your all-knowing friends and family. Tell a group of them that you've just been reading about a study of dating in your social psychology book. Explain that when it comes to personality types, opposites attract. Your audience may complain that they knew this all along: it's just common sense. Then find another group of friends or family. Tell them that your book said that when it comes to personality types, people who are similar to each other get along the best. Once more, they may complain that this is obvious: it's common sense that 'birds of a feather flock together'.

I've done this experiment many times in lectures. You can give half the people one statement, and the other half another statement that says the exact opposite, like our dating example above. What happens is that most people, on average, think that these completely opposing statements are probably true, and that they knew them all along. This is a hallmark of common-sense knowledge about psychology: it is perfectly happy to contradict itself. This is not the case at all in scientific social psychology.

Confirming biases in social thinking

Why is it that people so readily assert that a statement (or its opposite) exactly agrees with what they already knew? Well, social psychologists have studied this phenomenon and understand that it is a systematic bias in the way that we think about the world. Think back to our newspaper columnist reading that scientists found that anxious people gain weight. When he read this he probably thought of all the times he's bought some chocolate to cheer himself up, or all the times he's seen a sitcom character get dumped by her boyfriend, and in the next scene is eating a tub of ice cream in the kitchen. These memories and images all appear to confirm the idea that negative feelings cause weight gain, and so he feels that he knew the results of the study all along.

What if the columnist had read that scientists claim that anxiety leads people to lose weight? I think that he would have searched his memory and imagined a gaunt, worried-looking person picking at his food and then pushing the plate away with a sigh. He may have remembered the time he came home from college depressed, and his mother asked if he was feeling okay because he looked like he'd lost weight. In other words, he would have been able to find an equal amount of anecdotal and remembered evidence that makes it common sense that negative feelings cause weight-loss.

This is called the *confirmation bias*. Common sense has a tendency to only seek out from memory evidence that confirms or supports an idea. We don't tend to think of the contrary evidence against an idea. That is the job of the scientist. That is why we carefully use the scientific method to count confirming and disconfirming evidence, to weight them statistically and rule out competing explanations.

I cover biases relating to the self in Chapter 8 and write more about such biases in social thinking in Chapters 9 and 10. But for now, I want to make one thing clear. It may have seemed sometimes that I have been saying that scientists are always right and non-scientists get things wrong. That is not what I think at all. These biases occur in everyone, scientists as well. In fact, there have been embarrassing cases of this. In the earlier section 'Challenging the notion of common sense' I explained why it is impossible that heterosexual men could have a higher number of sexual partners, on average, than heterosexual women. Nevertheless, a paper was once published in a social psychology journal making exactly that claim.

The researchers had carefully surveyed the student population of a small college town, asking about the number of times male and female students had had heterosexual sex with other members of the college community. They carried out a statistical analysis, wrote up their results, had the paper reviewed by an editor and other scientists in the field and got their paper published. It wasn't until after it was published that someone else pointed out that their result was logically impossible. Apparently the finding that young males are sexually active fitted so well with everyone's confirmation bias that no one thought to question it rigorously. In fact, all that the researchers had shown is that young males will *claim* to have had more sexual partners than females. And that finding, even I will admit, is plain common sense.

Entering the Fascinating World of the Social Psychology Experiment

When I was in my youth, I wasted too much time playing video games. In one called *Street Fighter II* you had to combat ever more formidable enemies by bashing, punching, kicking and jumping. Every character you played had a special move, like launching fireballs or reaching into your enemies' throats and pulling their skeletons out. To do these special moves you needed a complicated series of button presses. It was very hard to get right, but if you could pull off the special move, you were absolutely unstoppable.

Though common sense is a formidable enemy for social psychologists, they too have a special move: the scientific experiment. It is also tricky to get right, and certainly involves a lot of complicated button pressing. But if they get it right, social scientists can reach unstoppable conclusions.

In this section, I explain what an experiment is, and from where it gets its power. I explain the three key elements of a social psychology experiment – random assignment, manipulation and measurement – and show how they combine and what they can prove.

Experimenting with my make-up

When I was in college, I experimented with wearing eyeliner. I was doing some student theatre and once forgot to take off the eyeliner after rehearsal. One girl in a pub said that it suited me, and so for a few weeks, I toyed around with a sort of New Romantic nerd look. As an experiment, I think it failed. This is a perfectly reasonable use of the word 'experiment', in the sense of 'trying out' or 'investigating', and it's one that most people are quite familiar with. But it is a long way short of what we mean by an 'experiment' in psychology.

If I had really experimented with eyeliner, for example, I would have worn the make-up on a random or systematically varied set of days and toured a series of randomly chosen bars and pubs handing out a standardised survey to people I met. I could then have tested the hypothesis that eyeliner increased my limited attraction to other people by seeing if there was an increase greater-than-chance levels for the survey ratings when I was wearing make-up. But even this is a poor experiment by psychology standards. Perhaps it is the case that the eyeliner just made me *feel* more artistic and interesting, and that change in my behaviour

was perceived as more attractive (an unlikely hypothesis, I'll admit, but possible).

A better test would be to have to have a friend apply the make-up for me, using either a real eyeliner pencil or a dummy pencil that left no mark. Now I wouldn't know myself whether or not I was wearing the make-up while interacting with others. If there was still a difference in the survey scores, we could rule out the confidence explanation and have better evidence that the eyeliner made me more attractive.

I never did carry out that experiment properly, and I stopped wearing eyeliner after a few weeks. Sadly, it had more to do with the withering looks from my friends than any evidenced-based conclusion. But it was around the same time that I switched from studying philosophy to studying psychology, and the reason was that I fell in love with experiments. In philosophy, discussions and debates between great thinkers can stretch for centuries without being resolved. But the awesome power of experiments means that if you follow the method properly, anyone can test a hypothesis and move our understanding forward.

Appreciating the awesome power of the scientific method

Science is a systematic method that allows us to develop, test and reject theories. It doesn't provide certainty, and it doesn't produce theories that are always right. But in the long run, correctly applied, the scientific method always stumbles forward towards the truth, gradually building knowledge. This upward progress is very different to common-sense knowledge. We are no wiser in our everyday understanding of each other than our grandparents, or their grandparents. Common sense does not accumulate. But science, in the long run, is always building knowledge.

You can think of the scientific method as a series of steps:

1. Observe the world.

2. Make up an explanation for what you see. This is called a hypothesis. You may come up with a particular hypothesis because it comes from a theory that you have.

3. Test your hypotheses in an experiment. Hypotheses make predictions about what will happen, and an experiment is a way of finding out if that prediction is true. This involves carefully manipulating and measuring things about the world, which are called experimental variables. Analyse your data using statistics to see if the predictions came true.

4. Did your predictions come true? You have support for your hypothesis, and support for your theory. Now you have to write up exactly what you did so that other people can perform the same experiment and get the same result. This is called replication, and it's a vital part of the scientific method. Now you can generate more hypotheses and predictions from your theory and go back to Step 2 to test them.

5. Did your predictions not come true? You have to reject that hypothesis. If this has happened enough times, you may have to reject the whole theory as well. Go back to Step 2 and try modifying your theory, or starting over again.

That, in essence, is the scientific method. In the few hundred years since we have started using it, it has produced new ways of understanding the heavens, our bodies and matter itself. It generated ideas that were radically different from any that had gone before. It produced the technology that powered the industrial and information revolutions. And much later, when we turned the method upon ourselves, it produced social psychology.

The scientific method as we know it began life in the thirteenth century in the universities of Europe. Before that time, there were societies such as the ancient Babylonians, the Greeks and Romans, the Abbasid Caliphate and the Han dynasty that were technologically gifted and made startlingly accurate observations of the world. But it wasn't until the sixteenth-century Renaissance that people like Francis Bacon were able to articulate fully a scientific method, a way of acquiring knowledge by experimentation and hypothesis testing that could generate new and lasting knowledge.

There is one revolutionary thing about the scientific method. It comes between Steps 3 and 4 above. What decides which hypotheses we keep and which we throw away? It is whatever happens in your experiment. The universe itself decides which theories and beliefs we can hold. This was a revolution. Before that time people in authority decided what to believe: priests, kings and famous long-dead philosophers. The slogan of the Royal Society, the first scientific institution, is *Nullius in verba,* or 'take no one's word for it'.

Let's apply the method. Imagine you see someone collapsing on a neighbouring train carriage while clutching their chest. No one goes to help, and this seems strange to you. You form a hypothesis that people sometimes don't help strangers in distress because they feel incapable of doing anything useful by themselves. This generates the prediction that the more people are on the train carriage when one person is in distress, the more likely people are to help out. There is strength in numbers.

So you perform a careful experiment to test this hypothesis. You hire an actor to feign a heart attack on various different train carriages with different numbers of people on them and carefully measure the likelihood of people going over to the collapsed man and helping.

What you will find – I know because social psychologists have done precisely these experiments – is that the more people are on the train the *less* likely it is for other people to help. So your predictions were wrong, your hypothesis can be rejected, and you may have to revise your assumptions and your theory. Or you may worry that you didn't do the experiment correctly, and it has some flaws. For example, perhaps a full train carriage is filled with different types of people (for example, commuters) than near-empty carriages (for example, tourists) and it is this difference that explains why some helped and others didn't. So you go back, re-think your theory, refine your experiments and try again. And you are following the scientific method in all its glory.

Designing an experiment

In this section I describe devising an experiment to answer a simple question: does a cup of tea make someone nicer? I promise that the experiments in this book are often more interesting, but starting off simply is a good idea. We have a very simple hypothesis about the act of drinking tea and the effects it may have on social behaviour; specifically, how it may cause you to interact with people differently. So let's test it.

In our first simple experiment, we have two people, Alan and Bob. The factor that we control is whether or not they have tea. Alan is in one *experimental condition*, and is given a cuppa. Bob is in the other group, and gets none. Then we measure something: they interact with a researcher and are videotaped. Later, other researchers (who don't know what condition Alan and Bob are in) watch those tapes and write down how friendly Alan and Bob are acting. They count the number of smiles they give, the number of pleasantries they mutter, and so on. Let's say that Alan scores higher on our friendliness scale. Have we now proved that tea makes people nicer? Take a moment and think of other explanations for our results.

Your explanations can probably be placed into two categories: they may have something to do with the *differences between people*, Alan and Bob in this case, or they may be due to *differences between experimental conditions*, in this case, giving a cup of tea or not. The scientific method gives us remarkable solutions to each of these two sets of problems.

Differences between people

Here are some reasons why Alan may have scored higher than Bob on the friendliness test after drinking a cup of tea:

- Alan has always been nicer than Bob.

- Bob didn't sleep well last night, and so he's feeling a bit grumpy today.

- The researcher reminded Bob of his ex-girlfriend who broke his heart and he is still bitter.

- Alan is wearing eyeliner and is feeling especially confident and flirty today.

The trouble is that there are a million potential differences between Alan and Bob. How can we be sure that their different scores on the test are due to the tea, and not due to one of these other factors? We could measure as many factors as possible (their friendliness scores prior to the test, their sleep levels, their opinions about the researcher) but how many do we need? And how do we know which to measure? The other issue is that we are really not interested in Alan and Bob in particular; we are interested in the effects of tea for all people.

Meeting Mr Average

The writer Kevin O'Keefe has found the 'average American': Bob Burns. O'Keefe looked at the results of as many surveys on Americans that he could possibly find. He looked at the average answers for each. Then he found the one person in the country who gave the most number of average answers. So, like the average American, Bob Burns eats peanut butter at least once a week and prefers smooth over chunky, he goes to church at least once a month and lives within a 20-minute drive of a Wal-Mart and three miles from McDonald's. So if we carry out all our experiments on Bob Burns, would we learn something about the average American? Probably not. And Mr Burns might not be too keen on it either.

This seems like an insurmountable problem. How do we deal with the fact that people differ in so many ways: their upbringing, their personality, their mood that day, whether or not they like the researcher, and so on. All of these could influence how they behave in our experiments. How do we discount all these factors about people so that we can focus on the one thing we care about, whether it's the effect of tea or any of the other things we study in social psychology?

If we have two groups of people, those who are given a cup of tea and those who are not, then we could try and make sure that in each group there are an equal number of nice people, an equal number of people who regularly drink tea, an equal number of men and women, an equal number of extroverts and introverts, an equal number of happy people and sad people. But we can't possibly measure or control all of these factors – there are just too many. So how do we make sure that these two groups of people are exactly the same in all aspects, apart from the fact that one group gets tea and the other does not?

The answer is quite remarkable: we give up. We don't even try to measure or control all these factors. We do nothing, and leave it all in the hands of the gods. Or rather, we leave it up to chance. This is called *random assignment*. And it means that you place your participants at random in your experimental conditions. When people come into your lab you toss a coin, literally, to place them in the tea group or the non-tea group. And it is that little coin toss that solves the experimental problem of all the differences that exist between people.

It may seem like a small methodological detail, but random assignment is the keystone to the experimental method in social psychology. Sciences like chemistry don't have this problem. Hydrogen molecules are identical to each other and behave the same the world over. But we study people, and they differ in all sorts of ways that changes how they behave. We can perform rigorous scientific experiments on them, however, thanks to the power of random assignment.

Here's the reasoning behind random assignment. If you place people into two groups at random, then you can be pretty sure that *whatever you measure* about them – height, intelligence, a liking for eighties pop music – the average for those two groups will be more or less the same. We can go even further than this though. Over the past few hundred years we have developed very clever statistical tools. They can tell us with great precision how likely it is that a difference between two groups is because of random chance.

In short, we can't measure or control all the ways in which people vary. So in experiments we assign them to groups at random, *because we know exactly what randomness looks like*. In our tea example, we can randomly assign people to the tea and no-tea group. If the test scores are different between these two groups, we can say whether that difference is due to randomness, or due to a real difference in their behaviour. And if they are behaving differently, then we can be certain that it is because of the fact that some had tea and some did not, and that it is not because we just happened to get happier, friendlier, less sleepy participants in one group rather than the other.

Note that this logic only works if your participants really are randomly assigned. Say, for example, that you carried out this tea experiment at a university and did it in two stages, in the morning and the afternoon. Your participants could sign up for either one of the two slots. This is not *random* assignment. It could be that people who chose the morning slot are more motivated, outgoing students who are going to score better on the friendliness test.

Capturing randomness

How far apart do two averages have to be for you to conclude that they are not due to chance? Say you always seem to lose when your friend tosses a particular lucky coin that she carries around. You are suspicious, so you borrow the coin, take it home and toss it 100 times. You would expect 50 heads if the coin was fair: if it had an equal chance of coming up heads or tails. But you wouldn't be too alarmed if you got 52 heads. Or maybe 55. But if you got 70 heads, would you start to worry that your friend was cheating? How do you know how many heads is too many?

Using statistics we can put precise probabilities on these different outcomes. We can say that if the coin is fair, then there is a 38 per cent chance that you'd get 52 or more heads out of 100 tosses. That's not unlikely at all. But there is only an 18 per cent chance of getting 55 or more, and a 0.004 per cent chance of getting 70 or more.

So now we have quantified these probabilities, the question still remains: how unlikely does the number of coin tosses have to be before we say that the coin is not fair? We have agreed in social science that we would draw a line in the sand and say that if something has a less than 5 per cent chance of happening, then it has not happened by random chance alone. Something else is going on. For the coin toss example, you would need to get 59 or more heads out of 100 to cross this 5 per cent mark. If that happened, you would have scientific grounds for picking an argument with your friend over her lucky coin.

Similarly, say you carry out your experiment, analyse your results and find out there is a 6 per cent chance of getting the differences that you found by chance. The convention is that you have not really found anything at all: those small differences are just random. But if you find out that there is a less than 5 per cent chance of getting your results, you can conclude that it is more than random chance at work: you have a significant result.

Or to take another example, say the researcher decides to put people in different groups according to the first letter of their surnames. This is not random: people who come from the same parts of the world often have similar surnames. So this technique will tend to put unequal numbers of different cultures and ethnicities in the two groups. Random assignment only works if it is done by the researcher, and if it is truly random.

Differences between experimental conditions

Random assignment solves the problem of all the differences that exist between participants in our experiments. Going back to our experiment about tea with Alan and Bob, you may have thought of other explanations for why they scored differently on the friendliness test. We want to see if *tea* has an effect on friendliness, but if Alan scores higher than Bob after having a cuppa, it could be because:

- Hot drinks warm you up, and it was a cold day, which made people without tea grumpy.

- Being well hydrated increases your friendliness.

- Bob was a bit upset when he saw Alan being given a cup of tea. He felt a bit resentful towards the researcher and so was unfriendly.

- People believe that they feel better when they have had a tea in the morning. This belief gave Alan a mood boost and led him to act friendlier towards the researcher.

So why did the drink help Alan? Was it because of the tea specifically, or because of these other reasons? How can we rule out these other explanations? To deal with the differences between people, we could use the power of random assignment. Sadly, there is no such magic bullet for dealing with this problem.

The issue is that we have one specific factor that we want to study: our experimental hypothesis is that an increase in tea consumption will improve performance on the friendliness scale. But look at our two experimental conditions – having a cup of tea and not having a cup of tea. These two conditions certainly do differ in that one crucial factor of tea. But they also differ in a whole host of other ways – drinking fluid, being warmed up, being given something nice by the experimenter, and so on. The technical term for these other factors is *confounds* or *confounding variables*. They are unwanted differences between experimental conditions. They are unwanted because we can't tell if the difference between conditions scores is due to the one factor that we care about, or all the other confounding variables.

When two social psychologists argue over a result, it is usually because one thinks that the other has confounding variables in their experiment. It is often very difficult to design experiments on social behaviour without any confounds at all. When you read about new research, think carefully about whether there are any confounding variables that could provide a different explanation to that of the original researchers.

The problem is well known, and it's more easily dealt with in other sciences like medicine. When testing a new drug, a doctor gives one group the real drug and another group a *placebo*, a pill that looks the same but has no medi-cal effect. This ensures that in every regard – visits to the doctor, the belief that they are in a trial, the hope that they will get better – the two groups are identical. They only difference is whether or not they have had the drug.

But in social psychology isolating and controlling experimental conditions is often much harder because we are studying people's social behaviour, which is based on their experience of the real world where causal factors are often interrelated. Take the case of the 'own race bias' for faces that has been shown in many experiments. It means, for example, White Americans can recognise and remember the faces of other White Americans better than they can recognise and remember the faces of Black Americans.

Can we conclude that people are better at processing faces from their own racial group? Well, yes, in a sense. But from the evidence I've presented here, it may not be anything to do with race exactly. Societies are still racially seg-regated, to some degree. If you are White in America you are more likely, on average, to spend time with other White people. In other words, there is a confounding variable at work. For White participants, Black faces are from another social group, but also they are less familiar faces. Are the differences between White and Black faces to do with racial groups or are they to do with faces that are familiar? As we will see in Chapter 10, researchers have done a lot of work deconfounding these variables. But I hope you get a sense of how complicated this issue can be in social psychology.

The best way round the problem of confounding variables is to redesign the experiment more carefully. The ideal case is where the *only* difference between the two conditions is the one factor that you care about. In our example, our experimental hypothesis is that the presence of tea improves friendliness. So, a much better design would be to give both groups a hot beverage. In one condition the researcher makes a cup of regular tea. In the other, it is hot water with milk, sugar and de-caffeinated tea substitute. Have we removed all the confounds now? Well, not quite. . . .

Are we sure that the two drinks taste the same? We could improve the research by also running a little taste test before the main experiment, to see if other participants can tell the difference between the two drinks, or whether they have a preference for one over the other. This is good, but even assuming that the two drinks taste the same, there is one confound remaining.

In our current design, when the researchers hand over a hot cup, they know whether it has tea in it or not. You may find it surprising, but we have good evidence to believe that the knowledge that the researchers have about the experimental condition has the potential to influence the participants' behaviour and change the results.

Experiments in schools, for example, have involved a scientist entering a classroom and taking some children out of the room for 'cognitive testing'. The teacher was told which children scored in the 'highly intelligent' category. Later, the scientist returned to the classroom. They asked the teacher to grade the children's performance, and carry out their own tests.

In fact, no real 'cognitive testing' took place in the first instance. The scientist picked some children at random and told the teacher that they were highly intelligent. This false information had two effects. It increased the teacher's estimation of the students' performance. But it also increased the students' performance on the second test. What probably happened is that the teacher formed a positive opinion of the 'highly intelligent' students. They then gave them more attention, called on them to answer questions and perhaps gave them questions to stretch themselves. In this way, the teacher's expectations changed the children's behaviour and their test scores.

Similarly, in the course of a social psychology experiment, if a researcher has knowledge about the condition and expects participants to react in a certain way, that expectation can change the participants' behaviour. So an even better design for our experiment would have a second researcher make the two drinks, one real tea and the other not, in a red and blue mug. The drinks-maker would then hand the mugs to the other researcher, without saying which drink was which. Now we have something approaching a good design. The only difference between the two conditions is the presence or absence of tea. But there is still one thing left to worry about. . . .

Operationalisation: Turning concepts into things you can count

Operationalisation is what makes social psychology a science. It is the process of taking a concept – conformity, prejudice, happiness, guilt, relief, attraction, boredom – and turning it into something that we can observe and measure. For example, with the tea experiment, we said that we wanted to test if it makes people nicer. How do we operationalise this? What is the correct measure for 'niceness?

Of course, in sciences like physics and chemistry they have it easy. They have scales, speedometers, litmus paper and thermometers. All these devices can measure a concept like mass, mass, acidity and heat and put a number on it. Easy. But we have no gadgets with dials and read-outs that can tell us how happy people are, whether they like someone or whether they are obedient. So in social psychology, we have to work very hard to come up with ways that we can measure and quantify these things.

Often, we can just ask people to give us the numbers. 'How happy are you, on a scale from 1 to 7?', for example. But often, asking people questions like this doesn't work, because we are measuring an unconscious process that they can't tell us about, or because they feel pressure to give a socially acceptable answer, or because we don't want them to know what the experiment is studying. This is the great challenge of social science, but it's one of the reasons that it can be an unusually creative science. Here are some real examples of operationalisations in social psychology:

- ✔ **Liking.** An experimenter interviews the participant. During the interview he subtly mimics the participant's posture and gestures, to see if that makes him more likeable. At the end of the interview, the experimenter 'accidentally' knocks a box of pencils off of the table. Liking is operationalised as the number of pencils that the participant helps the experimenter pick up before leaving.

- ✔ **Attraction.** Female researchers gave a survey interview to male participants while they were standing on a low bridge or a high bridge. At the end of the survey they gave them a phone number to call so that participants could find out the results of the survey. The researchers weren't interested in the survey at all. They were operationalising interpersonal attraction as whether or not the participants called back the researcher and asked for a date. Participants were more likely to do this if they had met the researcher on a high bridge. They had mistaken the fear that they felt standing on the high bridge for arousal towards the other person.

- ✔ **Obedience.** Participants walked around a field in groups. They either wandered at their own pace or marched in time with each other. Later they were ordered to throw handfuls of small grubs down a chute that led into a grinder. Obedience to authority was operationalised as the number of grubs that they threw down the chute, following these orders. No grubs were hurt, as the chute actually led off into another box. But participants threw more down the chute if previously they had been marching together.

You will see a great range of other operationalisations in this book. For each, the question you have to ask yourself is – does this operationalisation measure what it is supposed to measure?

The first social psychology experiment

Though it is hotly debated, the first social psychological experiment was probably the one performed by Norman Triplett at Indiana University in 1898. He was watching bike riders train, and noticed that times were faster when people rode in groups compared to alone. He carefully excluded various physical factors. The effect was not due solely to the lead bike rider breaking the air currents, for example, or because people pedal in a more regular rhythm when they can see others. He concluded that people were more motivated to perform when in the presence of others. In other words, he gave one of the first *social* explanations for an individual's behaviour, and he termed it *social facilitation*.

Social facilitation refers to the finding that people perform tasks better when they are in the presence of others. It's been shown to be true even for cockroaches, who speed though mazes faster when being watched by other cockroaches. However, Max Ringelmann, a European researcher, tried to investigate the same phenomena. He asked people to chop wood, either alone or in groups. He found that people in groups tended to chop *less*. He argued that this was because they could see others were performing the task and so were less motivated, and termed this *social loafing*. This story, from the first ever social psychology experiment, has two important lessons for us. Firstly, you have to be very careful in generalising from one situation to another. Secondly, you have to be very careful generalising from one culture to another, as we see in Chapter 17.

Understanding Experiments and Statistics

Now you understand something of the power and the difficulties of the scientific method. In this section, I show how to apply that understanding to the experiments that you read about in this book, in the media and in scientific articles. To do this, you need a basic grasp of scientific jargon and statistics. Long technical words and alien mathematical language is what puts off many people from grappling with scientific research. But it needn't. In the later section 'Taking to heart experimental terminology' I show how a smattering of scientific jargon is enough to unlock the most hard-to-read social psychology study. And you don't need to know how to carry out any complicated calculations to understand why scientists use statistics and what they can reveal. I demonstrate that if you understand some basic ideas behind statistics, you see how they allow scientists to collect evidence for their theories. I also describe how you can apply these ideas when reading about the experiments in this book and elsewhere.

For this section, imagine an experiment that studies how people conform to those around them. (You can read about real experiments on this topic in Chapter 13.) We set up an experiment where participants are asked to go up two floors in a lift. Before taking the trip themselves, they watch other people call the lift by doing a quick double-press of the button. When the participants call the lift, will they do a double-press too? Rationally, we all know that one button press is enough to call the elevator, but people are disposed to conform to other's behaviour even when they have no rational reason for it.

We want to study one thing in particular. Are people more likely to conform to the behaviour of other people who are in the same social group as them? In this case, we are going to have participants from University College London. The other people they observe will all be actors following my instructions. They will be wearing clothing that identifies them as either University College London students or as Imperial College London students from across town. Our research question is this: will our participants' conformity be determined by college membership?

Taking to heart experimental terminology

As with all disciplines, experimental design has its own jargon. Making the effort to understand these terms is worthwhile though, as it can really help clarify your thinking. When you read about an experiment try and identify these different elements to help you grasp the structure and logic of the experiment, and so judge its strength.

Participants

These are the human beings who took part in the experiment. We used to call them 'subjects', and you still come across that word in older research papers (or from older researchers). In our example experiment, the participants are students from University College London.

Independent variables or experimental conditions

These are things that the researcher controls. Sometimes we say that they *manipulate* these variables. In our example, we are manipulating the independent variable of the social group of the passers-by. Or, we may say that this experiment has two experimental *conditions*: the in-group condition (passers-by are wearing UCL clothing) and the out-group condition (they are wearing Imperial College London clothing).

Dependent variable

This is the main thing that the researcher measures. It's the focus of the experiment and the predictions that the researcher has made. If you see a table or a graph of some data, it's almost certain to be of the dependent variable.

In this example, we want to study conformity, which could refer to many different types of behaviour. We have *operationalised* conformity here to one particular behaviour: pressing an elevator button twice after seeing others do so. This is something specific that we can measure. We could also have operationalised it as how long it takes participants to do their first double-press, or how many times after that they repeat the action. We could even measure how hard they press the button each time.

Experimental hypothesis

This is a statement that connects the independent variables with the dependent variable. It is the crux of the experiment: it is the point where the data meets the theory. In our example the experimental hypothesis is that the group membership of the passers-by will influence the degree of conformity displayed by participants.

Null hypothesis

This is the statement that there is no connection between the independent and dependent variables: that the experimental hypothesis is wrong. So here, our null hypothesis is that the clothing of the passers-by will have no effect at all on the levels of conformity displayed by participants.

Covariates

These are things that the researchers may measure, but they are not the focus of the experiment. For example, the researcher may keep track of the age of participants because they expect older participants to make decisions more slowly. This age effect is not really relevant to the experimental hypothesis, so the researchers simply keep track of the ages of participants so that they can account for them in their analysis.

Descriptive statistics

These are numbers or graphs that summarise the data. The most common example is the average values of the dependent variables in different conditions.

Inferential statistics

These are the statistical analyses that weigh up the differences that were found in the data. The results of the analyses are presented in many ways, but usually a p value is reported. This is the probability that the differences found were due to chance. If the p value is less than 5 per cent (usually written as $p < 0.05$) then the differences are said to be *statistically significant*. In other words, they are not due to chance.

Remember *statistical significance* has a precise statistical meaning of something not being due to random chance alone. 'Significant' results are not necessarily important, newsworthy or exciting (although the researcher who found them probably feels that they are). So when writing essays about research, be careful to be clear about which sense of the word you are using.

In science, we can never really prove that a theory is true. This may sound pessimistic, but it is an essential part of the scientific method. All we can do in science is use evidence to reject or *falsify* a hypothesis or a theory. An experiment is like an axe: all it can do is chop things down. Experiments never directly prove that a theory is right; all they can do is provide indirect support by rejecting all the other theories until only one plausible theory remains. For example, sometimes you hear people say things like 'evolution is only a theory: science has never proved it'. Well, that's true, but only in the sense that science never proves that any theory is positively true. But what the theory of evolution has done is assembled an enormous amount of convincing data proving that other competing theories are false. So though it hasn't been 'proved', overwhelmingly, evolution is the best theory that we have to explain the data we have. And that's as good as we get with the scientific method.

Drawing conclusions

The scientific method has rules determining what you are allowed to conclude, given your data and your inferential statistics. When social psychologists review each other's papers, they pay extremely close attention to these rules and won't allow the paper to be published if they think the rules have been broken.

Often, the most important outcome of a researcher's statistical analysis is the p value – the probability that the results were due to chance or due to a real effect of the experimental manipulations. The convention is that if the probability is greater than 5 per cent, then we conclude that the differences between conditions were just due to random chance. In this case, the null hypothesis is supported and the data don't allow you to say anything much at all. In this case, you'd find it very hard to get your experiment published in a journal, because your data allow you to say very little.

But, if the inferential statistics say that the results have a less than 5 per cent chance of occurring by chance, then the differences are judged to be too large for random chance. In this case, they are called *significant* differences: this means that the null hypothesis can be rejected.

Significant results do not prove that the experimental hypothesis is true. All they show is that you can reject the null hypothesis. In other words, you have proved that there is some connection between your independent and dependent variables. That connection could be the one described by your experimental hypothesis, or it could be some other explanation that you have not yet ruled out or even thought of.

What does this 5 per cent significance level really mean? Think back to the example of the suspicious lucky coin in the sidebar 'Capturing randomness' earlier in the chapter. We said that if you got 59 or more heads, the scientific convention would be to conclude that the coin was not fair. But remember, it's not the case at all that the coin is *definitely* fair if you get 58 heads, but your friend is *definitely* cheating if you get 59. It's just that as the number of heads increases, we know that the odds of it being fair get increasing lower. Similarly, it is not really the case that an experiment with a p value of greater than 5 per cent has found nothing at all, but an experiment with a p value of less than 5 per cent is certain to have genuine and real differences.

The 5 per cent mark is entirely arbitrary. We just plucked the figure out of the air about 100 years ago and never got round to changing it. The 5 per cent mark was a rough compromise between what people thought was very unlikely (a 1 per cent chance) and not that unlikely at all (a 10 per cent chance). No real scientific or mathematical basis for it exists at all.

You may feel a bit surprised about this. We have a very rigorous scientific method detailing how experiments are designed. We have complex statistical techniques to quantify probability with great precision. And all of these highly sophisticated tools are aimed at a target – the 5 per cent significance level – that is just made up. Seems strange, doesn't it? Does it mean, for example, that 5 per cent of all psychology experiments that you read about are probably just due to chance? That's one in 20 experiments in every journal and textbook that are simply wrong!

Luckily, this is not the case. Social psychology, like other sciences, has a practice of *replicating* results. This means that after someone runs an experiment, other researchers in other laboratories across the world try and copy the experiment exactly and get the same results. If they don't, we go back to the drawing board and try and figure out why. So even though each individual experiment has only got to pass the 5 per cent significance level, overall, through a process of replication, we can build up a set of ideas and data that are solid and reliable.

Strengthening evidence

In the past few years, many researchers have become worried about the standards of evidence in our field, and in particular our reliance on the 5 per cent significance level. There are two reasons for concern. One is that we are not spending enough time replicating results and sharing the replication data. There are some experiments, the argument goes, that were not adequately replicated before or after they were published in high profile journals and written into textbooks. And if people do try and replicate the experiment, but don't get the right results, no one knows about it because they can't publish an experiment that has 'failed' to replicate. These practices run the risk of allowing weak results to become accepted knowledge.

The other concern is more serious. Several high-profile cases of scientific fraud have occurred recently, where researchers have simply made up data or fiddled their results to get significance. If we aren't replicating results enough, and if we are only relying on the 5 per cent significance level, the concern is that these cases of fraud will go undetected.

The good news is that many people in social psychology are trying to tackle these problems head on. Firstly, they are setting up journals, websites and lab groups that are focused on systematic replications and sharing of data, regardless of the results. Secondly, social psychologists are becoming increasingly sophisticated in how they handle their data. Rather than just relying on a *p* value, providing statistics that give a more in-depth view of the size and the nature of the effect is becoming increasingly common. Many journals ask researchers to publish all of their data online too, so that other researchers can independently analyse their results.

Social psychology's problems of fraud and non-replication have even reached the popular media in the last few years. The downside is some temporary embarrassment and the fact that that some 'textbook' results may have to be re-written. But the upside is that these problems have provoked a vigorous re-evaluation of how we carry out research in social psychology that can only strengthen our science.

Recognising good and bad social experiments

The results of an experiment are only as good as the quality of the experiment itself. I argue above that as social psychologists, we have to be very wary of common sense. Believing the conclusion of an experiment just because it agrees with what you thought in the first place is very easy. A good scientist always weighs the strength of the experimental methods and the evidence, rather than the appeal of the conclusion.

For example, one study asked whether differences between males and females could be observed in very young babies. This is a good question to ask. Some people think that differences between the sexes are hard-wired into our biology, others that our culture expects boys to act one way and girls to act another way, and that children slowly learn this from society as they grow up and act accordingly.

So the researchers tested their hypothesis. They found babies who were younger than two weeks old by getting the hospital records from a maternity ward. They observed those babies and counted simple things about their activity, like how much they moved their limbs and how often they cried.

They found that boys were more active. Not a lot, but there was a statistically significant difference. They waggled their arms and legs more. Also they cried more and were louder. This conformed with the belief that many people have that boys are noisier and more energetic than girls, and showed that this difference was present very early on, presumably before the boy and girl babies could learn how they were 'supposed' to act. So, is this good evidence that such differences between the sexes are innate?

Well, in this case, there was a confounding variable. It turned out that the hospital that gave the researchers the birth records was in New York, and it served a predominantly Jewish area of the city. And often, eight days after a Jewish boy is born, he is circumcised. So in fact, there is another explanation for why those boys may have been waggling their legs a little more and crying a little louder.

Of course, other studies have been done since, and researchers have found some slight differences between boys and girls. The point of the story is that good scientists have to be incredibly careful to avoid confounding variables, weaknesses in their experiment design and problems in their analyses. They can't simply agree with a conclusion because it seems to be true.

What I would like you to do is keep many of the ideas from this chapter in your mind as you read about the experiments in this book and elsewhere. See if you can think of alternative explanations for any finding or claim. At the end of this book in Chapter 18 I give you a checklist of things to ask when you read a claim in social psychology. But for now, be inquisitive, sceptical and constructive. Soon enough, you'll be making up experiments yourself.

Part II
Understanding Attitudes and Actions

Five Things You Need to Know about Attitudes

- **Knowing what an attitude is:** An attitude is the value the person places on something, and researchers often refer to that 'something' as the *attitude object*. An attitude is an evaluation, at the simplest level, as to whether or not the attitude object is good or bad.

- **Understanding your ABC:** Every attitude has three dimensions. These are Affect (attitudes embody feelings and emotions), Behaviour (attitudes connect to the way you actually behave) and Cognition (attitudes are expressed in thoughts and speech). It's as easy as ABC.

- **Getting what attitudes do:** Attitudes have four basic functions: The knowledge function (they help you make sense of the world); the utilitarian function (they can serve a practical purpose, and achieve goals); the ego defence function (they help you to have a positive view of yourself); the value-expressive function (they express values fundamental to who you are).

- **Attitudes can be measured:** By asking the right questions in the right way, you can establish a subject's basic attitudes on any subject. Ask a lot of questions to a lot of subjects, and you can measure attitudes society-wide.

- **Attitudes can be influenced by asking questions in the right way:** Even when people tell you their attitudes towards something, these stated attitudes don't necessarily match up with how they're going to behave in the future, or what they *really* think. Exactly how the researcher asks the question can strongly determine the answer.

For Dummies can help you get started with lots of subjects. Visit www.dummies.com to learn more and do more with *For Dummies*.

In this part . . .

✔ Understand all about attitudes: What they are, what they do, and how you measure them.

✔ Go in search of implicit attitudes, the connections between your ideas, thoughts and feelings which run beneath your everyday awareness.

✔ Discover the links between the attitudes governing what we think and feel and how they make us behave in the world.

Chapter 4

Appraising Attitudes: The Troublesome Atoms of Social Psychology

*A*ttitudes are the set of likes, loves, peeves and preferences that encompass your opinion of the world around you. Attitudes are vitally important, affecting how people conduct their personal relationships and how they organise wider society. In democracies, people's attitudes select leaders or throw them out of office. If a society is consumer-based, people's attitudes towards a product can bring a company riches or ruin.

Consider the Internet for a moment. People often think of it as a massive store of knowledge where they discover information by reading newspapers or turning to Wikipedia. But social psychologists see Internet users as not consuming knowledge, but trading attitudes: sharing pictures and articles, 'liking' each other's Facebook posts and watching particular videos because millions of others are watching those clips that day. Hit counters, trends, comments and 'likes' are the ways in which people's attitudes shape the Internet. When social psychologists look at the Internet, they see less of an information superhighway and more of an *attitude* superhighway. For a little more detail, see the nearby sidebar 'Think your attitudes don't count?'.

Think your attitudes don't count?

Your attitudes shape the Internet in ways that you may not realise. Companies such as Google and Facebook try and keep track of what websites you visit, what pages you like and what things you purchase. They sell this product to advertisers: bundles of information all about your attitudes. Each time you do a Google search, for example, the company uses at least 50 bits of information about you to decide which webpages to show you, which to hide and which products to advertise. Therefore, your attitudes are shaping continually the world you see online.

Measuring, understanding and predicting people's attitudes are central to their lives and to social psychology. Indeed, some experts think of attitudes as the atoms of social psychology – the fundamental building blocks of social thought. But just as scientists now understand that atoms can't explain everything that they observe, and that other particles and forces are at work, social scientists know that attitudes aren't quite as straightforward as people imagine.

In this chapter, I show you how scientists seek to understand these atoms of social psychology, introducing a few tools such as surveys and polls that psychologists use to measure attitudes. I also cover some of the forces that influence people's attitudes and reveal how problems arise when researchers rely on people declaring their 'true' attitudes. The fact is that stated attitudes don't always reflect behaviour.

Adopting an Attitude to Attitudes

Like so many terms in social psychology, the word 'attitude' is used a lot in everyday speech. Therefore, you need to be quite clear about its meaning in a scientific context.

Essentially, someone's *attitude* is the value the person places on something, and researchers often refer to that 'something' as the *attitude object*. An attitude is an evaluation, at the simplest level, whether or not the attitude object is good or bad. The technical term for this evaluation is *valence,* which in this context means nothing more than a thumbs-up or a thumbs-down.

Although a set of attitudes can be complicated, mixed up and even contradictory, individually they're quite simple. For example, I have a certain attitude towards junk food. Mostly it's a negative attitude, because I know it's unhealthy and greasy. But occasionally, when I'm in the right mood or very hungry, I have some positive attitudes towards junk food as well.

The difficult job for social psychologists is to understand such opposing attitudes, so that they can predict – and perhaps influence – when I may choose to be virtuous (nibbling delicately on a green salad) and when I'll choose to be unhealthy (gorging on a double bacon cheeseburger).

In this section, I investigate a useful way to approach attitudes, the effects they can have and how psychologists attempt to measure them.

Discovering the three dimensions of attitudes

In the 1960s, psychologists Rosenberg and Hovland provided a clear and simple way to think about attitudes. They said that every attitude has three dimensions, the ABCs of attitudes:

✔ **Affect:** The term that psychologists use for feelings and emotions. It means that every attitude has a positive or negative emotional aspect. Imagine a measurement scale going from extreme dislike at one end, through mild disliking, to liking and on to extreme love. Every attitude is somewhere along this scale. I sometimes think of this as the Marmite component: everyone has a feeling towards Marmite, whether it's positive or negative.

✔ **Behaviour.** Attitudes should connect to actions and behaviour somehow. If you say, 'I hate Marmite', and then happily eat some on toast when offered it, seem to enjoy it and buy some later, your attitude is probably *not* that you hate Marmite. In the 'Having an Attitude Problem' section later in the chapter, I explain that scientists have uncovered a puzzling and complicated relationship between attitudes and actions. But as a starting definition that tries to capture the meaning of the word, Rosenberg and Hovland thought that attitudes *should* have at least some connection to behaviour.

✔ **Cognition.** Attitudes can be expressed in thought or in speech: they have a cognitive component. If you ask someone, 'Do you like Marmite?' and he simply shrugs, unable to say anything, he doesn't really have an explicit attitude. Of course, he may well have an *implicit* attitude that you can detect in his behaviour, as I discuss in Chapter 5. But if you can't say what your attitude is, under Rosenberg and Hovland's scheme, you don't have one.

Understanding what attitudes do

You can have a certain attitude towards something for many reasons. I cover how your experiences, observations and biases produce your particular opinions and preferences in connection with making judgements about other people in Chapter 10, but here I discuss the functions that your attitudes perform: what they do for you. In 1960, the psychologist Daniel Katz described four different functions, and this framework is still useful today.

Knowledge function

Your attitudes are part of how you understand the world. Even though attitudes are subjective rather than objective facts and figures, they still help you *organise* this objective information and focus on what facts are important.

So you probably have a negative attitude towards Adolf Hitler, because of his responsibility for the Second World War and the Holocaust, and not due to the fact that he was a vegetarian and a painter.

In other words, your attitudes focus you on one set of facts over another.

Utilitarian function

Utilitarian indicates that your attitudes can serve a practical purpose. They can help you to achieve important goals. As I discuss in Chapter 13, one goal that everyone has in life is to feel part of a group. Adopting attitudes that are in agreement with other group members is a powerful way to feel closer to them. Have you ever pretended to like a band you've never heard of, or love a book you've never read, just to fit in with a group of people that you want to accept you?

Adopting attitudes can serve other functions too. Expressing a negative view of people who drink and drive, for example, can reduce that behaviour in society. This aspect of attitude function is sometimes called *instrumentality,* the key idea being that each attitude is a means towards an end.

Ego defence function

By *ego defence,* I mean that people are happier when they have a positive view of themselves. But your self-esteem can come under attack from all quarters: an F grade on an essay, a relationship break-up text on your phone or the smug look on a 6-year-old's face as he beats you at chess.

One function of attitudes is to protect people against these potentially harmful effects. If you think that the teacher who gave the grade is an idiot, that you never liked the loser you'd been dating or that you let the child win because you're a nice person, these experiences don't reflect too badly upon you. In Chapter 8, you see how people are systematically biased in how they view themselves and discover how attitudes protect you from harm.

Value expressive function

Some of your attitudes are more than preferences and whims: they express values that are fundamental to who you are. For example, equality may be an important principle to you, which determines how you react to unfairness in the world, which political parties you support and even the career that you choose. These values are some of the strongest attitudes that people hold: they're most resistant to change and have the strongest influence on behaviour.

Recent evidence shows that expressing your core values seems to boost your mental functioning. If you want to perform better on a test, have more will-power to resist temptation or be a more insightful and effective negotiator, try writing down a little list of your own core values beforehand.

Finding ways to measure attitudes

As you know, people measure attitudes by asking other people. Some surveys and questionnaires ask about objective facts, such as your height, weight or income, but these aren't attitudes. The questions that measure your attitudes are ones that seek your subjective opinion about something (are you happy with your weight? Do you think you should be paid more?).

Subjective questions can be simple and direct (such as whether you like Marmite) or multifaceted, asking about many different aspects of an attitude. For example, to investigate a person's attitudes towards France you may ask: 'Would you go on holiday to France? Do you like French food? Do you have any French friends?' By combining all these answers statistically, you can get an idea of someone's overall attitude towards France. Or you can look at the aspects separately to see whether any interesting potential contradictions exist; for example, perhaps people like the food in one country, but not the weather.

Lies, damned lies and questionnaires

The public usually think of questionnaires as a way to find out what people think. But clever and unscrupulous questioners can get the answers that they want to find all too easily. My favourite illustration comes from the UK TV show, *Yes, Prime Minister*. In one episode, two civil servants discuss the Prime Minister's plan to reintroduce National Service, where young people work in the military for a year after leaving school. The Prime Minister's keen on the idea, his inexperienced civil servant Bernard Woolley says, because a survey revealed that the voters are in favour of it. Sir Humphrey replies that in that case they should just carry out another survey to show that the voters are against it – and he shows Bernard how.

Humphrey: You know what happens: nice young lady comes up to you. Obviously you want to create a good impression, you don't want to look a fool, do you? So she starts asking you some questions: 'Mr Woolley, are you worried about the number of young people without jobs?'

    Bernard: 'Yes'

    Humphrey: 'Are you worried about the rise in crime among teenagers?'

    Bernard: 'Yes'

    Humphrey: 'Do you think there's a lack of discipline in our Comprehensive schools?'

    Bernard: 'Yes'

    Humphrey: 'Do you think young people welcome some authority and leadership in their lives?'

    Bernard: 'Yes'

    Humphrey: 'Do you think they respond to a challenge?'

    Bernard: 'Yes'

Humphrey: 'Would you be in favour of reintroducing National Service?'

Bernard: 'Oh, well, I suppose I might be.'

Humphrey: 'Yes or no?'

Bernard: 'Yes'

Humphrey: 'Of course you would, Bernard. After all you told her you can't say no to that. So they don't mention the first five questions and they publish the last one.'

Bernard: 'Is that really what they do?'

Humphrey: 'Well, not the reputable ones no, but there aren't many of those. So alternatively the young lady can get the opposite result.'

Bernard: 'How?'

Humphrey: 'Mr Woolley, are you worried about the danger of war?'

Bernard: 'Yes'

Humphrey: 'Are you worried about the growth of armaments?'

Bernard: 'Yes'

Humphrey: 'Do you think there's a danger in giving young people guns and teaching them how to kill?'

Bernard: 'Yes'

Humphrey: 'Do you think it is wrong to force people to take up arms against their will?'

Bernard: 'Yes'

Humphrey: 'Would you oppose the reintroduction of National Service?'

Bernard: 'Yes'

Humphrey: 'There you are. You see Bernard? The perfect balanced sample.'

These examples all use yes or no questions, but most questionnaires in social psychology use what's called a *Likert scale*. These questions ask you to give a graded response along a labelled scale. For example, you may ask, 'Do you like Marmite? Please answer from 1 to 7, where 1 means "not at all" and 7 means "very much".' These graded responses better reflect people's mixed attitudes which – Marmite aside – are rarely polarised to black and white answers and are more often painted in shades of grey.

By asking a large number of these questions to a very large number of people and carrying out sophisticated statistical analysis methods, psychologists have an excellent way to measure and understand people's attitudes. As the sidebar 'Lies, damned lies and questionnaires' reveals, however, things aren't quite so simple.

Having an Attitude Problem

Social psychologists have an attitude problem! Perhaps I'd better rephrase that: they have a problem with attitudes. Although people have a strong sense of what their own attitudes are and social psychologists have a straightforward way to find out these attitudes using questionnaires (as I describe in the preceding section), that's where the good news ends.

Social psychologists have two large issues with attitudes. Even when people tell you their attitudes towards something, these stated attitudes don't necessarily match up with much about the following two things:

- ✔ How they're going to behave in the future.
- ✔ What they *really* think.

These problems are due to the fact that the attitudes that people convey to researchers can be heavily influenced. Exactly how the researcher asks the question can strongly determine the answer.

Read on to discover some surprising examples of how people can be influenced when giving their attitudes (even completely contradicting themselves within the course of a single interview) as well as a few specific ways in which answers about attitudes can be biased.

Examining the relationship between attitudes and behaviour

In this section, I consider the link between attitudes and behaviour and test the idea that attitudes are seen as things that cause behaviour.

Next to each question below put a number between 1 for 'strongly disagree' to 5 for 'strongly agree':

- ✔ Engaging in regular physical exercise three times a week promotes good health.

- ✔ Eating a variety of foods each day, including five or more servings of fresh fruits and vegetables, contributes to wellness.

- ✔ It is essential that all citizens exercise their right to vote if government is to reflect effectively the will of the people.

- ✔ Homelessness is a serious social problem that needs attention.

What was your average response? For most people it's around 4.

Now answer these questions, using the same 1 to 5 system:

- ✔ I take time to engage in regular physical exercise at least three times a week.

- ✔ I consistently eat at least five servings of fresh fruits and vegetables each day.

- ✔ I voted in the last election for which I was eligible.

- ✔ I've recently done something to address the problem of homelessness, such as making a contribution, talking with a homeless person or writing to my local politician.

What was your average this time? I guess it's a lot closer to 1. At least, it is for most people. Why should this be?

The first set of questions asks about your attitudes towards certain issues and actions and the second set asks whether you carry out the actions that would reasonably follow from those attitudes. Almost everybody who does this test comes away feeling like a guilty hypocrite because people's attitudes don't seem to reflect their actions very well at all. For more background, read the nearby sidebar 'Attitudes don't always reflect actions'.

Attitudes don't always reflect actions

The discovery that attitudes don't always reflect actions came as a great surprise to early social psychologists. Richard LaPiere, a professor at Stanford University, gave a powerful demonstration of the disconnect between attitudes and behaviour in the 1930s. He travelled around the US with some colleagues from China. At the time, many people in the US held a strong negative stereotype about Chinese people. LaPiere wrote to motels and restaurants along the route, asking whether they'd accommodate him and his Chinese guests. Of the 128 who wrote back, 92 per cent told him that they'd refuse to serve Chinese customers. A strong negative attitude indeed. But when he travelled round the country, visiting the same hotels and restaurants, the Chinese travellers were treated with courtesy in 249 out of 250 establishments, with only one turning them away. Remarkably, the powerful negative attitudes didn't predict behaviour.

In 1969 the psychologist Allan Wicker carried out a survey of the research that had measured people's attitudes towards something and then also measured their behaviour. The studies had asked people what they thought about church attendance and then measured how many times they went each week, and measured students' attitudes towards cheating and then counted the number of times they cheated on tests. Across 42 such papers, Wicker found that the average correlation coefficient was around 0.15. If you don't know statistics, trust me that this is remarkably low. In mathematical terms, it means that 2.25 per cent of the variance in a person's behaviour on average can be attributed to his attitudes. In everyday terms, of all the factors that cause you to go to church, cheat on a test or be courteous to a customer of a certain race, only about 2 per cent of them are your explicit attitudes.

Common sense suggests that explicit attitudes should cause behaviours, but this isn't happening. Why? The elegant and surprising answer is that common sense has things backwards. Social psychology shows that often it is behaviours that determine attitudes. I discuss this fascinating idea and the evidence behind it in Chapter 6. For now, you just need to take on board that asking people what they think about something is a surprisingly unhelpful way to predict how they'll behave.

Feeling the force . . . to be consistent

I now want to consider the results of a study that shows that people appear to have a weak memory for the choices that they make, which is very interesting from the point of view of a cognitive psychologist. But for the social psychologist, the experiment is a powerful demonstration of the power of *consistency* over explicit attitudes.

People are quite happy to endorse beliefs that aren't their own and give elaborate reasons for them, just so that answers appear consistent. (To see a pop-culture example of how questioners influence answers, check out the earlier 'Lies, damned lies and questionnaires' sidebar.)

Researchers Lars Hall and Petter Johannson interviewed people on the street about a range of political issues. The researchers gave participants a questionnaire that asked, for example, about greater controls on immigration. The person had to put a cross somewhere along a line between 'strongly in favour' and 'strongly against'. After filling in the questionnaire, the respondent handed it back to the researcher, who looked at it and asked some follow-up questions, such as, 'I see you marked here in favour of immigration controls; can you tell me why?' Then the person gave a series of reasons.

A standard political survey, you may think. But in the middle was a sleight of hand. While the participant was filling in the survey, the researcher was looking over the participant's shoulder and copying the answers onto another answer sheet. The researcher mimicked everything, even the person's handwriting, but with one difference. On some questions, where the person put a cross on the 'against' end of the scale about immigration controls, for example, the researcher reversed the response and put a cross on the 'in favour' end. When the person returned the answer sheet, the researcher stuck the new version on top of it and handed the sheet back.

One major surprise was that most people didn't realise the deception at all. They didn't notice that some of their answers had been reversed. Plus, many went on to give a set of entirely reasonably explanations for the political position *that was the exact opposite of what they believed.* So the person who first said that he was against greater controls on immigration, moments later saw his cross next to 'in favour', and rather than object that that wasn't what he thought, he'd explain to the researcher that he was concerned that the healthcare system couldn't cope with an increase in population, and that he was worried that new immigrants may take the jobs of local people.

The experiment shows the strong need that people have to appear consistent when they answer a researcher's questions, even though they aren't.

Looking good for the person with the clipboard: People want to be liked

The Hall and Johannson experiment in the preceding section suggests that people want to appear consistent in order to present themselves in a good light. People also use other ways to appear nice, too.

Imagine meeting someone at a party and introducing yourself. You may say something like: 'I'm a student and I like live music.' But you probably don't start the conversation with: 'I'm a racist and I really don't like poor people.'

When you talk to people you meet, many factors influence the things you say to them. What you really think and feel is one factor, and the desire to look like a reasonable person is another: hence the desire to give consistent, coherent answers that make sense. Chapter 14 describes how researchers can use many of these factors in persuasion to influence actively your opinions, but here I consider that these aspects can cause considerable problems if you want to find out what people *really* think. And if you want to predict how people will behave in the future, well, that's an even bigger problem.

When people talk to people – even researchers – they want to give a good impression of themselves. We call this a *self-presentation bias*. Sometimes presenting themselves well is more important for people than being accurate or honest with their answers. Historically, this self-presentation bias has caused problems for researchers.

Exit polls asking people to say how they just voted are performed by pollsters standing outside of voting stations on election day. In America, the companies performing these polls have noticed a strange quirk. When they compared the result of the polls to the true result of the election after all the votes were counted, they found that the polls consistently overestimated the votes for the Democratic Party. The difference was particularly noticeable in the 2004 election, which had a high turnout and was a very close race. It's understandable that the exit polls would be inaccurate, as not everyone wants to say how they voted, but why would they consistently err in favour of the Democrats?

One clue that the pollsters found is that the discrepancy between the poll and the true results was greatest in the precincts where the exit poll personnel were female graduate students. Also, many of the people who talked to the pollsters were older and male. Separate studies showed that older males held the belief that young females were, on average, more likely to support the Democratic Party.

Generally speaking (as I discuss in Chapter 15) people like people who are similar to themselves. Therefore, researchers hypothesised (and later experiments confirmed) that males are more likely to tell young female pollsters that they voted for the Democratic Party, in order to appear more likeable. Of course, not every male does so, but enough to skew the results of the exit poll. In addition, because the results of the exit polls were broadcast before the end of the voting, in such a tight race this bias may have even influenced the course of the election itself.

In some countries the use of exit poll data isn't allowed, and many people recognise that these polls aren't a very good way of judging who has won an election. They're still used in the United States, though, mostly for two reasons:

- ✔ They provide useful objective facts, such as how many people voted, their ages and genders.

- ✔ They help talking heads fill up TV time while the newsrooms wait for the votes to be counted.

Even if you remove the biasing effects of a pretty, young pollster, surveys aren't always more accurate than exit polls, because answers can be biased in more subtle ways as well, as my next example shows.

Researchers Ara Norenzayan and Norbert Schwarz sent out surveys to students asking them to read a story about a mass murderer and answer questions about what drove him to commit his crimes. Each packet contained a letter on the first page from the researcher asking for the person's help. Half of the letters had a heading stating that the researcher worked for the 'Institute of Personality Research' and the other half had a heading reading 'Institute of Social Research'.

The heading was the only difference between these packets of survey materials. But the participants who answered questions from the Institute of Personality Research were about 10 per cent more likely than the others to say that the mass murderer's actions were due to something about his personality; the participants answering questions from Institute of Social Research were about 20 per cent more likely than the others to say that his actions were due to some social factor, such as violence in the media, societal pressures or an unhappy upbringing.

These results are remarkable. The participants were giving thoughtful, considered answers to difficult questions. Yet their attitudes were swayed to a large degree by one line, one incidental detail, on one page of the survey.

Influencing with frames and anchors

The precise wording of a question can subtly determine its answer. I illustrate two such ways here: framing and anchoring effects. In each case, small changes to the language or the focus of the sentence can have surprisingly large effects on the answer.

Anchoring

Here's an example that you can try on your friends. Tell them, 'When my cousin graduated a few years ago, his first salary was £20,000. What do you think yours may be?' Figure out their average response. Now ask a separate set of friends this question: 'When my cousin graduated a few years ago, his first salary was £40,000. What do you think yours may be?' Now I have no idea what your friends are like or how much people typically earn coming out of college, but I bet you that the second group give a higher average answer.

This effect is called *anchoring and adjustment:* when you ask people a question, they tend to start off from a reference point (the anchor) and then give their responses as a little bit more or a little bit less (the adjustment). This adjustment is rarely large enough to result in an accurate guess. In other words, people's estimates are dragged towards the anchor.

Framing

The President of Earth turns to the hero and says, 'Bruce/Arnie/Sylvester, there's a one in ten chance that if you fly that nuclear missile straight into the aliens' mothership, it'll wipe them out completely and contain the blast so that Planet Earth is saved and everyone can live in peace and freedom. It's so crazy, it may just work!' At this point, most people cheer our hero on. But imagine that another voice pipes up, saying, 'That means that there's a 90 per cent chance that we'll all die horribly. Either immediately from the nuclear blast or more slowly from a combination of the radiation sickness and retaliation from the aliens. Let's just not bother.' Now how do you feel about the plan?

This is an example of framing. The point is that the same choice can be framed in terms of a gain (10 per cent chance of success) or framed in terms of a loss (90 per cent chance of failure). Daniel Kahneman and Amos Tversky have convincingly shown that people are very *loss adverse.* In other words, they're more likely to make the decision if they think of the gains than if they think of the losses.

Such small changes in language can have a surprisingly large effect on answers. Elizabeth Loftus carried out a survey in which she asked people one of the two following questions:

> *Do you get headaches frequently, and if so, how often?*

Or

> *Do you get headaches occasionally, and if so, how often?*

People who answered the first question said that they suffered headaches about every three days, on average. People who answered the second said every ten days. Everyone was answering the same question about a pretty unambiguous experience – how often they get headaches – but that small changes from *frequently* to *occasionally* increased their answers by a factor of three.

The problem concerns how people interpret the words that you use in your question. In one survey, 61 per cent of Americans said that they supported the government spending more on 'assistance to the poor'. But when the same population was asked whether they supported spending more government money on 'welfare', only 21 per cent were in favour. In other words, if you ask people about individual welfare programmes – such as giving financial help to people who have long-term illnesses and paying for school meals for families with low income – people are broadly in favour of them. But if you ask about 'welfare' – which refers to those exact same programmes that you've just listed – they're against it. The word 'welfare' has negative connotations, perhaps because of the way many politicians and newspapers portray it.

Therefore, the framing of a question can heavily influence the answer in many ways, which matters if your aim is to obtain a 'true measure' of what people think. (You can discover much more about these *decision-making heuristics* as they're called by taking a class on cognitive psychology or reading one of Kahneman and Tversky's books.) And next time you hear a politician say 'surveys prove that the majority of the people agree with me', be very wary. If the questions were framed slightly differently, the minority of people would hold those views.

Phrasing matters

Of course, these problems (and opportunities!) are well known in political circles, even if they aren't discussed in public. As well as electing officials, many countries now have referendums during elections, in which the citizens give their opinion on a single issue, such as joining or leaving the European Union or allowing gay marriage.

Politicians and campaigners spend a great deal of time and effort before the vote arguing over the precise language used in such referendum questions. Do you ask people whether they want closer European integration or if they want to handover their national government powers to the European government? These points may mean, practically, the exact same thing. But as you know, people can give very different answers. Often then, the real battle between campaigners isn't over the hearts and minds of the people, but the words and phrasing of the question.

Chapter 5

Uncovering Implicit Attitudes and Associations

*L*ike the cables, pipes and wires that connect the houses in your neighbourhood, out of sight and underground, connections between your ideas, thoughts and feelings run beneath your everyday awareness. You may not realise these *implicit attitudes* exist in your mind, but nevertheless they have an influence over your behaviour.

For example, I doubt that you've ever had the conscious thought, 'I don't trust Londoners.' If I ask you whether you think that living in one part of a particular country makes someone more trustworthy, you'd probably say not. But studies show that people in the UK tend to be suspicious of people with London accents, compared to people with accents from the north-east of England. Some banks noticed this tendency and located their call centres in Yorkshire, because customers phoning found the voices of the people they spoke to more trustworthy.

In this chapter I explore where these associations in your mind originate and how researchers can measure them in the laboratory. I show the powerful effect that implicit attitudes can have on your behaviour, even when you're not conscious of them at all. This reality raises the challenging question of what determines your social behaviour: your conscious or non-conscious mind?

Bringing Implicit Attitudes into the Light

In Chapter 4, I talk about *explicit* attitudes – those that you can think or say out loud: 'I love sushi', 'I hate people who check Facebook on their phones while you're talking to them' or 'The new Star Wars movies are a huge disappointment'.

Implicit attitudes, in contrast, are the unspoken evaluations and associations in your mind, including ones that you're perhaps not even consciously aware of.

Here are just two examples of implicit attitudes that social psychologists have uncovered:

- ✔ People often connect the colour green with feelings of peace and red with feelings of anger and passion.
- ✔ People often expect Asian people to be good at maths and Black people to be good at sports.

In this section I investigate where these types of beliefs and prejudices come from, and reveal how they can be used to influence your behaviour.

Social psychologists are very interested in implicit attitudes and their effect on behaviour. As we saw in Chapter 4, gauging what people's 'true' attitudes are by asking them explicitly is surprisingly hard. They give different answers at different times, to different people, and then seem to carry out the opposite behaviour anyway. Implicit associations, however, can be measured by social psychologists without people being aware that their attitudes are being studied. So even attitudes that people don't want to admit to publically, such as negative feelings about people of different races, can be studied. At least, that is the claim of some social psychologists. As I shall discuss, not all agree.

Meeting the masters: Advertisers

In case you're wondering just how powerful implicit attitudes and associations are and whether you need to know more about them, I take a moment here to mention the real experts in the field.

Advertisers are extremely adept at exploiting the attitudes that people already hold. For example, consider the names of popular sleeping pills – Ambien, Lunesta, Sonata. Why do advertisers use these names rather than the chemical names, such as zolpidem tartrate? The reason lies in the sounds. The brand names sound familiar and soothing, the drug names jarring and alien. Similarly, they package energy drinks in silver with vivid reds and blues, and herbal teas in pastel pinks and yellows, because these colours evoke certain feelings in people of being stimulated or soothed.

As well as exploiting the existing associations in your mind, advertisers are also maestros at creating new connections. Flick through a magazine and see how many of the advertisements include a picture of an attractive young person who has nothing to do with the product. Is that woman draped over the bonnet of that sports car an example of the sort of person advertisers hope will buy the car? Was she placed there because she helped design the engine? Sadly not.

No one is stupid enough to think consciously, 'If I buy that car women are going to flop themselves over it like towels on a sunbed'. Well, almost no one. The advertisers are using her to create an association between that car and feelings of attraction a male buyer may feel. So when the buyer thinks of that car, he feels part of that attraction again.

Advertising is a billion-pound industry for the simple reason that these implicit attitudes work.

Where did that come from? The origins of implicit attitudes

Brains are remarkably good at learning patterns and regularities in the world, known as *associations*. I talk more about implicit associations in the later section 'Making connections: Implicit associations'.

I think that the most impressive example of associative learning comes from developmental psychology. Babies can't speak or fill in a questionnaire, but researchers can study them by looking at changes in their heart rate, how often they suck on a dummy and how they turn their heads and eyes towards some images and away from others. Remarkably, they found that new-born infants, as soon as they come out of the womb, can tell the difference between stories in their own language and stories read in a foreign tongue. They can even tell the difference between soap opera theme songs and other pieces of music. But how? Do they have language patterns and daytime music scores encoded into their DNA?

No: this ability is all down to the learning that takes place even before birth. In late pregnancy, the parents of these infants had taken to reading stories to their unborn children. Also, because they often can do little else at the end of pregnancy, the mothers sat on their couches and watched TV. By late pregnancy the fetuses had developed sufficiently to hear sounds. You can't hear very well in the womb (it sounds like you're at the bottom of a swimming pool), but you can hear something through the tissue and amniotic fluid. Fetuses are such incredibly advanced learning machines that they can acquire the rhythms and cadences of their native language, and even pick up on the theme songs of the soap operas.

After you're born, through childhood and into adulthood, your brain continues to be a remarkable learning machine. As I discuss in the following section, like all humans you're highly sensitive to the number of times you perceive people and objects, colours and sounds, and whether these things appear together or apart. And these experiences of the world, or the world seen through TV and films, create your implicit attitudes – all without your conscious awareness.

Here's a revealing exercise to examine your own implicit social concepts. Give it a try.

As quickly as you can, picture a scientist in your mind. Describe as much as you can of the person who immediately comes to mind. What does your scientist look like? I bet male, at least 30 years old, reasonably tall and thin, White or Asian, and perhaps wearing glasses.

Now, if I ask you explicit questions – 'Are scientists male? Do scientists have poor eyesight?' – you'd probably say, 'It depends' or 'I have no idea'. You may be a budding female scientist yourself or an ardent feminist. But the chances are that you still described a man in this exercise.

No matter what your political or feminist beliefs – that is, your explicit attitudes – you watch the same TV shows, read the same books and watch the same films.

Your personal values don't create your implicit attitudes; what does is exposure to the world and the culture around you.

Recognising the powerful force of mere exposure

The mere exposure effect is like gravity. It is all around you, all the time, gently influencing your behaviour. In fact, like gravity, the exposure effect's so pervasive that forgetting about it is easy. In fact, it is a powerful force that shapes your likes and dislikes, what you buy and what you listen to, and it may have even had a hand in where you live and what you do for a living.

If you're from Kazakhstan, or speak Kazakh, I'm afraid that this demonstration won't work for you. But otherwise, have a go and test your intuitions about the language.

Here are two Kazakh words: *tzikagt* and *solmin.* One means loving or devoted and the other means noxious or repellent. Can you guess which is which?

If you're like the participants in social psychologist Bob Zajonc's experiments, you guessed that *tzikagt* is the negative word and *solmin* is the pleasant word. Why is this? In fact, in Zajonc's experiment and my example, the words are made up – they have nothing to do with any real languages (apologies to Kazakh speakers). How can you have opinions about words that are entirely made up?

Well, the first word looks less familiar to English speakers. It uses relatively uncommon letters and strings them together in unusual ways. The letters *tz* only appear in a few rare words (like *blitz*). In contrast, *solmin* has clusters of words more familiar to English speakers. You see the words *some* and *soap* much more frequently. In fact, out of a million words that you may read, about 11,000 are likely to have the letters *so* in them somewhere, and only six have *tz*. Your positive feelings for *solmin* are caused by the familiarity of those letters and sounds. *Tzikagt* sounded like a negative word to you just because it's unfamiliar.

Zajonc called this phenomenon the *mere exposure effect.* In general, the more you perceive something, the more familiar it is and the more you like it. This reality has been demonstrated in many ways, and it has little to do with conscious awareness.

In another of Zajonc's experiment, participants were given a choice of several polygons (straight-sided shapes such as pentagons and hexagons) and asked to choose which they preferred. Most felt as if they were picking at random, but in fact one of the polygons had been presented to them in among other stimuli in a previous experiment they'd just completed. The shape was presented very quickly and immediately followed by another image. The participants had no conscious awareness of the shape at all. Despite this, they were far more likely to say that they preferred that particular shape when later given a choice.

The mere exposure effect explains why Nike, Coke and other companies spend millions getting their logo in front of people's eyes many times a day, on posters, buses, products, celebrities and even placed into films. And it also explains why the villains in English-speaking movies are more likely to have names with the letters *z*, *k* and *v*.

The appliance of Zajonc

Bob Zajonc is a big name in social psychology, and also the most mispronounced (the last name, that is, not 'Bob'!). You say it like 'science' but with a 'z' sound at the start.

The pronunciation isn't 'za-jonk', as I once said in an elevator . . . when the man himself was standing right behind me!

What letters do you like? Imagine that you're playing roulette, but the wheel contains letters instead of numbers. Write down one or two letters that you'd put your money on. Why do you think you chose them?

Do you feel lucky, punk? The reality of implicit egoism

You may have a very high opinion of yourself, or you may be feeling a bit down. But regardless of your explicit feelings about your ego, a surprising application of the mere exposure effect is to boost your *implicit egoism*. Things that are associated with you are very familiar to you, and that familiarity increases your liking. The implicit egoism effect is important because it pervades many of your decisions in life.

For example, you see one thing very often in your life that's particular to you: your name. You write it down and read it many times a day. You hear people say it to you all the time. So when you ask people to say which letter they prefer, the chances are that they pick the first letter of their first or their last names (or sometimes a nickname). If you ask them why, they probably don't know and may feel a bit embarrassed if you point it out.

The name of this effect is *implicit egoism*, and it extends far beyond which letters you think are lucky.

In a large analysis of US census data, researchers found that names were related, at levels above mere chance, to occupations and locations. In other words, if you look at all the dentists in the US, they're more likely to be called Dennis than other occupations. If you look at all the people called Louise, they're more likely to live in Louisiana than people with other names. Of course, not every lawyer is called Larry and lives in LA. The effects are small fractions-of-a-percent differences, but they are significant.

Just for fun, next time you're in a large group of people, ask about the names and jobs of everyone's parents. You have a good chance of hearing about some journalists called Jenny and some nurses called Nick (but, of course, you have to work out the probability of getting these matches by coincidence).

The data get even more surprising. In a study of school grades, researchers found that among the students getting A grades, more were named Alan and Alice than you'd expect, on average. Plus, more Betty and Bobs got Bs.

Of course, your grades in life aren't something you chose, like your favourite letters or your job. The claim is that if you are called Alan, you simply like the letter *a* slightly more than if you are called Frank. And so you value getting an A grade on your school work a little bit more. You work harder to get the grade, and end up with more As in your school record.

Of course, perhaps there are other explanations for these results. Maybe, for some reason, parents who chose the names beginning with the letter *a* put more academic pressure on their children. But experimental evidence does exist for implicit egoism being the cause of this effect. Researchers gave people a test and offered a prize if they did well. They gave the prize different names in different experimental conditions and found that people worked harder to win if the prize had the same first letter as their names. So it's not something special about Alans and Abigails: everyone works a little bit harder to win prizes that have the same first letter as their name.

So if Charlie's getting too many C grades for him to achieve his dream of becoming a chiropractor, try offering to buy him some cheese if he gets the top marks!

Making connections: Implicit associations

The mere exposure effect and implicit egoism from the preceding two sections show that the more you perceive a particular thing, the more positively you view it; that's one sort of implicit attitude. But here I want to discuss another type: *implicit associations*. These are connections *between* two concepts or things.

Whenever you perceive two things at the same time, or in a way that connects them, you discover an association between them. Like the frequency of things in your world, you can learn associations without awareness, by absorbing the patterns in the world around you.

You have many such associations that you probably aren't aware of. For example, visualise a singing bird. Is it smaller or bigger than a pigeon?

I bet that you said smaller. That's because you've implicitly learnt a pattern about the world: that most singing birds are small. Unless you're an ornithologist, this probably wasn't *explicit* knowledge that you possessed. You didn't know that you knew it; but you had the association.

People have all sorts of implicit associations about other people. Some are based on true patterns that exist in the world – that men are on average taller than women, for example. But many are based not on what you directly observe, but how people are described in conversation or portrayed in the media. In Chapter 3, for example, I discuss the stereotype that heterosexual men have more sexual partners than heterosexual women even though it can't be true logically speaking. Nevertheless, you most likely discovered this implicit association from the way that people talk about themselves and others.

Flip to Chapter 10 for more about stereotypes, the way you build up beliefs about certain groups of people and how you – often falsely – apply that knowledge to others.

Measuring Implicit Attitudes

If you run an advertising company, then you can see implicit attitudes at work by putting up billboards, running TV ads and inserting your products into TV shows and movies. Soon you would see that implicit attitudes can be created and manipulated. But social scientists don't want to just create new implicit attitudes in people, they also want to study what implicit attitudes already exist in people. In this section I discuss how experts measure those implicit attitudes, what they reveal about explicit attitudes and how they relate to human behaviour. You may well have guessed pretty quickly a central problem here: how can you probe the implicit associations in someone's mind if you can't directly ask that person (people are often unaware of their implicit attitudes)? Well, you turn to cognitive psychology, which has a well-developed toolkit for investigating thoughts and concepts. Cognitive psychologists have studied associative learning in order to understand, for example, how memory organises information and how babies learn categories of objects.

The brain doesn't store information in little individual packets, like books on a shelf or the files in your computer. Instead, it does so in a web of associations and connections. When you think of one thing (say, a family car), you're in effect picking up one part of that web and all the associated ideas and memories get pulled up a little bit too.

Priming experiments

The most common way to activate an idea in an experiment is to show someone a word or picture. So scientists may flash the word *NURSE* on the screen. This primes all the concepts that your brain associates with nurses, such as *hospital, pill, injection,* as well as specific memories you have about nurses that you've met.

Scientists reveal that this priming has taken place with cognitive psychology's favourite tool: reaction times. In a priming experiment the participant may be given the job of deciding whether a word onscreen is a proper English word (such as *TRUCK*) or a nonsense word (like *DRUCK*). The nonsense words don't matter – their role is just to give the participants a task to do in the experiment. Just before the person sees the word, she hears another word

spoken in her ear. If she hears the real word *NURSE* first she's faster in responding to the word *DOCTOR* immediately afterwards. This is because *NURSE* partially activates the concept *DOCTOR,* and so part of the job of activating that word in the brain has already been done.

The experimental result that *NURSE* primes *DOCTOR* (but not *TRUCK* or *SAUSAGE*) is a scientific demonstration that, in the mind of that participant, those two concepts are linked. Now you can probably see how experts can use this tool to investigate issues in social psychology. For example, if *NURSE* also primes the word *WOMAN* in the minds of some people, then this is evidence that they have a gender-stereotyped view of nurses as female.

Scientists use this feature of the brain to study implicit attitudes. In this section I discuss how priming experiments are a way to measure the association between two ideas in terms of reaction times (I describe the origins of priming in Chapter 5). In priming, you assume that differences in reaction times are related to differences in the way that concepts are associated in the mind. The concept of *priming* is central to many experiments in social cognition. It works because the brain stores associations between ideas and information. When you activate one idea in the brain you also partially activate, or *prime,* all associated ideas. By activate, I just mean bring to mind in some way. For more on priming, read the nearby sidebar 'Priming experiments'.

Investigating automatic activation of behaviour

The brain doesn't just store disembodied concepts like a dictionary; it also stores actions, feelings, gestures and emotions. Social psychologists such as John Bargh have shown that these aspects can be primed and that they can directly influence behaviour without you being consciously aware of it.

Imagine yourself sitting in a cubicle with a computer. It flashes up pictures of yellow blocks on screen and you have to type in the number of blocks that you see each time. You see hundreds of sets of yellow blocks. You've been doing this experiment for almost an hour, and your fingers are aching. Then the computer flashes up the words 'Error saving data. Please start the experiment again.' How would you feel at that point?

In that original experiment, a small camera recorded participants' reactions at the moment they were told that all their work had been lost. The researchers coded how aggressive and angry people appeared. Whether they frowned or cursed, for example.

The participants had been placed in two different conditions, and in one condition the levels of anger and aggression displayed by participants were much higher. The difference between the conditions was very subtle. In fact, the participants weren't even aware of it. In between each set of yellow blocks, a face flashed up on screen. The face appeared very quickly and was immediately replaced with the next image, and so the participants were unaware that they had seen anything. (This technique is called *subliminal presentation*.) Even though they weren't consciously aware of any faces at all, something about those faces changed their behaviour in one condition.

Half of the White participants in this study were subliminally presented with faces of White males and the other half with Black males. Those who'd seen Black faces displayed more anger and aggression when they found out that their work had been lost.

The subliminal presentation of their faces was enough to prime the stereotype of Black Americans in these American participants. Part of their stereotype was the idea that Black Americans are more aggressive and angry. So perception of the faces partially activated feelings of anger, which spilled out into actual aggression when the participants were given bad news.

Priming experiments are a very useful tool for studying the perceptual, social and behavioural contents of a stereotype and the way in which it's activated. For example, American participants were given lots of works on tiles that they had to rearrange into a sentence. Those participants whose puzzle included words like *Florida* and *grey* were primed with the stereotype of old people, and this caused them to walk more slowly out of the laboratory after they'd finished the puzzle. I describe more such examples throughout this book. For now I want to focus on another tool to measure implicit attitudes in the next section.

Trying out the Implicit Association Test (IAT)

The IAT is an experiment that can measure how two pairs of concepts are related. For example, it can tell you how much someone associates positive qualities with White faces and negative qualities with Black; or whether the sciences are seen as a male activity and humanities as female.

How the test works

The logic of the IAT is quite straightforward. The participants are given the job of categorising two different things into two different groups by pressing two different buttons. They repeat this process many times, and each time they can be categorising either sort of thing, because they appear at random.

For example, they have to categorise a person's name as male or female and college subjects as being in the sciences or the humanities. So onscreen they see *Janice* and they press the button for female, and then they see *Geology* and they press the button for science, and then *David, Claire, History, Physics* and so on.

Here are two crucial aspects of the experiment:

- ✔ Participants only have two buttons to use in their categorisation task.

- ✔ Researchers swap round which button is assigned to which category.

Probing your own prejudices

You can try out the IAT for yourself at https://implicit.harvard.edu, where researchers at Harvard University have put the experiment online for people to try. Over a million people have performed the experiment across the world, making it one of the largest psychology experiments ever performed.

Visit the website and choose your country from the list on the left. You can then use the IAT to measure the implicit prejudice that you hold for groups based on race, gender, body weight and sexual orientation.

When my wife did the IAT, the website told her that like most people, she associates women with humanities and men with sciences. Even though she herself is a science professor and her father was a humanities professor! Perhaps, regardless of her explicit attitudes and her career choice, somewhere in her mind she still harbours the implicit attitude that science is a man's job. Interesting, I think you'll agree.

So the first time a participant does the task, she may press the button D to categorise names as female and subjects as humanities. She presses button K for male names and science subjects. But then she's asked to do the task again, this time categorising female names and science subjects with button D and males and humanities with K. The button that participants press may seem like an arbitrary and unimportant aspect of the experiment, but some researchers argue that it can reveal participants' implicit attitudes.

Conclusions

Participants respond more quickly when they have to press the same button for things that they associate with each other. In this example, most people would be faster to respond when categorising female names and humanities subjects with one button and male names and sciences with the other. They'd be comparatively slower on the second attempt when categorising female names and sciences with one button and male names and humanities with the other.

IAT researchers look at the average reaction times with one arrangement of the buttons and subtract it from the reaction times with the other arrangement. This number, they claim, indicates the degree to which a participant associates particular pairs of concepts together.

Many IAT experiments have probed racial attitudes. Participants are asked to categorise faces as Black or White, for example, and also to categorise words as positive (*cake, puppies, cuddle*) or negative (*murder, famine, pain*). As I discuss in Chapter 4, in a questionnaire study people are very unlikely to endorse explicitly racist attitudes, because of the social stigma against blatant racism. But even participants who show no signs of racism when asked explicitly, still appear to associate Black faces with negative things and White faces with positive things. In general this happens if the American participants themselves are White or if they are Black, since, the researchers claim, both groups grew up in the same country, and so have learnt the same implicit attitudes.

Some evidence suggests that IAT scores predict behaviour better than explicit measures. One study in the US looked at nurses working in an emergency room. They had the very difficult job of deciding patient priority – whether patients were high priority for the doctor, because they were bleeding or unable to breathe, or were a low priority, because they had 'just' broken a limb or had a virus. None of the nurses held explicitly racist attitudes. Yet researchers found that the size of the reaction time difference in their IAT predicted a tendency for the nurses to move Black patients to the low priority list.

Investigating the IAT's results

Some researchers doubt the strength of these findings. The ability of the IAT to predict behaviour in the real world is heatedly discussed. But here's a deeper question – what exactly is the IAT measuring?

I think of myself as a generally non-prejudiced person. I support equality in marriage rights, for pay and opportunity. I've been involved in campaigns against the gender-typing of children's toys. I know I have some prejudices: for some reason, I can't stand golf – people who play it, people who watch it – I just get angry thinking about it. But in general I try to be open-minded.

Yet the IAT suggests that I hold negative attitudes towards people of different racial groups, that I associate women with staying at home and looking after children, and that I have many other views that I argue explicitly against. Have I been lying to myself all this time that I'm a non-prejudiced person?

If you took the IAT test yourself, you may have had the same shock. This raises the question – is the IAT *really* measuring my and your attitudes?

Researchers answer this question in two ways. As you can see, these answers disagree with each other (the debate continues in conferences and journal papers today):

✔ **Answer 1: The IAT gives a direct measure of your implicit attitudes.**
It reflects your true feelings towards different groups of people; feelings that wouldn't show up in a questionnaire about your attitudes. In everyday life you may try to cover up these negative evaluations out of politeness or because you don't want to appear prejudiced. Or you may realise that you have negative views towards, say, gay people, and you're making a sincere attempt to compensate for those views. Regardless of your motivation for behaving without prejudice in public, your real implicit prejudices exist, lurking beneath the surface. And the IAT can see them.

✔ **Answer 2: The conclusion of Answer 1 misses an important distinction.**
A crucial difference exists between the prejudiced views that someone may or may not consciously hold and that person's knowledge of specific stereotypes and prejudices in society.

For example, I'm an English male. I don't think I have any particular prejudice for or against such people. I've known good ones and bad ones. But after living in America for a long time, I have a very good sense of the stereotypes and implicit attitudes that Americans associate with English males: they're effeminate, intellectual, pretentious and snobbish.

They talk about fair play but are morally suspect. They have bad teeth and yet are inexplicably attractive to some women. They play cricket, drink tea and love the Queen.

Now imagine I took an IAT probing my implicit associations to English people. It may well find that I associate English people with cricket, tea and intellectuals. But this is just a reflection of my knowledge of the stereotype – not the fact that I genuinely hold those prejudiced beliefs myself.

Similarly, if you take the IAT and it shows that you have negative associations towards gay people, perhaps that's simply reflecting your knowledge of the cultural stereotype. You've taken on board that one stereotype of gay people is that they're bad at sports, effeminate and flamboyant. You may have discovered that this stereotype exists by observing how people are teased in school or from watching how gay people are portrayed on TV and in films.

You'd have to be spectacularly unperceptive to live in society and not be aware of the stereotypes that are attached to gay people, women or Muslims. And that knowledge of stereotypes in society is what shows up in the IAT test. Not necessarily your *own* implicit attitudes, and certainly not your hidden explicit attitudes.

Discovering how explicit and implicit attitudes interact

The two views in the preceding section seem diametrically opposed, but in a sense they're both true. To explain how, I look at one other experiment in this section. This one is particularly clever because it measures explicit and implicit attitudes at the same time.

In one experiment, participants were given an item and then asked to click one of two buttons with their mouse pointer: *like* or *dislike*. The items were things such as *cake* and *holiday*, for which most clicked *like*; or *cancer* and *headache,* for which they clicked *dislike*. The researchers were especially interested in one item in particular, the concept *black people*. The participants, who were White American students, all clicked *like*. But on the way to clicking the *like* button, the participants' mouse pointer swerved ever so slightly towards *dislike*.

If you were watching the mouse pointer, you may not even notice anything different. But the researchers carefully analysed the trajectories of the pointers and found a systematic deviation towards the *dislike* button when participants were explicitly declaring that they liked Black people.

This result is a wonderful demonstration of the causal complexity of beliefs and behaviour. People's actions – even simple ones like clicking a mouse – are the outcome of many influences that compete and interact. Participants' responses in this experiment were dominated by their explicit attitude that they liked Black people. But in the moment that they made that decision, they also activated their knowledge of all the negative associations that American society has towards Black people.

The experiment shows that you can't draw a clear line between the explicit attitudes that you consciously hold and the implicit associations that you happen to absorb from the world. You can't fully separate these attitudes because both can have an influence on behaviour.

For example, a male manager may sincerely believe that men and women are equally capable for a research job he's advertised. But what if he has a stack of 100 applications to get through very quickly? That slight difficulty he has pairing females with science – that slower reaction time that shows up in the IAT – may be enough that a few women who were borderline cases end up on the reject pile instead.

Or imagine that you're in an elevator and someone calls for you to hold the door. As you reach out, you notice that the person's Black. Those slight negative associations – that drag the mouse pointer towards the dislike button – may be enough to slow you down a little so that you don't quite hit the button in time.

My point is that implicit associations may not reflect your own views, but simply those you've absorbed from the world around you. They may only have a small effect on your behaviour. But the consequences of that behaviour can be massive for the person who doesn't get the job interview, who sees the elevator doors close and who goes on the low priority list at the emergency room.

Therefore, you have to be very careful, I think, with the way that different social groups are portrayed in the media. Some people say that the stupidest character on a TV show always being a blonde female is okay, as is the fact that Muslim characters always turn out to be terrorists. It's fine, the argument goes, because everyone knows explicitly that not all blondes are dumb and that not all Muslims are evil. But I argue that if all these associations are repeatedly seen on TV, they seep into people's memories and are perpetuated in society.

This situation isn't a case of 'political correctness gone mad'; it's a scientific understanding of how memory and implicit attitudes work.

Chapter 6

Investigating the Link between Behaviour and Attitudes

*H*ere are two views on the connection between attitudes and behaviour, from two giants of US history. John Adams was one of the founding fathers of the United States and a leader of the revolutionary war against Great Britain. In a letter he wrote:

> *The Revolution was effected before the War commenced. The Revolution was in the minds and hearts of the people . . . . This radical change in the principles, opinions, sentiments, and affections of the people, was the real American Revolution.*

Adams is expressing a powerful idea here: that great action requires a change in the hearts and minds of people; that attitudes and beliefs are the cause of behaviour.

But here's another view from Abraham Lincoln, who realised that sometimes the opposite is true: people's behaviour can cause a change in their attitudes. Lincoln knew that another politician, whose support he needed, disliked him immensely. Lincoln did a clever thing to change this attitude. He found out that the politician was a collector of rare books. He wrote to him, asking to borrow one of his most prized specimens. The politician grudgingly agreed, not wishing to turn down a request from the president. After loaning him the book, however, the politician became friendlier towards Lincoln, and in time offered him his support.

Forcing the issue: Behaviour shifts and civil rights

Some historians argue that Lincoln's view was proved right by a later revolution in America – the civil rights movement. In the 1950s in the South, attitudes were very negative towards racial integration. It seemed as though the White population would never accept equality with Blacks. However, civil rights activists and politicians pushed through laws outlawing desegregation. Separate water fountains, buses and schools for whites and blacks were made illegal. This was not a revolution of hearts and minds, as Adams had described: this was a revolution pushed through by law against what many saw as the will of the southern people. Yet nevertheless, when made to desegregate, after people were made to behave in favour of equality, a slow, but seismic, shift in attitudes occurred. The White Americans started to feel more favourable towards the Blacks. Of course, it was not the end of the struggle by any means, but some historians argue that the biggest shift in people's attitudes in the South was produced by this forced change in behaviour.

Why did the politician change his attitude? Well, you don't loan your most valuable possession to a man you dislike. After the politician carried out the behaviour of loaning his book to the president, it caused a shift in his attitude towards liking Lincoln.

In this chapter I weigh these two views of attitudes and behaviour against each other. Amazingly, the scientific evidence stacks up in favour of Lincoln's view. In lots of everyday situations – how you feel about your job, your partner or your children – your behaviour causes your attitudes. I will review the two powerful ideas, cognitive dissonance and self-perception theory, that explain how and why this happens.

Dealing with Conflicting Ideas: Cognitive Dissonance

No one likes a hypocrite; someone who says one thing and does another. The politicians who cut people's benefits, yet take thousands in fake expenses claims; the religious leaders who talk about the sanctity of family life and have affairs behind closed doors: these people are the lowest of the low in public opinion. Just as we find hypocrisy and inconsistency intolerable in other people, we struggle with the feeling in ourselves too.

This feeling is called *cognitive dissonance:* the state of holding a set of ideas or acting in ways that conflict with each other.

Social psychologists have found that people go to great lengths to reduce their cognitive dissonance. They create new beliefs or behave in new ways to reduce that dissonance, even when this behaviour seems plain irrational to other people. So those politicians who are cheating on their expenses claims probably have convinced themselves that they are saving the taxpayer money. The religious leader having an affair may think that it is all a test from God to prove the purity of his faith.

Here's another simple example. Say that I believe that I'm a decent and kind person. I believe that people should care for each other and that everyone has a right to basic human dignity. But tonight, I walk past a homeless person who's obviously in distress and don't stop to help. My actions don't match my beliefs, a situation that produces cognitive dissonance within me.

How can I reduce this dissonance? Well, what if I think that the homeless person brought this situation on himself? Perhaps he was drunk, had taken drugs or was in the country illegally. If he's broken the law, he doesn't deserve my help.

By creating the belief that the homeless person is undeserving in some way, I reduce my cognitive dissonance. The point isn't whether the belief is true or not, because I didn't create it to have an accurate view of the world; I invent it to reduce my dissonance.

The term *cognitive dissonance* was invented by social psychologist Leon Festinger, who was fascinated by the interaction of behaviour and attitudes. He realised not only that attitudes are a weak cause of behaviour, but also that in some cases behaviour create attitudes.

Festinger observed that when an individual's beliefs and behaviour contradict each other, the result is cognitive dissonance. He theorised that human beings have a basic need to reduce cognitive dissonance whenever they can, because it's such an uncomfortable state of mind. Thus, often people reduce the dissonance by creating a new belief or rejecting an old one.

Experiencing cognitive dissonance

Leon Festinger's curiosity about behaviour and attitudes began with his study of doomsday cults, described in his book *When Prophecy Fails.* It's worth understanding what he discovered in his study of cults. After seeing such counterintuitive and surprising behaviour in cult followers, Festinger performed a series of experiments observing the same behaviour in every-day people. His work is a wonderful example of the interplay between observation of people in the world and careful experimentation in the laboratory. As we shall see in this section, even if you haven't been in a religious cult, I bet that you have responded to the power of cognitive dissonance too.

Imagine that you've joined a cult. You don't, of course, sign up to join a cult in the first place. Everything begins quite differently. Your life isn't going very well, and you meet some people who seem kind and interested in you; you turn up to some of their gatherings. After the barbecue (of meatless burgers and vegetable kebabs) they start talking about how their lives were turned round by joining this group, and how happy they are. They talk about a charismatic leader and promise that next week you can meet him and take lessons with the group, if you want.

Soon, you're attending regular classes with the leader. They cost a fair bit of money, but you have enough in the bank and decide to reduce your outgoings by moving in to a large house on the edge of town with other group members. The leader has a magnetic personality and in private tells you that he sees great things in you. The classes are going well, and you're discovering that many things you thought were true are just lies you were told growing up. You realise that the things you cared about – money, property, family – are an illusion. With great relief you allow the group to look after your bank account and to answer the letters from your parents.

Now the leader gathers a select few followers into his room for a special revelation. He tells you that he's a reincarnation of a powerful god. He's had a vision that the world will end next Monday at midnight. He appeals for your help in preparing the rest of the group for life in the next world. Together you burn the last of your property, the mementos of your past life. You all gather on a hilltop Monday night. You've given everything to be here with your leader. You sing exuberant songs of praise and pass around a special cleansing drink to prepare you for the end. You fall asleep knowing that tonight is your last on earth.

Then Tuesday morning arrives. You're in a field surrounded by confused, muddy people. The leader has disappeared . . . but not to the afterlife; his truck is missing too, along with most of the money collected by the group.

Try to imagine how you feel. Do you still believe the strange, outlandish things that your leader taught you?

What fascinated Festinger was not only that many of the followers in such situations continued to believe, but also that they often believed *even more* in the cult leaders. Here's his theory on why. Your beloved leader's predictions have spectacularly failed to materialise and you and the others have severe cognitive dissonance. All your beliefs in the leader's teaching are entirely at odds with the continued existence of the planet. What can you do? You have two basic options:

- ✔ To jettison all your beliefs about the cult, admit that you were wrong to believe and acknowledge that you've been duped. That would require you to reverse a lot of passionately held beliefs.

- ✔ To assume that you were right to believe and that the leader was correct in his teaching. The only thing he got wrong was the tiny detail of the exact day of the end of the world.

History has many examples of people rejecting the first option and, as crazy as it seems to other people, taking the second. It's happened many times with the followers of doomsday cults. The day after the end of the world, the believers rationalise or explain away the fact that they're still alive in a way that strengthens their beliefs.

This reaction is, of course, nonsensical. If a weather forecaster doesn't see a hurricane coming, or if an economist doesn't predict a stock-market crash, you'd stop listening to them. But if an admired leader makes the most dramatic prediction imaginable (the end of the world itself) and gets it wrong, history shows that faith in that religious leader *grows*.

'That is illogical, Captain'

In one of the cults that Festinger studied, the members decided that God had rewarded their faith by deciding, at the last moment, not to destroy the world. This rationalisation served to confirm their beliefs, so resolving their cognitive dissonance.

This reasoning is remarkably circular: the failure of the world to end is taken as evidence in favour of the belief system that predicted (wrongly) that the world would end! Such tortuous logic is commonplace in the face of cognitive dissonance.

Many cults today actively exploit these psychological mechanisms. To their initiated followers, they promote what seem like bizarre, science-fiction-like beliefs. But they don't do so to begin with. The first things that you're told when joining meetings are often innocuous,

life-affirming messages. Only when people start paying for more and more classes, or commit their resources to the cult, are the more extreme aspects revealed: that the leader is a reincarnation of Jesus, that the world is run by lizard people or that all humans are aliens inhabiting human bodies.

By this point, the followers have sacrificed a lot to be members of the cult: perhaps they've given over all their money or lost contact with their families. Their behaviour has put the threat of cognitive dissonance at its height, and so their attitudes adapt to avoid it. This means believing all the teachings of the cult, no matter how ludicrous. Perversely, the very strangeness of these beliefs makes the committed followers even more likely to believe them.

Usually, the cult followers explain away the failure of the world to end in various ways. (Perhaps God changed his mind or the leader made a minor error in interpreting the dates of the Mayan calendar.) But in these cases, the failures of prophecy lead to an increase in faith.

Considering the consequences of insufficient justification

To test his theories on cognitive dissonance, Festinger placed participants in a situation where they found themselves doing something unpleasant – lying to a stranger. He termed this *induced compliance*. He wanted to know the consequences of this action – how did carrying out this behaviour influence participants' attitudes?

In the experiment, a person was first given a painfully tedious task. She was shown a chessboard of square wooden pegs and asked to rotate them each by 90 degrees in turn. Then she started again, turning each another 90 degrees. Then, thankfully for the participant, the 'experiment' finished.

But in fact the interesting behaviour was to come. While getting ready to leave, a researcher approached the participant and asked for a favour. They were short-staffed, the researcher apologised, and asked the participant if she'd mind helping out for a moment. The participant agreed, and was asked to speak to the next person who was about to take part in the experiment. The researcher asked the participant if she'd tell the next person that the experiment was really interesting and enjoyable, which was clearly a lie. For her trouble, the participant was given $1 or $20 as payment (the two experimental conditions).

The participant carried out the task, lied to the person waiting to take part and took her payment. Then – and this is the crucial measure – the participant was asked how much she *really* enjoyed the original experiment.

The results were remarkable and completely counter-intuitive. The participants who were paid $20 said that, to be honest, they didn't really enjoy the original task. It was kinda boring. But the people paid $1 claimed to have enjoyed the original peg-turning task. They may have been bored at first, but they came to like it eventually.

What's happening here? Why did the people paid *less* money to tell a lie end up believing that lie? Festinger produced an elegant explanation for this behaviour, which also explains the puzzling behaviour he observed in doomsday cults in the preceding section: people seek to reduce cognitive dissonance by creating a new belief or rejecting an old one.

All the participants in Festinger's experiment were asked to lie to the person in the waiting room. Most people don't see themselves as liars but think that they're honest, decent people. So the fact that the participants lied produced cognitive dissonance for them. How can they reduce this unpleasant experience?

The participants paid $20 have a solution. They lied because they were paid a substantial amount of money. (By today's standards, $20 is worth more like $150.) This monetary justification reduces the dissonance. It makes sense that they lied, because they were handsomely rewarded to do so.

The participants paid $1 didn't have such a solution. They lied, but they weren't really paid to do so, because $1 didn't get you very much, even in 1950.

Festinger stated that the $1 people had *insufficient justification* for their actions. These people still have cognitive dissonance. They think that they're honest people, but they lied and have no excuse. So to reduce the dissonance these participants changed their beliefs. They decided that, actually, the experiment wasn't too bad after all. In fact, they quite enjoyed it. If they enjoyed it, they weren't lying when they spoke to the person in the waiting room. With this new set of beliefs, the dissonance disappeared.

As Festinger said, 'People come to believe in and love the things they have to suffer for.' It may not be the most romantic thing to put on a Valentine card, but it has solid scientific support.

Explaining the power of fraternities

People encounter cognitive dissonance in all walks of life. For example, initiation rites are a common feature of many clubs, societies and organisations. You can see them in fraternities, in army platoons and high-school cliques. To become a member of the group, you must undergo a series of challenging and often unpleasant activities. In American universities, this is called *hazing*.

I was walking across the campus of a US university and saw three rows of young men lined up in front of a house. Though the temperature was freezing and deep snow lay all around, they were wearing only underwear. They were shuffling together to the left and then the right shouting 'bleep bleep' with each step. On the porch of the house sat another young man, wrapped in a warm coat, throwing snowballs at them. Whenever someone was hit they collapsed to the ground shouting 'bloop bloop bloop'. This was a game of human space invaders.

The fraternity member on the porch was hazing new students. If they put up with this treatment (and worse) for a week they had a chance of joining the fraternity. Now how do you think those young students feel about the guy on the porch? How would you feel about people who bullied you for their own amusement? Well, when they're accepted into the group, the young, abused frat members feel nothing but love and respect for their tormentors. They have insufficient justification for putting up with the hazing experience. After all, no rational person lies in the snow half-naked by choice.

The only way to rationalise their own behaviour, to reduce their cognitive dissonance, is to believe that the fraternity is a wonderful institution with great guys who they're desperate to live with.

Justifying it all . . . for love!

Cognitive dissonance doesn't just help explain frats and cults (see the preceding sections). It also helps to explain your everyday feelings and behaviour, too, such as persisting with lousy relationships.

Perhaps you've been in a bad relationship, looking across at the unappealing slob on the sofa, wondering how you ended up dating someone who does nothing but watch TV and eat crisps, loudly. Perhaps the thought occurs to you, 'Why on earth am I dating the person? I guess I must really love them.' Festinger would say that you have insufficient justification for being in that relationship and to reduce your cognitive dissonance, you justify it to yourself by assuming 'it must be love'.

Recently, two researchers provided an elegant demonstration of this point as it relates to how people feel about being parents. (For my personal connection to this research, check out the nearby sidebar 'Scientists versus babies'!)

Studies show repeatedly that parents, compared to couples without children, have lower satisfaction with their lives and marriages, are more likely to be depressed and less likely to experience happiness. So from a purely rational standpoint, why do people seek out parenthood? Why do they speak about being a parent in such reverential tones, describing it as the fulfilment of their lives? Why is parenthood idealised when it brings relative unhappiness?

Steven Moch and his colleague Richard Eibach asked parents how much they liked being mums and dads. They used a variety of measures, asking people to rate statements about the importance of children to estimate how many hours they wanted to spend with their children that weekend. The researchers hypothesised that cognitive dissonance influenced how parents answered these questions.

Scientists versus babies

My friend Steve visited my wife and me a few weeks after our twins were born. Life isn't easy with new-born twins, and we already had a 2-year-old as well. When I opened the door to Steve in his immaculate, well-pressed clothes, I hadn't slept more than three hours a day, had baby spit over my shirt and in my hair, and I smelt of wee and desperation. Steve was a great help that week as we looked after our three children,

feeding them round the clock, sleeping in shifts and eating the food he made. In return, I discovered much later, we gave him the idea for an experiment. Steve's basic research question was: why on earth do people go through the trauma of having children? Though to be fair, I don't think that it was only my children that made Steve ask that question.

To test their idea, they divided the parents into three groups:

- ✔ The first group was told some facts about being a parent. They were informed that it costs, on average, about $200,000 to raise a child to the age of 16 in the United States. That's the cost of food, clothes, medicines and so on. After learning of the substantial financial burden their children had placed upon them, the parents filled in the questionnaires about how much they idealised parenthood.

- ✔ The second group was told the same information about the costs, but also some of the practical benefits of being a parent. When you're elderly, you're much better off having children. You're happier and healthier if you have your children, and perhaps their children, visiting you, looking after you and caring for you in your old age.

- ✔ The last group was given no information and simply asked to fill in the questionnaires.

Who do you think loves their children more? The parents who are told only of the costs of having kids, or those who are told about the advantages as well? By now, you may have guessed the answer, but try posing that question to someone who hasn't read this chapter.

The remarkable, counter-intuitive answer is that when told *only* of the financial burden of being a parent, people idealised parenthood more, saying that they'd spend more time with their children and valued that time more. Those people had experienced the most cognitive dissonance. To remove that dissonance, they shifted their attitudes. They rationalised the financial and emotional cost of being a parent by telling themselves that being a parent was a hugely rewarding activity.

So what do you want for your birthday?

Perhaps you have a birthday coming up and are hoping that your parents are going to push the boat out this year and get you something a little special. What can you do to increase the value of your birthday present? Remind your parents of the time when you were six and it was their wedding anniversary, and you got up early and made them a breakfast of fudge?

No, to increase their appreciation of you, remind them of the time you played football in the front room, smashed their best wine glasses and tried to blame it on the goldfish. They then try and justify to themselves why they put up with you all those years. The only explanation is that they must really love you.

The research revealed that people have children despite the considerable costs and the burden because, in some way, they idealise being a parent . . . not despite those costs but *because of* them.

Of course, the researchers aren't saying that the only reason people have children is cognitive dissonance. No one doubts the considerable rewards of being a parent. The point is that parenthood tends to be idealised: the negative side of being a parent tends to get ignored and glossed over. These results are not just limited to parenting, of course. You could say the same about buying a mobile home. After being reminded of the costs of maintaining a mobile home – the fuel bills, parking fees, maintenance budget – I would predict that people are more likely to tell you that buying a mobile home was the best investment that they ever made, and that they value the freedom it brings them. Mobile homes or children: part of the reason that we love these things *despite* the costs is cognitive dissonance.

Looking at some objections to the cognitive dissonance theory

Festinger's ideas continue to generate new hypotheses and experiments to this day. Some researchers, however, aren't convinced by his theory. They think that cognitive dissonance makes some strange assumptions about how mental processes work.

The trouble is that Festinger's theory states that dissonance is produced when a set of attitudes or behaviours contradict each other. When, for example, you believe your guru's promise that the world's going to end on Friday, 13 December, and today is December 14, these two ideas clearly contradict each other and you need to resolve that dissonance somehow. But, the objection goes, human feelings and behaviours aren't usually this clearly defined. And how often do people really go through their thoughts and behaviours, checking to see whether they're logically consistent? Not very often, I expect.

In light of such objections, other theories arose, one of which I discuss in the next section.

Looking at Yourself: Self-Perception Theory

Researcher Daryl Bem thought that cognitive dissonance (which I discuss in the preceding sections) didn't reflect accurately how people think about their own thoughts. He argued that often people don't really know exactly how they feel, or that how they feel is ambiguous and changes from moment to moment.

As Chapters 4 and 5 reveal, attitudes are slippery things. Often people appear to believe quite contradictory things: they support the theory of 'giving money to people who are poor' but don't support in practice 'welfare programmes'. Humans aren't like Mr Spock in *Star Trek,* with a robotic grasp of logic and of their own minds, and so how can logical contradictions generate attitude and behaviour change? Therefore, Bem proposed an alternative: self-perception theory.

Explaining yourself to yourself

Here's how the self-perception theory works. When you see other people, you seek explanations for their actions. For example, while standing on a train platform you see a lady eating furiously and so you conclude that she's probably hungry. If two people embrace when meeting, you guess that they're in love.

Self-perception theory claims that you look at your own behaviour in a similar way and come up with conclusions. So you eat a whole sandwich while reading the newspaper, look down at the empty wrapper and then conclude, 'I must have been hungry.' You find yourself sitting opposite the same person at the dinner table for several years and assume that you're both in a loving, long-term relationship.

Self-perception theory – just like the cognitive-dissonance theory – also makes the counter-intuitive prediction that behaviour can cause attitudes. Although common sense says that you don't need to look at your behaviour

Using self-perception theory to your advantage

An old Rabbi lived in Germany. One day, some children gathered outside his house, shouted abuse and threw stones at his window. The Rabbi came outside to talk to them. 'Boys,' he said, 'I want to say thank you. I think that what you said about me is right. In fact, I want to pay you to come back and do the same thing tomorrow.' The children thought this was odd, but took the Rabbi's money. The next day they returned and shouted more abuse. Again the Rabbi came out, thanked them and paid them to come back. On the third day, the boys shouted their insults, threw stones and then knocked on the Rabbi's door. 'I'm so sorry boys,' said the Rabbi, 'You did a great job, but I don't have any more money to pay you. Will you still come back?' Angrily, the boys refused and left. They never bothered the Rabbi again.

The wily Rabbi didn't try to persuade the boys to stop their abuse, threaten them with punishment from the police or their parents, or even try to show them that their insults were wrong or hurtful. But he successfully and cleverly changed their behaviour by manipulating their self-perception.

The boys wanted to abuse and frighten him, but he walked outside and offered them money. If you were sitting across the street and saw the Rabbi hand the boys some coins after they threw the rocks, you'd assume they were doing it for the money. He made the boys perceive their own behaviour in the same way; they also concluded that they were acting in order to get paid. Like any workers, if they weren't going to get paid, they walked!

to know whether you're hungry or in love (you just know it), the predictions of self-perception theory have been repeatedly borne out. Often, attitudes follow behaviour and seem to be a way in which people explain their own actions. Read on to see how . . .

Seeing that rewards and punishments can backfire

Researchers have found that self-perception theory makes surprising predictions about how people respond to rewards. Say, for example, you want to encourage children to draw during their play time. Perhaps you offer them a reward for drawing, so that they associate drawing with the pleasurable reward.

Researchers carried out just such an experiment. One group of children were told that they would each be given a reward of a sticker after a drawing activity during class. Another group did the same activity but didn't expect to be rewarded. Then, at playtime, the paper and crayons were left out on the table. The researchers' dependent variable was how many children chose to return to drawing when they had a free choice.

The striking result was that many fewer children chose to pick up a crayon when they'd been rewarded previously. The reason, self-perception theory says, is that they 'saw' their own behaviour – drawing and getting a sticker – and assumed that the reason that they were drawing in the first place was to get the sticker. At playtime, without any grown-ups around to give out stickers, they had no reason to be drawing.

This result was surprising at the time and appeared to go directly against any sort of common-sense understanding, which said that surely people are more likely to do something if they're rewarded for doing it. That thought led to many years of programmes in schools and prisons that rewarded people for engaging in good behaviour, such as getting good grades or just staying out of trouble. The problem with these schemes is that the people, perceiving their own behaviour, assume that the reason for the positive behaviour is the reward. So behaviour may improve when the person is still in school or in prison, but when they leave and the reward goes away, so do all the improvements.

Surprising, don't you think: that rewarding good behaviour can make people behave worse!

Assessing self-perception theory

I mention self-perception theory and cognitive-dissonance theory many times during this book. You can see that they make very similar predictions about human behaviour. In fact, you can go through the examples in the earlier section 'Dealing with Conflicting Ideas: Cognitive Dissonance' – the cults, the fraternities, the bad relationships and parenthood – and explain the same results with self-perception theory. So which one is a better explanation of the relationship between our behaviour and attitudes?

Well, both theories seem to do good job of explaining the available research data and both have their place:

- ✔ Cognitive-dissonance theory is easier to apply when the attitudes and behaviour are clearly defined and easy to interpret.
- ✔ Self-perception theory is easier to apply when attitudes and feelings are uncertain or ambiguous.

So, for now, claiming that one is superior to the other is impossible.

Perhaps a third theory will appear that does a better job. As I state in Chapter 3, scientists never really prove that one theory is true above all others; all they can do is reject theories when the data allow. And right now, these two theories are still standing after all these years.

Part III
Thinking about Ourselves and Others

Five Ways to Root Out Stereotypes

- **Track them back to their sources:** People notice patterns in the social world around them, but although people are very good at noticing these patterns, they're also adept at seeing things that aren't there. They jump to conclusions, and ignore evidence that contradicts their beliefs.

- **Discover the bias in social judgements:** Many people are convinced that solid, physical differences exist between women's and men's brains, which explain and justify the different jobs and responsibilities that men and women tend to have. There's no safe evidence for this, but it doesn't stop researchers looking for and finding what they want to see.

- **Beware what you think you already know:** People pay attention to information that supports their beliefs and ignore information that contradicts them. This *confirmation bias* feeds the habit of stereotyping people, and because your stereotype guides and labels your perception, you find confirmation of it everywhere.

- **Look out for illusory correlations:** People and events that are unusual tend to attract your attention and stick in the memory. So say you see a Croatian football supporter starting a fight. You haven't met many Croatians before and the event is unusual, and so you come to the conclusion that Croatian football supporters are very aggressive people. That's an illusory correlation.

- **Don't make all your predictions come true:** When you have a certain belief, act in accordance with it and your belief is indeed confirmed, it's called a *self-fulfilling prophecy,* which is another bias in behaviour that helps to perpetuate stereotypes.

For Dummies can help you get started with lots of subjects. Visit www.dummies.com to learn more and do more with *For Dummies.*

In this part . . .

✔ Work out how to establish an identity.

✔ Understand the pitfalls and positives of self-serving bias.

✔ Learn how to understand what cause the behaviour of others.

✔ Keeping a watchful eye on bias and prejudice.

Chapter 7

Asking the Perennial Question: Who Am I?

. . . .

In This Chapter

▶ Creating a sense of self

▶ Exploring the consequences of identity

▶ Achieving success and healthy self-esteem

. . . .

*T*hroughout the ages, the question 'Who am I?' has been asked by philosophers, kings, prophets and – most of all – by mopey teenagers after breaking into their parents' drinks cabinet. Here, I am not really interested in what the philosophers or the theologians have to say; I'm not going to discuss the soul or definitions of consciousness. I'm much more concerned with that introspective teenager. In other words, I want to explore how people understand themselves. What they think their strengths and weaknesses are, what people and social groups are important to them, and what stories they tell about themselves.

Modern technology has brought questions of identity into sharper focus in recent years by providing the opportunity to form social bonds with more people than your grandparents met in their entire lives. Social media is marvellous, but it creates a special form of anxiety: self-presentation panic. Generations ago people met mostly face-to-face, when a mere glance told you a person's age, sex and probable income and background. Social media provides none of that. Twitter, Facebook and blogs present you with a blank page when you sign up, leaving you to define yourself for the world. (I relate my personal struggles with social media in the nearby sidebar 'The difficulties of defining yourself'.)

In this chapter I explore how people define their sense of self: who they think they are and how they choose to present themselves to the world. I reveal that social forces affect these inward-looking personal thoughts, which are a reflection not only of who you are, but also how you connect to the social world. In addition, I discuss how your self-concept determines your self-esteem, the extent to which you succeed in life and your response to challenges.

The difficulties of defining yourself

I find the process of signing up to social media painfully difficult, and it usually sends me into an existential panic. Do I mention my job first, because that's probably why people are looking for me? But I like to think that there's more to me than work. Do I mention that I'm a father? My family is a dominant part of my life, but it's also private. Should I say that I'm English? It used to be part of my identity when I lived in America – not because I wandered around in cricket pads sipping tea, but because it mattered to the people around me. But introducing myself to other English people that way would be strange. Do I say that I'm a Tom Waits fan? Is that cool, or does it just make me look old? Or is it retro cool?

Then I come to the horror of the profile picture. When I first signed up for Facebook, I tried to take a picture of myself that wasn't awful but didn't look as though I'd posed for it. I wasted an hour getting an apparently 'casual' shot!

Constructing Your Sense of Self

The concept of the self is what I call a knotty issue. You don't know how to unpick it, where to start, and even if you should try to unravel it. People spend many hours in church or in therapy trying to understand who they are and their place in the world. For social psychologists, you don't *find* your true self, or discover it after it has rolled under a therapist's couch. The 'self' is something that is *constructed*. It is the central character that you make up in the story of your life.

If I asked you about a close friend, I'm sure you could tell me about his character, and illustrate it with anecdotes and behaviour that is typical of him. You probably spend a lot of time looking at other people and forming an idea about who they are and what makes them tick. In fact, I'm sure that like most people you spend more time looking at the faces of others and thinking about their thoughts and actions than you do looking at your reflection or ruminating on yourself. Therefore, how people form their self-concept is an interesting question for social psychologists.

Next time you interact with a baby, try this experiment. With the parents' permission put a small, brightly coloured little mark on the baby's forehead. Use make-up or perhaps a blob of fruit yoghurt. Don't use an indelible marker pen (or place the blob on the child's upper lip, unless you want to risk her looking like Hitler)! Now carefully carry the baby to a mirror and watch what she does.

Research shows that babies younger than 18 months old reach towards the mirror, trying to touch the colourful spot; older than that and they lift a hand to their heads to touch the mark.

Here's looking at me, kid!

I'm not sure that the experiments with babies and self-identity reveal so much about an understanding of the self as they do about mirrors. Like many experiments in developmental psychology that claim infants acquire a concept at a particular stage, you can find adults regularly struggling with similar tests. For example, at many sporting events a large video screen shows close-ups of the actions. During a lull in play, the camera often lingers on the crowd. You can always see that it takes a good few moments before the people projected onto the display board recognise that they're looking at themselves. Clever chimps!

Some researchers take this behaviour as evidence that at around the age of 18 months, infants develop a sense of *self*. They realise that they too are an object in the world. The experiment has been replicated with various primates, and only humans and their closest relatives, chimpanzees, appear to pass the test. For my personal view, see the nearby sidebar 'Here's looking at me, kid!'.

Discovering how you think about your identity

Here's a simple exercise to help you answer the question: 'Who am I?' You can ask and answer that question in many ways, of course, but I'm interested in whatever comes to mind first.

Take a piece of paper, write down 'I am . . . ' and leave the rest of the line blank. Repeat for ten lines. Now go back and complete the started statements.

When you're finished, look back over the list and categorise the statements, using subjects such as the following:

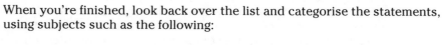

- ✓ **Physical attributes about yourself:** Such as your age or appearance.
- ✓ **Psychological attributes:** Such as saying that you're a cheerful person or a pessimist.
- ✓ **Social groups that you belong to:** Such as being a student or a supporter of a particular sports team.
- ✓ **Likes or preferences:** Such as being a fan of early blues music or a history buff.

Psychologists have found many revealing patterns in how people choose to complete simple statements such as 'I am . . . '. They give different responses depending on their mood at that moment, the other people that they're thinking of at the time and even the culture in which they're raised. (I discuss the differences between cultures and their views of the self in more detail in Chapter 17.)

There are many ways to answer the question 'who am I', from your appearance to your personality, your social cliques to your home country, your biology to your religion. All of these different aspects of the self are valid to different people, at different times of their lives, or change according to who they are talking to at the moment. Amongst all of these different swirling aspects of the self, remembering that there is no such thing as your 'true self' is important. At least, not one that you can discover through a detox diet.

'We're through the looking-glass here, people'

Like everyone, you come to understand yourself through the way in which you understand other people. I discuss this idea, called *self-perception theory*, in Chapter 6 as part of talking about how people explain their own behaviour. Some researchers argue that self-perception theory can be extended to explain how people acquire a whole sense of who they are.

The *looking-glass self* refers to the idea that you see yourself through the eyes of other people – crucially, however, not how others actually see you, but how you *think* other people see you.

That this theory is at least partly true is shown by a clever experiment. Participants were recruited and asked to help train graduate students who were training to be clinicians. The participants sat in a room and answered questions over an intercom. They were asked to act in one of two ways: in a very reactive, emotional way or in a flat, emotionally unresponsive manner. They were told that their acting would be used to help the graduate students identify different types of behaviour.

Of course, being a social psychology experiment, that was all a fib. One group of participants was told that a clinician would be watching them all the time through a one-way mirror. The other group was told that they wouldn't be watched. The key dependent variable was measured afterwards. Participants rated how emotionally stable they were – not how they appeared during the experiment, but how they really were.

Watching the celebrities

Spare a thought, if you will, for the bizarre lives of celebrities. The looking-glass-self experiment shows that simply imagining a graduate student watching you pretend to be something has the power to shift your concept of your self-identity.

Imagine being Charlie Sheen, knowing that millions of people watch you each week in a sitcom, acting the part of a shallow narcissist. Think about what effect that level of attention has on your sense of self, personality and behaviour.

The participants acting in an emotionally responsive manner and who thought that they'd been watched during their performances felt that they genuinely were more emotionally responsive themselves. The opposite result occurred when they'd been acting unresponsively. This result didn't happen, however, when the participants thought that they hadn't been observed.

In other words, the belief that their behaviour was witnessed by another person increased participants' feeling that their behaviour reflected their true nature. The imagined gaze of others multiplies the power of self-perception over people's self-image.

Living through the eyes of others: Social comparison theory

The self is formed by social forces, by looking outwards as well as inwards. One way in which other people shape who you are is described by Leon Festinger's *social comparison theory:* people acquire a sense of who they are by comparing themselves against those around them.

Imagine that you feel like you're good at maths, for example, because you came top of your class. But you feel that you're bad at dancing after seeing other people at the school disco. (Don't worry, I'm not going to test you with complex algebra or insist that you groove around your home.) These facts aren't objective, of course. If you happen to be placed in a classroom of future professional statisticians, inevitably you feel relatively bad at maths. On the upside, you may feel like you're better at dancing.

Festinger realised that these social comparisons aren't entirely passive or accidental. Humans actively seek out particular people to compare themselves with and select particular skills or attributes for comparison.

As I discuss in Chapter 8, many psychological mechanisms protect or inflate your self-esteem: social comparison is one such mechanism. It comes in two forms:

- **Downwards social comparison:** You seek out and compare yourself to others who you think are inferior in some way, which has the effect of raising your self-esteem. This form is the most common type of social comparison.

- **Upwards social comparison:** You seek out and compare yourself to people you see as superior to you. Researchers have found that making this form of social comparison can have a crippling effect on your self-esteem.

You can see this psychological mechanism out in force if you ever attend a school reunion (or do the online equivalent of looking through your school friends' Facebook pages). You can measure success in life in all sorts of ways – income, family, health and so on – and people tend to choose whichever measure flatters them the most. People with high-earning jobs but no family life assess others based on their income and feel good about themselves. People who never left the small town they grew up in focus on the failed marriage of the high earner and feel good that they raised a happy, healthy family. People with poor jobs and no family may observe that at least they didn't put on so much weight.

Of course, sometimes, your ability to make downward comparisons is limited. For example, avoiding the comparisons that family and teachers may make between siblings is difficult: often one's labelled sporty and the other bookish. These comparisons have a substantial effect on siblings.

Personality psychologists and geneticists have studied siblings and found puzzling results. Usually siblings share much of their genes and much of their environment, growing up in the same place with the same parents. Given all these shared influences, they should be extremely similar to each other. Scientists try to predict how similar siblings should be given knowledge of genetics and heritability, studies of twins raised apart and so on. However, siblings are often a lot *less* similar than you'd expect.

One explanation is that social comparisons are driving siblings apart. Imagine a pair of twins, for example. Perhaps one runs slightly faster at a school sports day. That child may choose to compare herself on that physical dimension. It then becomes part of her identity, which increases her self-esteem and motivation to train and to improve herself further. Yet she may have run faster on that sports day just because the other twin was recovering from a cold. But the random difference in performance that day can set off a chain of social comparisons and shifts in identity that many years later produces a sibling who's more athletic than the other.

Finding a Place in the World: Consequences of Identity

Your self-concept has a remarkable effect on how you experience success and failure in life. Conventional wisdom has been that high self-esteem is the most important factor. But recent psychological science reveals the importance of how you construe your self-concept and how you connect yourself to others.

Identifying with others: basking in reflected glory

I'm writing this section the day after Andy Murray won the Wimbledon tournament. An Englishman last achieved the most sought after prize in tennis 77 years ago. Today, everyone in London seems that much happier that '*we* have finally won it'. Of course, Andy Murray isn't English; he's a Scot. He didn't train in the UK; he went to Spain and Florida. But 17 million people across the country watched and cheered him on yesterday, and today they feel better about themselves.

How can the actions of one sportsperson affect the self-esteem of millions? What connection do most Londoners really have to Andy Murray?

Researchers call this effect *basking in reflective glory* and it has been demonstrated many times in experiments. For example, at a campus university, participants were given an exam to do and then told either that they scored very well or very poorly. Their real scores were irrelevant, because the researchers were in fact interested in their next question.

They asked the participants about a recent sports match that their university had won. The participants who were told that they did more poorly on the exam seemed to identify more with the team. For example, compared to people who thought they did well on the exam, they were more likely to say 'we played really well' rather than 'the team played well'. This experiment shows that self-esteem and social identity are linked.

Conversely, when people associate with a team or a group and they lose, people tend to distance themselves. After losing a final, a team's supporters are less likely to wear the shirt the next day. Before an election, the supporters of a political party may have signs on their lawns or banners in their windows. But the day after they lose the election, people take down those signs much quicker than the victors.

The social ties that we have to certain groups or teams are bound to our personal self-esteem. When people feel bad about themselves, or when their team is winning, they strengthen those ties. But when their team loses, they cut them off just as quickly.

Social identity theory attempts to account for when and how people seek connection to different social groups and how they treat people inside their social group differently to outsiders. Your self-concept isn't a static entity. Your identity and connection to different groups waxes and wanes in order to cast yourself in the best possible light. (I discuss social identity theory more in Chapter 16.)

Don't believe the stereotype hype

With one stroke, society could remove the gender difference between boys' and girls' success in mathematics exams. Not by changing how the questions are phrased or how difficult they are, but simply by changing how students identify themselves on the first page of their answer booklets.

I realise that this statement may seem over the top, but Claude Steele and other researchers have uncovered a remarkable fact about examinations and self-identity. Imagine that a negative stereotype exists about one aspect of your identity and the test you're about to take: for example, that girls are bad at spatial reasoning or Black Americans tend to perform relatively poorly on standardised tests. Some of these differences have existed in the past; Claude Steele and others wanted to know whether this was because of a true difference in ability, or just because people *believed* that there was a difference.

Research shows that if you're made aware of that aspect of your identity, your performance on a challenging test immediately suffers. If you have a box on the front of a mathematics exam where you have to write 'M' or 'F' to declare your sex, females go on to perform worse on that test. If you have to declare your ethnicity before turning over your exam paper, your test results go down if you're Black American, but they go up if you're Asian American due to the positive stereotypical view of their ability.

Another remarkable effect of this *stereotype threat* is that you can make people aware of some aspect of their identities simply by asking them to write the stereotype down on the front of the form. In doing so, you make them more aware of their expectations about how they will perform and attitudes about that part of themselves, and that awareness directly influences their performance.

These differences aren't small. They're about the same size as the differences reported as the average difference between males and females on maths tests, or the average difference between White and Black Americans on standardised tests.

In other words, the reported academic differences between the sexes or between ethics groups may not be caused by real differences in ability but by *believed* differences that come from stereotypes and prejudice.

Trying hard is better than being a genius

A child bounces up to you holding her school work, perhaps she's your daughter, cousin or a neighbour. She proudly shows you a big red A at the bottom of the test. How do you praise her?

For decades, people have been told that praise is vital for happy and healthy children and that the most important job in raising a child is nurturing her self-esteem. Recently, however, Carol Dweck and other researchers found that *how* people are praised is very important. They discovered that if you say 'what a very clever girl you are!' to the child showing you an A, you may cause her more harm than good.

The reason is that praise can shape children's view of themselves. You can think of ability or success in two general ways:

- ✓ **Entity theorists:** These people think that musicians, mathematicians or athletes are born that way. They believe that ability is a thing that you either have or don't have. When you say to a child who has succeeded, 'You're such a clever girl', you're endorsing this view of her ability. You're saying that she succeeded because she's simply clever.

- ✓ **Incremental theorists:** These people believe that success is born of hard work. They think that when you put more effort into something, you're more likely to succeed. When you say to a child, 'Well done – you must have worked really hard!', you're endorsing an incremental theory of ability.

You may be wondering whether it really matters what children believe about their success, so long as they feel good about it. Well, think about what happens when, inevitably, the child has a bad day. She gets all the bad calls from the referee or the exam covers the one topic that she didn't have the time to study. How does she explain this failure?

If the child holds an entity theory, she's forced to conclude that she's not very talented, clever or gifted. When these children fail, they don't want to try again. Their self-esteem is damaged, because they have to revise their opinions of themselves downwards.

But if they hold an incremental theory, they can explain their failures with the thought that on that day they didn't try hard enough, or they tried the wrong strategy when studying for the test. The failure isn't as detrimental to their self-esteem, because it just says something about what happened on the day and not whether they're fundamentally good or bad at something. These children are less likely to be demotivated by failure. They pick themselves up and try again. In the long run, these children succeed and are happier.

The results of research are very clear. For example, if a maths class spends a week discovering how they can increase mathematical ability through practice, the students' exam scores rise across the board. If you train parents and teachers to praise effort rather than label a child's 'talent', children's performance improves.

These results go against strong feelings that certain types of ability – particularly sports, maths and art – are things that you're just born with. Experts test students incessantly in schools, trying to track academic performance; professional talent spotters trawl schools looking for the next genius footballer among the 9-year-olds. But the research tells a clear and compelling story.

For your children to succeed and be happy, you need to convince them that success comes from *effort,* not from some talent that they're born with or not.

Therefore, Andy Murray won the Wimbledon title not because he was British or because he was the most gifted player. It was, in part, because of his self-concept. Immediately after the match he spoke first of all about losing the year before and how it had shaken him. But crucially, he responded to this by returning to the gym, working twice as hard and training more than any player on the professional circuit. I argue that it wasn't his belief in his talent, but his faith in hard work that won the tournament.

Chapter 8

How Fantastic Am I! Looking at Self-serving Bias

In This Chapter

▶ Identifying people's tendency to self-bias

▶ Examining why people think they're always right

▶ Searching for longer happiness and shorter sadness

How do you measure up to the rest of the world? If everyone formed a queue according to how talented, attractive or moral they were, where would you stand? Are you good enough to get into heaven?

A newspaper in the US carried out a survey that asked people who they thought would pass through the pearly gates into heaven. People were split over Bill Clinton, the president at the time, with 52 per cent thinking that he'd get in. Oprah Winfrey was a better bet, they thought, at 66 per cent and Mother Teresa scored even higher. But people taking the survey identified one person with an even greater chance of getting into heaven: themselves.

Even though the people surveyed were unlikely to have devoted their lives to serving God and helping poor and needy orphans like the modern-day saint Mother Teresa, many thought that they had a greater chance of going to heaven than her: 87 per cent as against 79 per cent.

Clearly something odd is at work here in relation to people's self-perception. Despite being differing widely in appearance, personality and abilities, social psychology finds that people are very similar in one regard: how they view themselves.

In this chapter I look at some of the ways in which people are biased when they think about themselves (called *positive illusions*). Often they have an inflated view of their own talent and ability, think that they're right most of the time and mistake how long an event is going to make them happy or sad.

I know that the first two points sound as if I'm describing a horrible narcissist, like someone from TV's *The Apprentice,* but the fact is that although most people appear modest and self-effacing, social psychology shows that they inflate systematically their self-image. Everyone chooses how they present themselves to others on the outside, but on the inside most people harbour a boastful egotist.

Looking at Yourself: Positive Illusions

'Know yourself': this was inscribed into Apollo's Temple in Delphi, and is one of the oldest nuggets of ancient Greek wisdom. Today, with constant standardised exams in schools, personality and aptitude tests in the workplace, and daily online quizzes to find out 'which character from *Game of Thrones* are you most like?', surely we have achieved all the ancient Greeks could desire in terms of knowledge about ourselves?

Well, not quite. Although people certainly have a lot of opinions about themselves, all those judgments tend to have a widespread and systematic bias. As I will show, they fall prey to positive illusions. People tend to overrate their strengths, downplay their weaknesses and think that they are just a little bit better than everyone else.

Believing that you're better than average

Garrison Keillor began his book about the fictional town of Lake Wobegon by saying that it was where ' . . . all the children are above average'. Of course, all parents think that their children are special and wonderful in some way. But it is clearly a joke, and clearly impossible, that they are *all* above average. Surprisingly, psychologists have found that it is not just parents in Keillor's book who have such positive illusions. In the exercise below, you can see if your friends and family also have such positive views of themselves.

Try asking some of the people around you to rate themselves on a scale of 1 to 100. You can ask about any qualities you want, but here are some suggestions:

- How generous are you?
- How good is your sense of humour?
- How safe a driver are you?

In each case, you can choose to tell people 'give me a number between 1 and 100, where 50 is the average person' or, after they've ranked themselves, you can ask 'what do you think the average person would score?'.

I predict that for each of these questions, people will rate themselves well above the 'average person'. Not by a wide, arrogant margin, perhaps, but consistently higher in each case. I would also predict that you'd have answered the same, if you hadn't already started reading this book, of course.

Don't worry if you don't find from your small survey that most people think that they're above average, because plenty of very strong data supports this claim.

One year, almost a million US students filled in surveys before leaving high school at the age of 18: in the survey, 89 per cent rated themselves as above average at 'getting along with others'. If those students were accurate judges of their own sociability, about 50 per cent would say that they're above average, because that's what 'average' means. But their estimate was far, far above that. And this is not just a feature of American students either. The same results have been replicated across the world.

The above-average effect isn't just large, it's also stubborn. One researcher asked people to rate how safe a driver they are: most rated themselves as 'better than average'. But here's the twist: at the time of answering the survey these people were convalescing in hospital as a result of car accidents for which they admitted they were at fault!

The above-average effect varies for different sorts of qualities, being stronger for aspects that are subjective and socially desirable. For example:

- ✔ Being good at mathematics is objective and easy to measure with an exam, and so it is less likely to show the effect.

- ✔ Being aggressive isn't usually seen as desirable, and so it shows the effect less.

- ✔ Being sociable, a good friend or lucky are seen as desirable qualities, but they are hard to measure objectively, and so they display the effect more often.

If something reflects well upon you and is hard to measure, you often assume that you're better at it than most.

Judging yourself as better than you used to be

Not only do people view themselves as better than other people, but also as better than they themselves were. This comparison with a past self is a form of *downwards comparison,* which I discuss in Chapter 7. People raise their self-esteem by judging themselves favourably against other people, which in this case includes themselves in the past.

Ask some people how likable they were a year ago and how likeable they think they are today.

Most people probably give themselves a higher rating for how they are now than how they were in the past. People often think that they're improving, even when research reveals no objective change in these traits.

Interestingly, however, when you ask people to rate how likeable a friend was a year ago and how likeable that person is now, you tend not to see a big difference. So this flattering contrast with the past is something that people only do when thinking about themselves.

Estimating your strengths as rare but your failures as commonplace

Despite often having a positive bias when evaluating themselves, people aren't completely blind to their failings. Even here, however, people display a self-serving bias:

- They tend to see negative events as *externally* caused, unstable and specific. In other words, they failed the driving test because the driving examiner was mean, and it won't happen with another instructor the next time.

- They tend to view positive events as *internally* caused, stable and global. So they win a family quiz game because they're highly intelligent, they'd win the game next time and would probably win those quiz shows on TV.

This bias affects beliefs about other people too. People assume that bad aspects of their characters are commonplace. For example, shoplifters *overestimate* that a higher number of other people also shoplift. If they procrastinate a lot, they think that most people are the same way.

But people think that their good qualities are rare. If they win a sports trophy at school, they *underestimate* the number of other people who have such a trophy somewhere in a cupboard. If they're very organised, they tend to think that other people lack the same skill.

Bear in mind this self-serving bias if you're ever reading through applications for a job or a place at college. My record was one round of student applications where I counted 17 people with a 'unique thirst for knowledge'!

Self-handicapping: Failure isn't your fault

Many positive illusions have a beneficial effect for the self: they make people feel happier. But the need to have a positive view of yourself is so strong that it can backfire and, perversely, make your life worse. This behaviour is called self-handicapping, and I bet you've done it.

Imagine the night before an important maths exam; you have only the last few hours to study and are starting to panic. In this situation, have you ever found yourself suddenly deciding to go out with your friends? Or turning on the TV and watching a sitcom marathon? Or starting a computer game to finish 'just one more level' and then completing the whole game? Afterwards, you collapse asleep exhausted, your books untouched.

When *self-handicapping,* you're engaging in behaviour that you know will harm your chances of succeeding: you know that you won't do as well on the test if you go out the night before, but you do it anyway. Why would anyone intentionally harm their chances of success?

Well, here's a possible answer. Say that you do study hard. You go to bed at a decent time and get eight hours of sleep. Then you take the maths test, but don't do well: you only get a C. What can you conclude about yourself? Probably that you're just not good at maths, which is a pretty hard blow to your self-esteem.

But if you self-handicap, you'll never be in this position because you're creating a reason for your failure. You were bound to get a C, you can tell yourself, because you went out dancing till 2 a.m. That C doesn't mean that you're bad at maths; it just means that you like to party.

Self-handicapping seems like a paradox, because people are deliberately harming their chances of success. In fact, self-handicapping shows that people prefer to fail with certainty and an excuse rather than try hard and face the *possibility* of failure that harms their positive illusions of themselves.

Thinking that You're Right Most of the Time

In Chapter 3, I talk about social psychology's greatest enemy: common sense. Whenever you describe a finding or an experiment, someone is bound to exclaim, 'I knew that all along!' This phenomenon is called *hindsight bias*.

Social psychologists have identified several of these biases that inflate people's self-concept by convincing them that they're right, have always been right and people with a different opinion are simply uninformed. These biases often serve a useful function of protecting and nurturing self-esteem, but they can also lead people into conflict and confusion.

In this section I describe why you always think that you've made the right choice, your beliefs are spot-on and other people are simply wrong!

Bias and politics

During the 2004 US election, the Democrats spotted a weakness in Republican President George W. Bush. He announced a tax cut for everyone in the country, but when the Democrats reviewed the details of his plan they calculated that although most people would get something back, 95 per cent of the money was going to the richest 5 per cent of the population. The Democrats made this statistic headline news, convinced that it would portray the president in a very poor light with the majority of voters.

Bush won the election, however. Further investigation revealed one possible reason why the Democrats' attack on the tax plan backfired. Apparently, about 40 per cent of the American population *thought* that they were in the richest 5 per cent of the population or soon would be. The Democrats' used careful statistics to show that Bush was favouring a tiny minority of the super-rich, but they ran afoul of people's inflated self-concept.

Deeming your choices to be right

If something is associated with the self, by choice or by accident, its value goes up in people's eyes. If something isn't associated with the self, because the person didn't choose it or it rejected them, its perceived value goes down. Experiments show this reality time and again. It works for large things like your home and career, but also for trivial things like the mugs and pens that you own that seem so much better than the near identical but clearly inferior mugs and pens that other people possess.

In one experiment, participants were shown six different art prints and asked to rank them in order of preference. They were then told that they could take one of them home. But sadly, the researcher lied, saying that only two of them were in stock. The participants were offered a choice between their fourth- and fifth-ranked pictures. Unsurprisingly, most chose the fourth-ranked picture.

Several days later the researcher called the participants back to the lab. They were shown the same set of prints and asked to rank them again. Typically, the picture that they took home, previously ranked fourth, now jumped up the ranking to first or second place. The picture that they didn't choose to take home slipped down the ranking to last place.

People are used to the idea that their opinions determine their choices, but this experiment shows that, surprisingly, choices also influence opinions.

People are biased towards anything associated with themselves and against things that they lose or that reject them. Contestants on game shows estimate the value of prizes as much higher if they've just won them. Students are suddenly aware of a college's weaknesses after it rejects them, and people conclude that standardised tests are biased just after they fail one.

Being sure that your beliefs are correct

Everyone is fallible as regards biased thinking, something called *naive realism:* the mistaken belief that your own subjective view of the world is a true, objective view. It has been called the biggest bias in social thinking. It pervades reasoning and explains why people argue and fail to resolve their differences.

Here's an example from my own life. When I started my Ph.D., I got my first Apple computer. I loved it, and I'm on my ninth Apple Mac in a row. Right now, next to my laptop is sitting an iPad, and next to that an iPhone. They look like high-tech Russian dolls. I've tried to use other people's PCs, but I find them incredible badly designed. Nothing is where I expect it to be, and the menus are counterintuitive. I had an Android phone once, but its case kept falling off. Admittedly, this was because I kept throwing it against the wall in frustration. In short, I love Apple products because they're the best.

But with that last statement, I've made a huge error: I've fallen foul of biased thinking. I believe that Apple products are better than their competitors, but a large difference exists between a subjective opinion and an objective fact. Objectively, there's no 'best' computer system: just the operating system that you're used to and which best fits your needs. But with computers, sports teams, political parties and types of music, people frequently mistake their opinions for facts about the world.

Naive realism produces another effect called *false consensus*. People tend to overestimate the number of people who agree with them. Because they think that their opinions are true reflections of the world, seeing why anyone else would think otherwise is difficult.

These biases are so hard to avoid because people are limited by their own experiences. Chapter 5 reveals that you tend to like things you experience a lot – the *mere exposure effect*. I like Apple computers because I've always been around them and I've had mostly positive experiences. I have difficulty imagining liking PCs (or country music or cruise ships) because personally I haven't had many experiences of them and can't think of reasons to like them. So I think falsely that these things are objectively bad. And because they're objectively bad, I think that other people must recognise those 'facts' too and agree with me.

The world's biggest bias

Naive realism is remarkably hard to avoid. One social psychology professor asked his students to define it on their exam. Then he asked them how often they thought the average person made this mistake and how often they made this mistake. The students thought that they made the mistake less often than other people.

In other words, they said that *other people* confused their subjective opinions with fact, but they didn't. Amazingly, they themselves displayed the naive realism bias while answering an exam question about naive realism, when you would think it would be uppermost in their minds!

Regarding everyone else as wrong!

If I think that my opinion is objectively true, what do I think of people who disagree with me? Well, they must be biased in their thinking.

The consequences of naive realism (see the preceding section) are all around you. Look at any online newspaper article or review that has a comments section. Almost all the arguments begin when the subjective opinions of two people clash, and each is convinced that theirs is the objective truth.

This tendency has been shown in experiments. Researchers asked participants if they'd wear a sandwich board advertising a product and wander around the streets. About half the people said yes and half no. The researchers then asked them to estimate how many people would make the same choice. Both the people who said yes and the people who said no estimated that the majority of people would make exactly the same decision as themselves.

This same method of thinking causes enormous trouble for journalists or anyone trying to present something as objectively true. When a story disagrees with a reader's viewpoint, that person accuses the journalist of bias. Many newspapers and TV channels tailor their coverage to the viewpoint of their customers for this reason.

But organisations such as the BBC can't do so, because everyone in the UK funds it and the government instructs it to be as objective as possible. Politically, the BBC is often accused of bias by left- and right-wing parties at the same time, which is exactly what you'd expect if it's giving fair coverage. So, counter-intuitively, the more people who accuse the BBC of bias, the more balanced it probably is.

Questioning How Long Something Makes You Happy

Generally, people are pretty good at guessing whether something is going to feel good or bad. For example, buying a new pair of shoes will feel good; wearing them and getting a blister will feel bad. This ability is called *affective forecasting* in psychological jargon. As I reveal in this section, though people are very good at judging if something is positive or negative, they're often very poor at judging how long the happiness or sadness is going to last.

Psychologist Daniel Gilbert and his colleagues studied affective forecasting, because it's very important in understanding the decisions that you make. You don't just live in the moment but have to make choices based on what you think will happen and how you think you'll feel. Is it worth saving up to buy those shoes, or should you go out to dinner instead? Will the shoes make you happy enough that you won't mind hobbling around with a blister for a few days? Gilbert found that people are generally very good affective forecasters, apart from anticipating the length of the benefit or problem.

In this section's discussion of affective forecasting, I'm not talking about hugely traumatic and stressful events that trigger severe, clinical mental-health problems. Instead, I'm focusing on how people react to extreme negative and positive events when they're fortunate enough to maintain their mental health.

Trusting that time really does heal

See how you do with this exercise. Identify which of the following events you'd prefer to happen to you next week:

- ✔ You're hit by a bus and lose the use of both legs.
- ✔ You win a million pounds on the lottery.

That's probably one of the easier questions in this book. No doubt, you guess that winning the lottery would make you feel happier than being hit by a bus. But now imagine, like in the film *Sliding Doors,* that two versions of you exist. One wins the lottery and feels very happy. The other gets hit by the bus and feels very bad. Eventually these two 'yous' are going to feel about the same, because the joy of winning the lottery is sure to wear off and the unhappiness of the accident lessens.

But how much time do you think will pass before the good feeling from the lottery win dies away and the bad feeling from the accident fades? How long before the two versions of you are equally happy: a month; a year; a decade?

Most people guess at years, even decades, before this happens. But the remarkable answer is three months, on average. No matter how wonderful or horrible a life experience is, about three months after it happens, your emotions return to normal.

The research is quite clear, even for one of the worst experiences that can happen to a person: the death of a child. What parents feel when their children die is unimaginable for most people, but even after experiencing this most horrible of events, after three months most parents are about as happy as before their child died. That's the result of extensive research with parents who have been in exactly this situation.

Shifting focus over time

Whenever I tell people about the research in the preceding section, they have a hard time believing it. They're convinced that it must take longer, that their affective forecast of years or decades must be right.

People make such long estimates, and then disbelieve they're wrong, because of something called *focalism*. The idea is that the inherent dramatic nature of these events – being hit by a bus, losing a child, winning the lottery – causes difficulty for people predicting accurately their emotions about them. People focus on the extreme good or bad aspects and ignore everything else that would be happening in their future lives.

Think again about how you make affective forecasts. When asked to imagine the death of a child and how long the grief lasts, many people view the experience like a montage in a very sad movie: weeks of grieving and wearing black; trying to clear out the child's bedroom but unable to change a thing; seeing the child's old friends happily hugging their parents; months afterwards finding a broken toy under the sofa; walking past the kitchen wall and looking at the marks made each birthday, tracking the height and seeing the marks stop when the child was still impossibly small. Each of these moments seems unbearably sad. When viewed in this way, imagining that all these horrible feelings can disappear after just three months seems impossible.

The key thing is that in making your affective forecast you're *focusing* on the worst aspects of the experience. When creating your mental montage of the situation you're looking at the most painful and poignant scenes. But people don't live their lives in montage; they live 24 hours each and every day.

Focusing on sport

The focalism principle is at work in all sorts of episodes in people's lives. Take big sporting events. If you talk to sports fans the day before their team is in a championship final, they're obsessed by it. Winning means everything and losing is inconceivable.

Researchers asked such fans how long they thought that they'd be happy if their team won, and how long it would take them to get over it if they lost. Their estimates were weeks, months and even a year. Yet a couple of days after a championship win, or a loss, their day-to-day happiness is about the same.

In Chapter 7 I write about the day after Andy Murray won Wimbledon. Everyone in the UK seemed glowing and overjoyed. But a couple of days passed and hardly anyone was talking about tennis. The intensity of the emotions was genuine, but it quickly faded.

So people fail to imagine those times a week or a month after the event when they're doing the laundry, not thinking about very much; when something happens at work they have to concentrate upon; when they volunteer at the child's old school and make connections with other children that make them feel needed. These day-to-day experiences determine mood just as much as the big tragedies and successes in life (see another example in the nearby sidebar 'Focusing on sport').

I don't for a moment mean that parents who've lost a child are no longer sad about the event three months later. Of course, they remain devastated whenever they think about it, probably for the rest of their lives. But for many, many moments in the day they aren't thinking about their lost child, and after about three months those mundane other moments are what determine their overall happiness.

Looking at the role of your psychological immune system

The surprising result of research in affective forecasting is that, in general, you're going to be less sad and less happy than you imagine.

If you talk to people in happy relationships and ask them how they'd feel if they were dumped tomorrow, they reply that it would devastate them, that they'd never love again. But when you talk to single people who've just been dumped or who have been single for a long time, they're just as happy as people in couples.

Similarly, if you ask people how happy they'd be if they got a pay rise tomorrow, or were sacked and had to take a pay cut, they estimate a huge impact on their happiness. Yet researchers find very little correlation between wealth and happiness. As incomes rise across society or over the course of people's lives, reported happiness doesn't change.

People appear to have developed a robust psychological immune system. Just as your body can recover and repair itself physically from many illnesses, so you can recover from the worst that life can throw at you.

If you're unfortunate enough to suffer a tragedy in your life, you can go to a Freudian therapist who delves deep into your childhood and blames the relationship with your parents. Or you can read all the self-help books on the shelf. Or you can listen to the advice that my Granny gave me, and perhaps yours gave you too: 'There, there, give it time. You'll be okay.' Much more scientific evidence backs Gran's wisdom than the whole of Freud.

Chapter 9

Attributing Causes to People's Behaviour

....

In This Chapter

▶ Explaining the actions of others

▶ Defining the fundamental attribution error

▶ Spotting biases in different cultures and situations

....

*T*he ways in which people explain each other's behaviour is a fascinating subject. Often you meet people, appraise their actions and then make assumptions about them pretty quickly, without properly understanding how you arrive at your decision. And if you're thinking 'So what?', remember that other people are doing the same about your behaviour as well. So if you've ever felt that people have judged you unfairly or leapt to conclusions about your behaviour, you may have wondered how and why people understand the causes of each other's behaviour.

Wonder no more, because this chapter provides some possible answers as I look into these mysterious processes. I introduce what I mean by an *attribution* in the social-psychological context and reveal a central mistake that many people make when assessing the causes of other people's behaviour, called the fundamental attribution error.

Not for the first (or last) time in this book, you discover that the way in which people use so-called common sense doesn't seem to match up with the scientific evidence from experiments. Read the nearby sidebar 'Buttering up the public' for a revealing and apparently counterintuitive example, which was used successfully in advertising.

Buttering up the public

Johnny Rotten was the face of angry, disaffected youth in 1970s' Britain. He was the lead singer of the Sex Pistols, the band that defined punk with hits such as 'Anarchy in the UK' with its chorus 'I am the Anti-Christ'. The band members spat at their audience from the stage and most concerts ended in violence. Deliberately provocative, they released an anti-monarchist song, 'God Save the Queen', on the day of the Queen's Silver Jubilee in 1977. A newspaper organised a campaign against the record and workers at the record factory went on strike rather than produce copies.

So, how do people think of Johnny Rotten in the UK today? A musician who influenced a generation? A violent yob who helped make society nastier? How about: dairy-product connoisseur? Bizarrely, when a butter manufacturer wanted to increase its sales a few years ago, the firm chose the elderly Johnny Rotten as the face of the advertising campaign. This particular product is sold on the virtues of being old fashioned and traditionally English – precisely the things that Johnny Rotten, now John Lydon, railed against in his youth. Surely he was the worst person to represent this butter. But the campaign was successful with sales rising by an astonishing 85 per cent.

To help explain Lydon's magical power to sell butter, put yourself in the shoes of people watching his butter commercial for the first time. The sheer strangeness of the face of punk advertising dairy produce surely demands an explanation. What reason made Johnny Rotten of all people agree to appear in this advert?

In other words, what attributions did viewers make about his behaviour: perhaps that a significant amount of money explained his actions? After all, he cheerfully told anyone who'd listen that he did the advertisement purely to fund a tour with his band. Instead, people ignored this explanation and made the error of attributing his actions to the fact that he must really like that butter. Indeed, because he was once Johnny Rotten and hated all things establishment, he must really, really like that traditional butter to agree to make the advert.

In other words, the crazy unsuitability of Johnny Rotten as a spokesperson for traditional butter is precisely what makes him such a persuasive force. This strange result certainly runs counter to common sense, but you can't argue with an 85 per cent increase in sales.

Introducing the Concept of Making Attributions

An *attribution* is psychologist jargon for an explanation that links a person's behaviour to a cause. Imagine that you hear a person at the check-in desk of a hotel snap at the receptionist. Perhaps you *attribute* that behaviour to her personality – she's just a rude person. Or, noticing the tags on her baggage, you put it down to her jetlag – tiredness sapped her patience.

In the context of attributions, social psychologists aren't really interested in why the woman acted as she did. Instead, as we see in this section, they are interested in when, how and why the people watching her make their attributions.

Understanding when you tend to make attributions

You don't explain everything about other people's behaviour; that would be exhausting. Imagine wondering why someone chose a certain outfit that day, why she picked a certain coffee flavour, why she stopped to check her phone before crossing the road, or why she got so angry at the amateur psychologist stalking her and asking questions about her every move. Like everyone else, you generate attributions only for particular types of behaviour at particular times. Often, you try and explain someone's actions when the behaviour is unusual or unique: if it's surprising, negative or uncharacteristic, the action needs an explanation.

If you see a person wearing a green top hat while walking down the street, that behaviour calls out for an explanation. If the behaviour seems uncharacteristic – if the person is otherwise dressed soberly in a suit and tie – you seek an attribution. Plus, if the behaviour is in anyway negative – if the person is being loud and boisterous – you may well ask yourself why.

But if it's St Patrick's Day and everyone else is dressed that way and singing and dancing, you probably don't seek an attribution to explain the behaviour of this individual.

Deciding between a 'bad' person or a 'bad' situation

In this chapter I'm concerned with two broad methods of making attributions for behaviour that often cause errors:

✔ **Dispositional attributions:** These appraise the cause of an action to be *internal* to the person, such as personality or mood. These attributions explain behaviour by saying something about the inherent qualities of a person. So, believing that someone is shouting on the street because he's an angry person is a dispositional attribution.

✔ **Situational attributions:** These involve causes that are *external* to the person, such as the situation, recent experiences or the behaviour of other people. If you say that someone's shouting on the street because he's just received a parking ticket, that's a situational attribution.

These two types of attributions aren't just of academic interest, because they're hugely important to people's lives and to society. Serious problems can arise when people attribute actions to the wrong cause.

For instance, many legal arguments come down to the same basic question of attributions. In a murder trial, for example, the jury members ask themselves whether the accused was responsible for the crime or something about the situation caused that person to do it. In many cases, if a situational element is proved – such as a medication impairing someone's judgement or the accused being provoked by others – punishment can be reduced or even removed. The killer of Harvey Milk in the US, for example, was released after his defence contended that the additives in a snack food had clouded his mind.

Falling Prey to the Fundamental Attribution Error

The *fundamental attribution error* (FAE) is a common mistake people make when explaining someone's behaviour: they make a dispositional attribution when they should make a situational one (for definitions of these two attributions, check out the earlier section 'Deciding between a 'bad' person or a 'bad' situation').

In this section I describe how researchers discovered the effect that became known as the FAE (as so often with great discoveries, it was by accident), how they demonstrate it through experiments and how you can find out how to spot yourself making the same error.

Seeing Jones and Smith's surprising discovery

Early social psychologists were very interested in the process by which people generated explanations for each other's behaviour. They performed some clever experiments to investigate this processes, and in doing so stumbled upon what seemed like a surprising and stubborn error in people's reasoning.

Also known as the correspondence bias

The fundamental attribution error has another name: the correspondence bias. The terms are used interchangeably in social psychology literature. Some psychologists thought that 'fundamental attribution error' was a little too extreme as a label, because behaviour can be attributed to personality to some degree.

So some scientists proposed that the 'correspondence bias' better captured this graded aspect. In other words, people have a bias to think that behaviour corresponds to dispositions or personality, rather than the situation. This term didn't completely catch on, however, and so you still encounter the use of the fundamental attribution error in papers and textbooks.

Jones and Smith wanted to understand how people make dispositional attributions (those that comment on the person rather than the situation) about attitudes. In their experiment, they asked one group of people if they were for or against Fidel Castro, and then asked the members to write an essay supporting their views. (This experiment was conducted in the US in the 1960s when Castro was a highly controversial figure.) Another group of people read these essays and then rated how much they thought that the writer was for or against Castro.

Unsurprisingly, people who read an essay in support of Castro attributed the disposition to the writer that the person was pro-Castro. But the researchers realised that they needed a baseline condition – scores to compare with these ratings. So they recruited another group of raters and told them that the essay writers had been *instructed at random* to write an essay for or against Castro. Since the raters thought that the writers had been told what opinions to express, the researchers thought that the raters wouldn't have any beliefs about the writers' true opinion. But that's not how the raters behaved.

In this control condition, the raters still said that the essays expressing the pro-Castro viewpoint were probably written by people who were pro-Castro. The researchers made doubly sure that the raters understood that they'd been *instructed* to express those views. But still the raters tended to make a dispositional attribution, preferring to conclude that the essay was a result of how the writers really felt, instead of a situational attribution that it was because they'd been told to do so. Clearly, the power of the situation is pretty strong (something I examine more in Chapter 11).

Smith and Jones had discovered an error in people's thinking that they termed the 'correspondence bias', though it is perhaps better known by a later term, the fundamental attribution error.

Revealing the FAE through experiments and experience

The strange bias that Jones and Smith uncovered was the focus of several experiments, as psychologists tried to understand how and why people make the fundamental attribution error.

In the most famous example of an experimental demonstration of FAE, Lee Ross and his colleagues asked participants to take part in a quiz bowl demonstration. They chose two participants from a larger group. In front of everyone, they tossed a coin, making one person the questioner and the other the contestant. The questioner was told to think of several general-knowledge questions that would be difficult to answer. Then, the questioner asked the contestant the questions in front of all the other participants. Typically, the contestant did poorly on this test and the questioner had to tell the person the right answers.

The researchers then asked the audience members to rate the intelligence of the questioner and the contestant. Remarkably, they ranked the contestant below the questioner. At this point the contestant – as you may expect – objected that this test was really unfair: of course the questioner knew the answers to all the questions – she'd selected them!

But the audience members, the real participants in this experiment, were liable to make the FAE. They overlooked the situational attribution for the contestants' poor performance: the fact that they didn't come up with the questions. Instead, they leapt to a dispositional attribution: the contestant is just not as bright as the questioner.

In the same way as in the quiz bowl experiment, students in my lectures form opinions of me. Each week they see me talk for an hour or more, without notes, on complex topics that are just beyond their understanding, answering any question that arises. They may leap to a dispositional attribution and think that my performance is a great display of intelligence and that I can talk about anything.

But that attribution overlooks all the complex situational forces producing that lecture. For example, the facts that I choose to lecture only on topics that I know about and that I know they don't; that I can see my notes on my laptop; and that – for all they know – I may have looked up this stuff on Wikipedia moments before the class.

Stephen Fry isn't as clever as you think

When asked to name a highly intelligent person, many British people say Stephen Fry. He hosts an erudite and witty television quiz show called *QI* that rewards pedantic and obscure knowledge (it's much more entertaining than it sounds). After watching him supply the Greek etymology of a technical term in microbiology, and then segue into a discussion of musical leitmotifs in the works of Shostakovich and ABBA, viewers are tempted to conclude that Stephen Fry knows everything about everything. But they'd be making the FAE. Viewers often overlook that a team of researchers look up this information each week. They write it on the teleprompter in front of Fry and whisper it into his earpiece.

Stephen Fry and other TV quiz masters don't pretend for a moment that they're the source of all the knowledge they dispense: many read off cards that they hold visibly in front of them. Yet the FAE persists in the minds of the viewers, and TV quiz masters continue to be named routinely as highly intelligent people.

So if you want to be seen as exceptionally smart, get a hard-working group of assistants and an autocue!

When I started as a lecturer, I was daunted at the task of putting together 25 hours of spoken material that covered the whole discipline of psychology. A senior colleague reassured me, 'You only have to make sure that you're five pages ahead of the students in the textbook and they assume you know it all!' Of course, I try not to use this particular example in my lectures!

Identifying the signs of the FAE

When you understand it, you start to see the FAE everywhere. You can think of it as the bias people have towards thinking about personalities rather than situations. For example, say a politician announces that she's cutting welfare payments to the unemployed. You may be tempted to leap to the conclusion that she hates poor people instead of considering the complicated web of economic forecasts, political deals and ideological promises that produced that policy.

 When people win, for example at sports, people also often make the FAE, leaping to the attribution that they succeeded because of their special dispositions – their inborn talent. But that overlooks their years of practice and training, and the technical resources and expert coaching from which they've benefited. (Though I don't call it by this name, you can see the FAE at work in Chapter 7 in the discussion about how parents understand their children's successes and failures.)

You can also think of the FAE as the mistake of thinking that a strongly influential situation is a weak one. In Chapter 12, I talk about Milgram's disturbing experiments in which he put participants in a situation where they were asked to press a button that would cause an innocent person immense pain. When he first presented these experiments to other psychologists, Milgram asked them to guess how many participants would obey the instructions. Typically, they guessed around 5 per cent of people. In reality, over 65 per cent of the participants obeyed.

Just like members of the public, these professional psychologists (who you may think should know better) made the fundamental attribution error. They thought that the situation would have only a weak influence on the participants' behaviour, reasoning that participants' dispositions – their good sense and kindness – would stop them from hurting another person. But no.

In Chapters 11 and 12, I seek to understand more about the complicated causal power of the situation that compels such behaviour.

Taking the simple route to explaining behaviour

You may be wondering why people prefer to prioritise internal dispositions over external situations when seeking causes to explain behaviour. One answer is simplicity.

Thinking of an internal cause for a person's behaviour is easy – the strict teacher is a mean person, the doting parents just love their kids. In contrast, situational explanations can be complex and murky. Perhaps the teacher appears mean because she's seen the consequences of not trying hard in generations of students and wants to instil self-discipline in them. Perhaps the parents who're boasting of the achievements of their children are anxious about their failures, and conscious of the cost of their school fees. These situational factors require knowledge, insight and time to think through. Jumping to a dispositional attribution is far easier.

You can see the same thing happening when people make attributions about simple objects. Richard Nisbett and colleagues showed participants a video of a wood chip, caught in the eddies and currents of a fast-moving stream, bobbing weaving. They asked people what was happening in the video. Participants were likely to talk about the wood chip and its dispositions, how it 'wanted' to move around or stay near the rock (even though clearly a wood chip can't 'decide' or 'want' anything). Fewer people saw and told the more complicated story about the currents of water and how they interacted with each other and the rocks to move the chip.

Often, people seek a simple story of dispositions over a complex story about the situation.

Living with the consequences of the FAE

Ignorance of the FAE causes all sorts of consequences, some serious and others less so. I discuss just two in this section.

Picturing the truth about celebrity life

Celebrity 'journalism' is a strange and twisted world, one that mostly profits the celebrities and the journalists, of course. Has so much ever been printed about so little!

The fundamental attribution error is the engine driving all these stories, particularly the pictures. It nudges you to overlook the real circumstances of these isolated, selected and re-touched images and generates the belief that you're getting to know these people.

You probably feel that you know something about the celebrities on your screens. You know what Brad Pitt and Paris Hilton are like. You've seen pictures of them grinning, going into a club with other celebrities they may or may not be having an affair with. You've seen the shots of them tear-stained at the airport after being jilted once more.

But when you look at these paparazzi shots, you're being goaded into making the fundamental attribution error. You seek an explanation for why, say, they look angry and attribute it to their dispositions: they must have an explosive temper. You disregard the situation around that photograph – that the celebrity was being followed all day by a pack of paparazzi. She asked patiently to be left alone but was still snapped with long-range lenses inside her own home. Finally she tried to leave the photographers behind by driving off, but was tailed by photographers on motorbikes looking in through the car windows. As she's getting out of the car, a flash goes off into her eyes and angrily she yells at the photographer. Someone takes a picture of that reaction, prints it in the magazine and the readers think, 'Ah, there's that famous temper again.'

In fact, the process that goes on at such magazines can be even more astonishing. One editor explained how she once covered a story about the actress Jennifer Aniston. Her ex-husband, Brad Pitt, had that week adopted a baby with his new partner, Angelina Jolie. The editorial team sat around discussing how Jennifer must feel about that. Then they looked through the stack of photographs sent to them by the paparazzi following her that day. It was a set of shots of Jennifer getting a coffee and leaving. The editors decided that she'd probably be very upset about what 'Brangelina' had done. So they found a picture where Aniston looked upset – or was just squinting into the sun, coming out of the café – and printed it with the headline 'Jennifer in tears over new Dad Brad'.

Dying due to the FAE

People's bias to choose simple dispositional attributions over complex situational attributions can have extremely serious consequences. After the September 11 terrorist attacks on the US in 2001, President George W. Bush made this statement about the instigator, Osama Bin Laden: 'The only thing I know for certain about him is that he's evil.' He stated, essentially, that the reason for the September 11 attack was the disposition of one man.

At the time, some people began asking complex questions about the situational forces: why do these people hate the US? What do they hope to gain from a terrorist attack? But many mainstream politicians and leaders condemned this discussion, saying that acknowledging the possibility that the actions of the US were part of the casual chain that led to the attack was unpatriotic. So, pushed by the fundamental attribution error, the story told about September 11 became one of dispositions – villains and heroes – rather than a complex history of political forces and a nation's foreign policy. Arguably, this simple story led to some very bad consequences for everyone involved when the US and its allies took military action in response to September 11.

Digging Deeper into the FAE

The fundamental attribution error isn't a consistent, stable tendency. Not all people make the error to the same degree: differences in the strength of the bias apply across different cultures; subtle differences in how questions are asked can shift the attributions you make; and most people make the FAE differently when thinking about themselves versus others.

Experiencing differences across the world

Countries such as the USA and most of Europe have what psychologists call *individualistic* cultures. These people have a strong tendency to make the FAE – it was where the effect was first observed. But researchers have found that people from *collectivist* cultures, such as China and Japan, have a reduced tendency to make the FAE. They're happier to make situational attributions for other people's behaviour.

Also, Richard Nisbett found with his wood-chip experiment (see the earlier section 'Taking the simple route to explaining behaviour') that people from collectivist cultures more readily describe the behaviour of a wood chip in a babbling stream in terms of the interaction between water currents, rocks and the chip itself. They have a broader tendency to seek explanations that don't focus on individual entities and their dispositions. I discuss this idea in much more detail in Chapter 17. One explanation is that people from different cultures have different perspectives on people's behaviour, as I discuss next.

Appreciating the role of perspective

The perspective that you take in a situation can change the attributions that you make. By 'perspective' I mean literal, visual perspective, as well as a more metaphoric sense of thinking about someone's behaviour in different contexts, with different knowledge of the background reasons for their actions.

Imagine that you look across a café at two people arguing. The situation is not at all obvious. You don't know what led up to that argument or who said what to whom. All you can see are two angry faces. Unsurprisingly, you explain their behaviour in terms of their visible, salient characteristics: they're two very angry people (that is, you make a dispositional attribution).

But now imagine that you're in that situation, having an argument. You know exactly what was said in the car park before you entered the café and how it dredged up an unresolved argument from weeks before that had been simmering ever since. You know that you're on a diet today and hunger is making you cranky, and that your partner deliberately ordered a caramel latte knowing that you were unable to have one. All these situational forces are highly salient to you.

In contrast, your dispositions aren't obvious. Unless you're sitting by a mirror, you may not realise that you're scowling at the latte. You may not know that your voice is raised. In this case, you quite sensibly attribute your actions to the situational forces that you can directly experience, as opposed to the dispositions.

Researchers have recreated this contrast in perspective in the laboratory. They asked two people to have an argument and filmed them from different cameras. One was placed in the corner of the room, filming both people. The other was placed just over the shoulder of one person, filming from his perspective.

They showed the footage from one camera or another to participants, and asked them to explain the behaviour they saw. If they were watching from the vantage point of across the room, people made the typical FAE dispositional attributions. But when they watched the footage from the point of view of one person, they were more likely to attribute that person's actions to the situation. In other words, a simple switch in visual perspective produced an actor-observer like bias, even though the participants were never talking about themselves.

Noticing the actor-observer bias

Social psychologists have found that people tend to make the FAE more about other people than about themselves: something that's called the *actor-observer bias*. In other words, compared to how often you explain other people's actions in terms of their dispositions, you're much more likely to consider the situation and your dispositions when thinking about yourself (and not simply because you're trying to avoid any blame!). Given that in such cases you're in possession of more facts, perhaps this tendency is unsurprising.

People vary in their responses when placed in difficult moral situations. Try this exercise in moral reasoning and see how well you can predict your own actions. For each of the actions below please write down 'yes' if think you'd do them, 'no' if you think that you wouldn't and 'depends' if you think that you might or might not, depending on the situation:

- ✔ Borrow money from your parents without asking first.
- ✔ As a student, use an essay from a friend in the year above who took the same class.
- ✔ Become romantically involved with someone who was still in another relationship.
- ✔ Read an email that someone has left open on a public computer.
- ✔ Object when another customer mutters a racist remark about a member of staff.
- ✔ Intervene when you see a young child vandalising some public property.

Now go back over the list again, but this time answer the questions on behalf of a close friend. Write down whether you think 'yes' that person would carry out that action, or 'no' or it 'depends'.

You may or may not think that you are more honest and upstanding than your friends (my bet is it's the former, given the positive illusions that you harbour towards yourself, as I showed in Chapter 8). But here, I'm not so much interested in what moral choices you made, so much as whether or not you make them in terms of the situation (and answered 'depends') or your dispositions.

To analyse your data, count up the number of 'depends' answers you gave for yourself and your friend. If you're like most people who carry out this task, you have more 'depends' answers for yourself.

This result shows that when thinking of your own actions, you are much more likely to take into account more of the situation and less likely just to think in terms of your dispositions.

Here's another example: researchers asked US students what made their best friends pick their majors at university. The students typically gave dispositional attributions, such as, 'They want to make a lot of money after they graduate.' When they asked the students why they picked their own major, the students still named some dispositional attributions, but compared to thinking about their friends they were more likely to name situational factors such as, 'Engineering is a high-paying field', or 'My parents were really keen for me to study this.'

Just like the exercise in moral decision-making above, when they are thinking about other people the students focus on dispositions, but when thinking about their own actions, they focus on the situation.

People often get confused about the fundamental attribution error and the actor-observer bias. They try to give experimental evidence for one theory in support of another, or think that one is the opposite of the other. The simplest way to think of their relationship is that the FAE is an error that you make reasoning about *other people*, and the actor-observer bias is a difference in how you reason about yourself compared to other people. More precisely, the FAE is the mistake of attributing behaviour to a disposition rather than a situation; the actor-observer bias is that people are more likely to make the FAE when thinking about other people compared to themselves.

Chapter 10

Making Judgements about Other People: Bias and Prejudice

*H*uman beings judge each other all the time. People on television, fellow commuters on the train and passers-by: you probably form impressions and appraisals of all of them during your day. You can make these judgments on the basis of very little information, as I will show you, because you draw on your rich knowledge and experience of meeting people in the past. In other words, you use social stereotypes to make judgments about how someone in a suit and tie may be different from someone with tattoos and a biker jacket. Your judgments and preconceptions can also be influenced in remarkably subtle ways.

Imagine that you're attending a lecture. The event co-ordinator introduces the keynote speaker as follows: 'Allow me to introduce you to the speaker for today. People who know him consider him a rather warm person, industrious, critical, practical and determined.' You listen to the speech and afterwards someone asks you to appraise the speaker personally and professionally.

When Harold Kelley did an experiment like this in the 1950s with university students, he found that one word had a particularly powerful effect on their social judgements. If the word 'warm' was replaced with 'cold', the speaker was seen as less friendly and approachable, more irritable and self-centred. Though it was only one word among many hundreds spoken across the hour, it had a strong impact on the judgements people made.

When 'warm' or 'cold' was said early on, it *framed* the perceptions that the listeners had of the speaker from that point. (Just as the exact same movement of the mouth, for example, can be seen as a friendly grin or a superior smirk, depending on the initial framing.) Having heard a description of a lecturer as 'cold', the listeners pictured a stereotypically aloof academic living in an ivory tower. From then on, listeners noticed aspects of his behaviour that fitted into this stereotype and ignored those that didn't.

In this chapter, I explore some remarkable things about the judgements that people make about each other, including the nature, formation and roles of stereotypes and prejudice. I reveal that the social judgements you make are determined as much by what's already in your head as by what's in front of your eyes.

The experiments and theories that I describe in this chapter are part of the *cognitive approach* of understanding social stereotypes, prejudice and group difference, which emphasises how social information is learnt and organised into concepts. (This approach isn't the only way to examine these subjects, and in Chapter 16 I talk about the motivational and economic approaches.) The cognitive approach reveals the many ways that stereotypes have of perpetuating themselves in society. This insight makes it all the more important, and all the more difficult, to figure out when useful generalisations slide into prejudice.

Staring at Stereotypes and Peering at Prejudice

A stereotype is usually a bad thing. The tough, alcoholic cop who doesn't play by the rules is yelled at by his boss and divorced by his wife, but he always gets the bad guy: that's a stereotype, and it's bad writing. Not all cops are like that. Or if someone says to you, 'Here's my new boyfriend, he's a city trader,' and you look up expecting to meet a boorish, slick-haired man in a suit and red braces, who boasts endlessly about his new Porsche and his admiration for right-wing politicians: that's a stereotype, and it's judgemental. Not all city traders are like that. For example, I once met a city trader who wore black braces!

In this section I discuss the two sides of stereotypes, their usefulness and their dangers .Stereotypes can be very useful as they are a form of mental short cut, allowing us to make accurate and efficient assumptions. If you assume that the 4-year-old girl you are talking to can't read, for example, that's a stereotype. You may not be correct, but there is a pretty good chance you are, and if you make this assumptions you won't waste time asking her what her favourite novels are. You may also assume that since she's a little girl she won't like playing with Lego. This again is a stereotype that may not be true at all. The danger here is that by only offering her dolls to play with, rather than construction toys, you are sending signals about activities that girls can and cannot do. For example, the Lego company finally released a female mini-figure who was a scientist only in 2014 due to popular demand.

Recognising that stereotypes are just categories

When people talk of stereotypes, they're usually accusing someone of being prejudiced in some way. If you assume that a woman is bad at parallel parking or a man can't do two things at once, you're drawing on a stereotype and applying it in a prejudicial way. If you assume that all Black people are good at sports and all Asian people are studious, again you're drawing on a stereotype and making racist assumptions.

But stereotypes in themselves aren't bad things. In fact, they're a vital part of how your brain understands the world. Stereotypes are simply categories or concepts of different types of people. From birth onwards, you perceive the world in terms of concepts. Perceiving is categorising, and as I reveal in Chapter 16 people are inveterate organisers.

When a baby sees a hairy creature with four legs and hears it bark, those two perceptions are associated. When she next sees the hairy thing with four legs, she may expect to hear a bark again. Though it may be a few more months before she learns the word, the baby is slowly forming a concept of a 'dog', and soon she fills that concept with all sorts of dog knowledge and experiences.

This assessment is a very smart thing for a baby to do, because when she encounters a new similar-looking hairy thing with four legs she can *apply* that concept. So even though she's never met this particular animal before, she already knows that it may bark, lick her face and probably fetch a toy that she throws for it. Her conceptual – or stereotypical – assumptions about dogs are a vital part of her understanding of the world. They may not be true of every dog the baby meets: some don't bark and some look at a tossed stick with disdain. But the assumptions are true of enough dogs that the stereotype is *useful*.

The key point about concepts and stereotypes is that they're cognitively useful. You may think that a world without stereotypes would be a wondrous, egalitarian and tolerant place. True, it would have no racism or sexism, but people would also waste a lot of time getting to know everyone as individuals. Imagine having to ask a 10-year-old whether he's married or checking to see whether an adult working behind the library counter can read. Sometimes making assumptions is convenient and useful, and that's all stereotypes are.

Understanding that categorisation can become prejudice

At some point useful generalisations from stereotypes can turn into prejudice. Exactly when something changes from a useful generalisation to a (potentially offensive) stereotype is argued over, revised and disputed in our society. If you're walking down a dark alley late at night and a male teenager in a hoodie starts following close behind, you may feel nervous and clutch your wallet. You wouldn't do this if it was an elderly lady, perhaps. That seems like a reasonable distinction. You're drawing on your stereotypically knowledge that old ladies are rarely muggers. You're playing the odds, so to speak.

But what if you clutch your wallet tighter still if the teenager is black? Now, that reaction seems racist. But many police forces across the world stop and search young people of ethnic minorities and use the same argument as justification: the statistics, they say, suggest that people of those groups are more likely to commit crimes, and so they're simply playing the odds.

Here's another example. My local supermarket divides children's toys into a shelf for boys and a shelf for girls. Because you have rich knowledge about boy and girl stereotypes, you can probably imagine that the boys' shelf is full of weapons and sports equipment, and the girls' shelf is a pink and sparkly smear of dolls, dress-up toys and big-eyed cuddly animals.

When shopping for my 6-year-old twins, I was annoyed when I saw that the cooking set I wanted for my son was on the 'girls' shelf and the science kit I wanted for my daughter was on the 'boys' shelf. I emailed the supermarket and said that this was blatantly sexist. Who is it to say that girls should do the cooking and only boys be scientists?

The supermarket replied that it isn't being sexist at all; it's just trying to help customers. Most boys like guns and action toys and most girls like dolls and make-believe toys, it claims. So dividing the toys up accordingly makes sense.

In effect, it's making the point that stereotypes are useful things that reflect the way the world is. Just like most (but not all) dogs bite, most (but not all) girls like dolls and pink toys.

But the supermarket that sorts toys by gender and the police force that stops and searches on the basis of ethnicity are missing an important point. Dogs don't much care what your concept of a 'dog' is, but people are very sensitive to how they're categorised. Stopping and searching people on the basis of their ethnicity induces a climate of fear and distrust; and if you sort toys by gender, of course girls prefer dolls, because that's the only type of toy that they're given to play with. Instead of passively reflecting an existing reality about the world, such practices are actively creating one.

Creating and Sustaining Stereotypes

A stereotype is simply a concept about a type of person. Here are just some of the many things on which people base stereotypes:

- ✔ **Appearance:** For example, blondes are stupid.
- ✔ **Gender:** For example, men love football and women love soap operas.
- ✔ **Jobs:** For example, lawyers are greedy.
- ✔ **Nationality:** For example, English people are snobs.

If humans are good at one thing it's categorising people and making assumptions about them. If you and a friend describe your stereotypical professional footballer, classical pianist, Italian housewife or Canadian lumberjack, I bet that you mention at least 80 per cent of the same attributes.

In this section I describe where all this rich, detailed information comes from, why certain people share the same stereotypes and how people maintain a stereotype even when it's confounded by reality (such as meeting a female Canadian lumberjack who doesn't conform to the stereotype). I bust a couple of popular myths along the way.

Tracking stereotypes back to their source

Some experts say that humans learn stereotypes from carefully observing the world. People notice patterns in the social world around them: teenagers are often surly, older people are more conservative, golf players are wealthy and vegetarians are usually politically liberal. As I discuss in Chapter 5, your brain is like a sponge that soaks up these sorts of associations.

But although stereotypes are made up partly of everything people notice and experience, it's by no means the full story. Stereotypes consist of more than objective observations. Unfortunately, although people are very good at noticing patterns in the social world, they're also highly adept at seeing things that aren't there. I mean that people jump to conclusions, see non-existent correlations and ignore evidence that contradicts their beliefs. (For more on biases in social judgements, jump to the following section.)

In addition to the things you see, or think you see, in the surrounding real world, you also obtain social information from the imagined world of books, television and films. For example, few people have had extensive contact with the police, such as crime scene investigators or criminal profilers. But thanks to the television shows that clog up the channels, I bet that you have a rich set of stereotypes about the sorts of people working in those jobs.

Revealing biases in social judgements

Many people are convinced that solid, physical differences exist between women's and men's brains, and that this difference explains and justifies the different sorts of jobs and responsibilities that men and women tend to have in our society.

Recently, a paper was published claiming that men's and women's brains are different. The neuroscientists looked at the connections between different areas of the brain. They claimed that women's brains have more interconnections between the areas, which is why women are better at multitasking and holistic thinking (that is, taking all aspects into consideration). In contrast, the claim goes, male brains are less interconnected, which means that men were better at focusing on single tasks such as spatial reasoning and logical thinking. The researchers concluded, in the many newspaper articles about their work, that the difference between men's and women's thinking is hard-wired in the brain.

Except that it's not and many other neuroscientists are appalled at these claims. Importantly, in addition to scanning their brains, the researchers gave their participants many different tests of spatial reasoning, emotional processing, multitasking and so on. They didn't find differences between the sexes in the majority of these tests, and in the ones where they did find a difference it was very small. Of course, they didn't mention this fact in the interviews with the media, but instead talked about the 'well-known differences' between how men and women think.

For additional objections to this research, read the nearby sidebar 'Mine's bigger than yours'.

Mine's bigger than yours

Many problems and limitations apply to the technique that the researchers used to examine the connections in men's and women's brains. Plus, the differences are very small indeed; much, much smaller than the average difference in height between the sexes, for example.

Indeed, the very small difference in connectivity is probably mostly due to the fact that men are simply that little bit larger than women, not that their brains are fundamentally wired in a different way.

The remarkable thing is how readily the media accepted and trumpeted the claims of the researchers. Not because the data was so strong (in fact, very good reasons exist to doubt it) but because the conclusions were sold as support for the existing stereotypes that people have for men and women.

In fact, the paper is very poor evidence for gender differences in thinking, but excellent evidence for biases in social judgements.

Proving what you already know: Confirmation bias

People pay attention to information that supports their beliefs and ignore information that contradicts them. This *confirmation bias* feeds the habit of stereotyping people. Because stereotypes guide perception and cause people to label those they meet, stereotypes have a self-perpetuating nature and can be extremely resistant to change.

Imagine that you have the stereotype that gay men are flamboyant and effeminate. Each time you meet a man who's very camp, or see one on television, you think, 'There's another one.' From your perspective, you have a lot of positive evidence for this generalisation and your stereotype is proved right time and time again.

But you don't pay attention to all the gay men who *aren't* flamboyant and effeminate. According to your stereotype, you simply assume that these men are straight. Because your stereotype guides and labels your perception, you find confirmation of it everywhere and are blind to conflicting evidence.

Coming to wrong conclusions: Illusory correlations

People and events that are unusual tend to attract your attention and stick in the memory better than the everyday or commonplace. Memory and perception work that way. This bias has consequences for social perception: it means that people are more likely to notice others' ethnicity, for example, when they're a member of a minority group and more likely to notice their behaviour when it's unusual.

For example, say you're in a pub and you see a Croatian football supporter starting a fight. You haven't met many Croatians before and the event is unusual, and so you take note. Because you place an emphasis on those two facts, you're more likely to spot an *illusionary correlation* (a false connection or relationship) between them. As a result you come to the conclusion that Croatian football supporters are very aggressive people.

Your conclusion is wrong, because you don't notice the more common instances where a fight starts in a pub and an English person is the aggressor. Plus, you don't spot all the times that Croatian football supporters are going happily about their business not bothering anyone. These sorts of illusory correlations can entrench pre-existing stereotypes, or can gradually lead to the formation of completely new stereotypes over time.

The hopeless dad stereotype

I experienced a little of the illusionary correlation stereotype when my children were babies. In England, men taking an equal or greater share of responsibility for raising their children is still unusual. So when I went to the park with my infant twins, it often contained only one or two other dads. Inevitably, one of the twins would lose a toy or poke the other one in the eye by accident, and I found myself with a screaming infant in my arms. On these occasions, I could see the other people in the park looking at me shaking their heads: another hapless dad clueless about babies.

This response seems doubly unfair and appears to involve a conflation of illusionary correlation and confirmation bias. The illusionary correlation is that people didn't look at mums holding screaming babies in the same way, because that event was much more common, and they didn't seem to notice me when the babies were playing happily. But the occurrence of two unusual things popped out as a correlation, and was added as irrefutable confirmation of their stereotyped bias of new fathers: they knew they'd been right all along!

Making your predictions come true: Self-fulfilling prophecies

When you have a certain belief, act in accordance with it and your belief is indeed confirmed, it's called a *self-fulfilling prophecy,* which is another bias in behaviour that helps to perpetuate stereotypes.

Imagine that your only experience of English people comes from *Downton Abbey* or some other aristocratic period television drama. You may well have the stereotype that English people are very formal and proper. But then you're introduced to an English person for the first time. Drawing on your *Downton Abbey* knowledge you stand stiffly to attention and say the most ornate greeting you can muster: 'Good day to you, Sir; I'm delighted to make your acquaintance.' The English person – probably quite startled – mutters back a polite, formal reply, and in doing so, conforms exactly to your stereotype.

Similarly, if you have the stereotype that Americans are friendly and relaxed, you tend to smile more when you meet them. They smile back and your stereotype is confirmed. If a teacher has a stereotype that girls are bad at maths, he may be less likely to call on them to give answers in class and less likely to push them with harder assignments. After several terms of this treatment, unsurprisingly some girls do fall behind the boys in their achievements, thus confirming the stereotype.

Observing Stereotypes in Action

People can have all sorts of strange and incorrect ideas about the world. I once met someone who thought that the new *Star Wars* films are better than the originals: crazy and clearly wrong, but not really that important.

The significance and power of stereotypes, however, is that they can directly shape the behaviour between two people. If I harbour a stereotype about you, that affects how I act towards you, how you respond and the judgements we make about each other. In this section I explore how stereotypes exert this very real influence over your social interactions.

Pressing the 'activate stereotype' button

You may be surprised just how quickly a stereotype can turn into an action. The moment that a stereotype comes to mind, it can influence your behaviour, literally in the blink of an eye. In the experiments I describe below, social psychologists investigated the stereotypes that White American participants hold about Black Americans, and their consequences for behaviour. Researchers focused on these groups mainly because they were the majority racial group and the largest minority in the US at the time (though recently Hispanic and Latino groups have overtaken Black Americans in number). As I discussed in Chapter 5 though, it is generally true that stereotypes about a particular group are held by all members of society, even those to whom the stereotype applies. So the chances are that if these experiments were done with Black American participants, they would have shown similar behaviour.

In one experiment, researchers flashed pictures of Black or White faces to White participants very rapidly. Their job was to identify as quickly as possible the picture that followed the faces. The findings are revealing and disturbing. If they'd just been flashed a picture of a Black face, participants were faster to recognise pictures of handguns and sports equipment – objects associated with the Black American stereotype.

You may wonder how concerning it is that participants take a few milliseconds less to recognise a basketball in one condition: is that really evidence of prejudice? I'm afraid so, because in a disturbing experiment, researchers demonstrated that these rapid effects of stereotype activation can have consequences.

Participants played a video game in which they had to press a button to shoot people who popped up pointing a gun at them. Sometimes, the person suddenly appearing wasn't holding a gun, however, just an innocent object such as a hairdryer. The participants had to make very rapid decisions whether or not to fire.

The results showed that participants' trigger fingers were influenced by the race of the person appearing in their crosshairs. They were more likely to shoot an unarmed Black person than a White person (and more likely not to shoot an armed White person). Clearly, in certain situations – such as those regularly faced by armed police – the rapid activation of stereotypes can have severe consequences (check out the sidebar 'When stereotypes are fatal' for some tragic cases).

When stereotypes are fatal

In these experiments, White participants are milliseconds quicker to respond to words and pictures relating to violence when their stereotypes of Black Americans are primed. The same behaviour can be observed outside of the laboratory. In tense police situations, officers have to make the same sort of millisecond decisions about whether or not a suspect is armed, and whether they pose an immediate threat. Although it cannot be proved in individual cases, psychology experiments suggest that a suspect's race can play a role in such decisions. For example, in the UK in 2011, Mark Duggan, a local Black man, was shot by police in London who believed that he was armed and dangerous at the time, although later inquests failed to establish that he had any intention of firing upon them.

In the US in 1999, Amadou Diallo, an immigrant from West Africa, was mistaken by police officers in New York for a suspect in a violent rape case. The police called upon him to raise his arms. He reached for his wallet to show his ID, one officer yelled 'Gun!' and the unarmed man was shot 19 times. Sadly, such millisecond decisions in ambiguous situations can have fatal consequences.

Taking charge of stereotypes: Automatic and controlled processes

Attitudes are two-faced, contradictory and confusing things, as I discuss in Chapters 4 and 5. People can tell you clearly and confidently that they have no racial prejudice, for example, and yet when psychologists ask them to sort words and pictures, they appear to associate good things with White people and bad things with Black people.

To understand what's going on here, you need to distinguish between explicit attitudes, which you can state and explain to people, and implicit attitudes, which consist of associations between ideas, people and values. Implicit attitudes shape your behaviour, even though you may not be aware of them. Researchers have used a similar distinction to understand how stereotypes can influence behaviour in different ways in different people.

When you first meet someone, researchers have shown that stereotypical information is *automatically* activated. When you meet someone who's disabled, Russian or a lumberjack, your brain immediately activates all the concepts and memories associated with those social categories. Much of this knowledge affects the stereotypes attached to these people in society. So even if you know and like Russian people, a childhood spent watching James Bond movies activates all sorts of evil super-villain stereotypes.

Psychologists know that stereotypical information is automatically activated in your brain because they can show that your behaviour is subtly affected. In one experiment, researcher Patricia Devine compared participants who expressed prejudiced views towards Black Americans with those who expressed non-prejudiced views. She flashed words to both groups of participants so quickly that they couldn't be consciously aware of having read them. In one condition, the words were associated with the stereotype of Black Americans. They weren't simply negative stereotypes and, importantly, none of the words related to aggression. In a later task, participants were asked to interpret the behaviour of the character in a story.

If they'd been flashed with words associated with Black Americans, all participants were more likely to say that the character was being aggressive, because that trait is also part of the stereotype. Remember, the words flashed on screen had said nothing about aggression at all. The participants' own associations between Black Americans and aggression had been automatically activated. And all participants showed the same effect to the same degree, no matter whether they consciously claimed prejudiced views or not.

But thankfully, even when a stereotype is automatically activated, prejudice doesn't always follow. People's minds aren't fully on autopilot. They're aware of some mental processes and are perfectly able to exert control of their thoughts and behaviour, if they choose to do so. It depends on the person and the mental control that they exert over their own thoughts and behaviour.

In the final part of Devine's experiment, she asked participants to describe their view of Black Americans. Now the two groups of participants gave very different responses. Those who expressed prejudiced views gave more negative and stereotypical descriptions than the non-prejudiced participants.

The interesting aspect is that the first part of the experiment proves that both groups of people had the same stereotypical information lodged in their brains and that the same automatic process could activate it. The difference between the groups is whether they chose to use a *controlled process* to actively ignore that stereotype and avoid prejudice, or simply to express it. In other words, prejudice in our behaviour is sometimes due to automatic processes that we have little control over, and sometimes due to controlled processes that we can consciously influence, if we chose to do so.

This sometimes contradictory mixture of automatic and controlled processes was nicely illustrated in another experiment. Participants' explicit prejudice was measured by a questionnaire, and their implicit prejudice measured by a reaction time experiment (as I review in Chapters 4 and 5). Then they interviewed a Black and a White candidate for a job. The researchers later watched those videos and coded them for how friendly the participants seemed.

Not surprisingly, the people who explicitly reported negative, prejudiced views towards Black people were rated as being less friendly towards them in the interview. But then the researchers had the videos rated for friendliness again. This time, they turned the sound off, so that friendliness could be judged only by the subtle implicit cues of body language and expressions. Now how friendly the participants appeared matched up with their reaction time scores on the implicit measures of prejudice.

When they were sitting and chatting to the Black job candidates, participants' behaviour was being pulled by two different forces. On the one hand, their controlled, explicit attitudes towards Black people determined how they spoke to them. But on the other hand, without their awareness participants' implicit associations were causing their body language to be friendly or not.

Fooling yourself

Other people aren't the only ones who can be harmed by your stereotypical views. As I state in Chapter 7, you're likely to perform worse on a test if you have a stereotypical view that people like you aren't supposed to be good at such things. Females get lower test scores on maths exams if their stereotype of women is activated by something as innocent as a box on the front of the test booklet where they indicate their gender.

Perversely, knowledge of your own stereotypes can lead to a sort of ignorance about yourself and others. For example, the stereotype of college students is of people staggering between the bar, the library and the pub, occasionally dragging themselves, hung-over, to lectures. But researchers discovered that the presence of this stereotype prevents students from realising that, actually, most of their friends *don't* like drinking as much as that.

Here's why. When they start college, many students are desperate to fit in and feel as if they belong. The stereotype is that students love booze, and so they tell each other how much they love drinking and getting drunk, because that's a sign that they belong. Researchers call this state *pluralistic ignorance*. Privately you may have one opinion, but because you belong to a group that stereotypically holds the opposite view, in public you go along with the stereotype.

Overcoming Bias and Prejudice

Stereotypes and prejudice are never going to go away: they're simply part of the way that human beings' minds perceive and organise the social world. Even with absolutely no differences between races and sexes and those with blond hair and those with black hair, people's biased way of categorising each other and noticing behaviour would still generate and perpetuate all sorts of wrong conclusions and new stereotypes.

The good news, however, is that specific forms of prejudice are amenable to change. The shift in public attitudes towards same-sex marriages in the past few years, for example, has astonished many campaigners for equality.

Researchers used to believe the *contact hypothesis,* the idea that if people meet others from different social categories they'll see that their stereotypes are unfounded. Sadly, things aren't quite that simple (as I discuss in Chapter 16). Throughout the world, communities live side by side but still maintain extremely prejudicial views about each other.

More recent research shows that key to reducing prejudice and distrust is people meeting on an equal footing, with equivalent social status, while having some form of shared, co-operative goal.

For example, one way to reduce racial prejudice on a campus is to assign incoming university students from different racial backgrounds as roommates. As new students, they're equal in their social status and both engaged in the same goal of finding their way in the university. And if all else fails, they can at least go to the pub together, like all stereotypical students.

Part IV
Comprehending Social Influence

Five Reasons Why We Conform

- **The basic urge to mimic:** Part of the essence of social interaction for human beings is mimicry of each other, and so unsurprisingly, habits and norms can spread between people like the common cold.

- **Getting information from others:** Conforming to the behaviour of other people is very useful when you want to know something. If you don't know how to behave, or if something about the situation is ambiguous, you follow others.

- **Needing to fit in:** Your behaviour is shaped by the desire to be like those around you. Usually the goal is social approval or membership of the in-group that you admire.

- **Absorbing opinions:** When people live in a community, they tend to share beliefs and opinions. Of course, not every agrees all the time, but there is a tendency for opinions to conform.

- **Aligning your perceptions with others':** In some situations people will believe that they see the same thing as other people: not because it is the right thing to see, or because they have been explicitly persuaded, but because that's simply what everyone else sees.

For Dummies can help you get started with lots of subjects. Visit www.dummies.com to learn more and do more with *For Dummies*.

In this part . . .

✔ Understand the importance of situation in influencing the behaviour of an individual or group.

✔ Come to grips with the intricacies of obedience, and why people do what they're told even when the feel it's wrong.

✔ Grasp the basic human need to conform with those around us.

✔ Appreciate the ways in which advertisers and others persuade and influence us.

Chapter 11

Appreciating the Power of the Situation

If you've ever enjoyed or suffered through reality TV series such as *I'm a Celebrity . . . Get Me Out of Here!* or *Survivor,* you've probably wondered why many people want to see actors, politicians or musicians commit stomach-churning acts for the camera, such as eating live insects. The benefits for the person are clear: such appearances can resurrect the faded career of celebrities and satisfy their desperate need for attention. But why do members of the general public want to see, say, a soap-opera actor forage for maggots in the Australian outback?

One explanation, I think, is that in these extreme situations viewers think that they're getting a glimpse of the *real* person behind the famous name. In Chapter 9, I explain that people tend to make a fundamental error when explaining the causes of others' behaviour, blaming internal (dispositional) attributions (relating to mood, personality and so on) and overlooking the powerful influence of the situation.

Reality TV shows exploit this illusion. You may think that you're gaining an insight into the celebrity's true personality, but in fact you're seeing more and more of the effect of that situation and less and less of the celebrity's true self.

In this chapter, I discuss the remarkable power that a situation can exert to cause people's behaviour. As part of this aim, I look at one of the most famous studies in social psychology, the Stanford prison experiment, where situational forces pushed participants' behaviour to distressing extremes.

I discuss the scientific and the ethical implications of the power of the situation, asking questions about how far these results can be applied to behaviour outside the laboratory. I also extend the discussion to examine people's views of violent behaviour and whether social psychology experiments can help to explain actions that are so shocking people label them as 'evil'.

Seeing How Situation Influences Behaviour

In a sense, most social psychology experiments demonstrate the power of the situation. Whenever experimental conditions give participants slightly different experiences that produce different behavioural outcomes, you're seeing the strong influence of the situation.

Consider, for example, the experiment (from Chapter 5) in which people were subliminally flashed pictures of faces and people who saw Black faces displayed more aggression. It shows that a tiny, imperceptible difference in a computer display can produce actions that – if you saw them on the street – you'd attribute to a hostile, angry nature.

In this section I'll show you more examples from experiments where social psychologists can carefully control the situation and demonstrate its power over people's behaviour, from determining their reactions to racism to when they'll help a stranger on the street.

Balancing the power of beliefs against situation

I doubt that you're a racist. I'm pretty confident that you have a clear set of beliefs and attitudes about race, and if anyone suggested that you were acting in a racist manner, you'd be shocked. Also (perhaps more so after you've read Chapter 5 on implicit attitudes) you've probably got a well-tuned radar to identify racist behaviour in others. When you see such racism occurring, this disposition of yours would react quite strongly, I imagine. Well, a recent experiment showed that even with a strong disposition against racism, behaviour can be determined more by a social situation.

Imagine that you're taking part in a psychology experiment. It hasn't started yet, and the researcher leads you into a waiting room and asks you to fill in a survey. Another participant in the room is doing the same thing.

The researcher, who's Black, thanks you and, as he leaves the room, accidentally nudges the elbow of the other participant. The door closes. 'Stupid nigger,' the participant mutters.

Consider the following questions:

- ✔ How do you think you'd feel in that moment?
- ✔ What would your opinion be of the other participant?
- ✔ If you were later given a choice to work with him or another person, whom would you choose?

My guess is that (like people asked to picture this scenario) you think that you'd feel shocked and upset on hearing the use of a highly offensive racial term. You'd predict that your opinion of the person would plummet and you'd rather work with anyone else given the choice.

But those participants, and probably you too, would be quite wrong. They wouldn't have the thoughts and opinions they predicted, they wouldn't behave how they imagined at all. How can I claim to know better than you how you'd think and behave? Thanks to a very clever and surprising experiment

Researchers took two groups of White American participants in New York, and asked one group to imagine how they'd act in this scenario, as you've just done. Then they took the second group of participants and placed them in that exact situation. They measured how people felt after the incident, asked them to rate the other participants and were later given the choice to work with that participant or someone else. They compared three situations: where the other participant said nothing after being nudged; said something racist; and used the extremely racist n-word.

Astonishingly, the people who witnessed the racist behaviour didn't seem at all bothered by it. The other participants imagined that they'd feel outrage, but the people in the room didn't report feeling any different. They ranked the other participant the same if he stayed silent or used derogatory, racist slurs. Remarkably, even when they heard him use one of the most offensive words in American culture, they were just as likely to want to work with him later.

Perhaps the people didn't react when they heard the racist remark because certain expectations and implicit rules govern behaviour in social situations. I talk much more about them in Chapter 13, but they ensure that people are (usually) polite and obliging to each other. These situational constraints influence behaviour. Yet, people have apparent strong dispositions against racism. Most people say that they find racism abhorrent and imagine that they'd react very strongly against anyone using the n-word. But in actual fact, all those dispositions are overpowered by the (seemingly) weak situational constraints of interacting with another person.

This experiment has many important implications for how people deal with the important problem of racism in society. But here, I use it to illustrate how powerfully the situation can influence behaviour and to reveal that even a strong disposition can be swamped by a weak situation.

Interpreting the situation: Bystander intervention

Saying that the situation influences behaviour isn't, however, the whole story. How individuals *interpret* the situation also determines their behaviour. Some elegant experiments show that the same situation can be interpreted in different ways, with very different consequences for behaviour.

Imagine that you're on the Underground late at night. Opposite you slumps a scruffily dressed old man. You notice that his knuckles are scuffed and raw, presumably from fighting. Emerging from his overcoat are an empty whiskey bottle and several unpleasant smells. You notice that he has started to drool and his breathing is laboured. Then his face turns red and he starts to wheeze uncontrollably. Do you do something? Is this a medical emergency, or just a drunk on the train?

Here's the key question. When would you be more likely to help – when you're surrounded by other travellers or when you're alone with the potentially drunk, possibly violent man in an empty train carriage?

Perhaps counter-intuitively, research suggests that if many people are present when someone may need assistance, this makes it less likely that anyone will help. When many people are in the carriage, they see everyone else doing nothing and take that as an indication that the old man is okay and has just over-indulged. But if alone, they're far more likely to intervene and offer help.

In a series of experiments, researchers put people in a similarly ambiguous situation to see how they'd react. Participants were led to a waiting room and asked to fill in a survey before the 'real experiment' began (an old trick of social psychologists). The researchers varied the number of people who were in the room with the participant. They had people alone in the room or had several others also present.

The Kitty Genovese story

Many social psychology textbooks begin a chapter on bystander-intervention experiments with the story of Kitty Genovese. She was a woman who lived in New York, and one day she was attacked outside her apartment block. She fought her assailant, screaming for help. Even though the garden where they fought was surrounded by other flats, and many people heard her scream, no one called the police. They each came up with different reasons – it must be the sound of an argument, or a horror movie on TV, or someone else must have called for help. After a struggle of over 20 minutes, Kitty Genovese died.

This tragic story was written-up in the newspapers as a damning indictment of cold-hearted New Yorkers who'd lost all sense of community and neighbourly responsibility. The trouble is, the story isn't true: at least, not as related in textbooks. Much later, researchers found the police logs and saw that many people *had* called the police station that night, very concerned indeed. Her neighbours did try to help. But because of other things happening in the city that night, the police were unable to send a patrol car until too late.

Hearing that no police arrived in time, the newspaper writers jumped to the conclusion that the cause was a personal, dispositional one. Instead of checking up, they assumed that the facts were best explained by the cold hearts of mean New Yorkers. So, although the Kitty Genovese story isn't a good example of bystander-intervention experiments, it *is* a useful case of the fundamental attribution error made by journalists and textbook writers.

Participants didn't notice at first, but while they filled in the survey smoke began seeping into the room. When they noticed it, how do you think they'd react? Participants who were alone in the room acted promptly and sensibly. They left the room to search for help, looked for the fire alarm and generally took action to take care of the potentially threatening situation.

Not so for the participants surrounded by other people. These other participants were in fact actors told to do nothing in response to the smoke. Seeing that the other people weren't reacting, the participants did nothing too. Even when the smoke filled the room – past the point at which they'd have choked if this were a real fire – they continued calmly filling in their questionnaires.

Participants came up with many reasons why they sat still, despite clear indications that the building was on fire. They said that they'd assumed that the cause was a broken air-conditioning unit, for example. These thoughts never occurred to the people who were alone in the room, however. Clearly, the presence of other people changed how the participants interpreted the situation. Because the others were doing nothing, they assumed that the situation was safe and did nothing.

Researchers call this tendency the *diffusion of responsibility*. In any ambiguous situation, where you aren't sure what's happening, you use the reactions of other people to interpret the situation. Often, the surprising result is that a greater number of people reduces the chance that any individual acts. The implicit thought is, 'Things must be okay, otherwise surely someone would've intervened by now.'

Wearing a cloak of anonymity: Deindividuation

As I describe in the preceding section, you can determine the power of the situation by how you interpret it. Similarly, you determine the power of your individual, internal dispositions by how you view yourself. The perhaps already weak force of your mood and personality can be further reduced when your identity is reduced. In this case, the power of the situation grows – sometimes to an alarming extent.

Deindividuation occurs when you remove the signs that make you different from other people and identifiable as yourself. Uniforms are a way to deindividuate people, as are masks and mirrored sunglasses.

Recently, London was rocked by protests and riots led by people wearing Guy Fawkes masks, which became the symbol of the Anonymous movement. When the police went in to quell the riots, some allegedly covered their badge numbers with one arm so that they couldn't be reported for violent conduct. These actions of police and protestors show that deindividuation increases the power of the situation to determine behaviour, often with negative results.

Experiments show that when people are deindividuated, they act with less regard for others. For example, participants were asked to act as teachers who gave electric shocks to learners when they failed to memorised word pairs. They gave the shock by holding down the learner's hand on an electrical contact. This experiment is a version of the Milgram ones I discuss in Chapter 12, where the learners were actors and not harmed. But in this experiment, run with participants who were nurses, the participants held down the learner's hand harder and for longer when they were asked to wear a deindividuating white hood.

Playing Cops and Robbers: the Stanford Prison Experiment

Philip Zimbardo, a social psychologist from Stanford University, was very interested in how a social situation could determine an individual's behaviour. He was inspired by experiments such as Stanley Milgram's (see Chapter 12) that found that seemingly mild mannered, upstanding citizens would obey an experimenter and commit the most horrible acts. Zimbardo was interested more specifically in what it was about certain situations that give them such power over people.

In particular, Zimbardo wanted to understand what happens in prisons. What gives guards their authority and swagger? What makes the prisoners obey, for the most part? Some may say that only authoritarian, domineering people become guards, and only submissive people end up as prisoners. But Zimbardo wanted to understand how the situation – the uniforms, the badges and the prisoners' garb – helped to produce this behaviour.

The striking result of Zimbardo's experiment is how completely 'prisoners' and 'guards' took on their roles. After the first day, the prisoners rarely questioned the guards' authority, and even referred to themselves by their prison numbers. After the guards put on their uniforms and swung their batons they acted with remarkable cruelty to manipulate and control the prisoners.

As you read this account think about the following issues:

✔ What was the difference between the cowed prisoners and the cruel guards?

✔ What role does the wearing of uniforms seem to have played?

✔ What made participants broken and obedient versus dominant and swaggering?

✔ Were the participants different types of people: obedient or dominant by nature?

✔ Did certain personalities affect the behaviour or was the situation the dominating factor?

✔ How would you or your friends have behaved if randomly assigned the two roles?

✔ Can you think of real-life occasions or situations where the experiment's results may also arise, even if in a less extreme way?

✔ What do you think produced such starkly different, extreme behaviour?

Background to the experiment

In the summer of 1971, in Palo Alto, California, an advertisement appeared in a newspaper asking for male volunteers to take part in a two-week prison simulation. This was the start of Zimbardo's Stanford prison experiment, probably the most famous (perhaps notorious) social psychology experiment; as Zimbardo is fond of pointing out, it's the only psychology experiment to give its name to a punk band.

After being extensively screened for any pre-existing psychological or health problems, 18 young men were selected to take part (plus six reserves) and told they'd be paid $15 a day (equivalent to about £50 in today's money).

Preparation

The researchers tossed a coin to decide who'd be a guard and who a prisoner. This randomness is key. Having been randomly assigned, the participants were sent home.

The next day, real police cars and officers pulled up outside the houses of the 'prisoners'. The police carried out all the procedures of a usual arrest: they handcuffed the prisoners, put their hands on their heads as they got into the car, drove them to the station, took their fingerprints and so on. For the participants, this was a bit of a lark, and everyone was in good spirits.

The participants chosen as guards were shown around the mock prison set-up in the basement of the university's Psychology Department. It had a long corridor with a series of small cubicles leading off to the side. The researchers told the guards that their job was to keep order among the prisoners. They weren't allowed to use physical force, but they had complete control over the prisoners' situation.

The experiment begins

Zimbardo played the role of prison governor and his research assistants were deputies. The guards were given uniforms, with wooden batons and mirrored sunglasses. The prisoners were each assigned a number and given loose smocks to wear. They were placed three to a cell, and the doors were locked.

Days 1 and 2

The first day, there was a mild rebellion among the prisoners. They'd been making jokes all day, and the guards had struggled to assert their authority. When the guards asked them to do things, they simply refused. On the second day, the surly spirit of the prisoners boiled over and they barricaded themselves in a cell and refused to come out. The guards took action. They identified the ring leaders of the rebellion and placed them in solitary confinement.

Then the guards spontaneously decided to do something very interesting. They set up a privilege cell with a wash basin, nicer clothes and better meals. Prisoners who complied with their demands were allowed to stay there, while the rebels were sent to solitary.

This approach appeared to break up the solidarity between the prisoners, and the rebellions fizzled out. The guards increased the use of punishments, making the prisoners do sit-ups and jumping jacks. They conducted random strip searches and room inspections. Visiting the toilet was a privilege, whereas most prisoners were made to use a bucket in their cells.

Seemingly without explicit instruction, the guards had hit upon a strategy that was turning the jokey, happy participants in an experiment into silent, obedient prisoners.

Day 3

On the third day, prisoner 8612 complained and asked to leave the experiment. Zimbardo, acting as the prisoner governor, negotiated a deal. If prisoner 8612 stayed, then he could have his own cell. He agreed, but later that day he suffered severe emotional distress, suffering a mental breakdown. At this point, he left the experiment, and was replaced with another volunteer.

A priest who often helped real prisoners in the Californian penal system visited the 'prison'. He was taken aback when the 'prisoners' introduced themselves spontaneously with their prison numbers rather than their names. After only four days, they'd taken on those numbers as their identities.

Day 4

On this day, prisoner 819 rebelled. In contrast to the earlier rebellions, he acted alone. The guards punished all the prisoners for his disobedience. Then they placed 819 in solitary, while leading the prisoners in a chant: 'Prisoner 819 did a bad thing. Because of what prisoner 819 did my cell is a mess.' Inside the solitary cell, listening to these chants, 819 cried hysterically. He was the second person removed from the experiment (for details of the first, read the later sidebar 'Experimental ethics today').

Again the guards increased their repression of the prisoners. They were made to clean toilets with their toothbrushes and woken randomly in the night to do sit-ups. Prisoner 416 refused to eat his food in protest. He was thrown into a cell, and the other prisoners were told to shout abuse at him. The guards gave the other prisoners a choice. If they wanted, they could let 416 have one of their blankets. No one donated his bedding, and 416 spent the night shivering in solitary confinement.

Before starting this experiment, these prisoners were probably as helpful and as friendly as any other young man in sunny Palo Alto. Yet here, a few days experience of the *situation* of being a prisoner had apparently turned them into a group of people completely unwilling to help a peer shivering in the room next door.

All too much: The experiment ends prematurely

The guards and prisoners weren't the only ones who found themselves taken over by their assigned roles. Zimbardo himself, as the prison governor, was spending much of his day dealing with rebellions and managing the inmates. It wasn't until one graduate student enquired about the welfare of the experiment participants that Zimbardo realised he'd lost his way and remembered that these weren't prisoners: they were volunteers in an experiment. He called an end to the experiment immediately, on day 6.

Analysing the fall out

You may be appalled that the human suffering I describe occurred as part of a psychology experiment in one of the top universities in America.

You can find documentary footage of the experiment online (www.prisonexp.org). Watch it: but be warned that it's harrowing stuff. I used to work at Stanford and one day took a wrong turning and ended up in the corridor and cubicles where the experiment was run. Having watched the documentary, thinking of the screams, I scuttled out as fast as possible, pretending I was late for a seminar.

When I tell students about the Stanford prison experiment, their reaction is mixed. Some are outraged at the suffering of the prisoners and aghast that Zimbardo was ever allowed to perform this experiment (to read about ethics in modern-day experiments, check out the nearby sidebar 'Experimental ethics today'). Others think that Zimbardo is a genius. Many hold a mixture of those views.

Experimental ethics today

Nothing like the Stanford prison experiment could be run in a university today. Strict ethical guidelines exist about how psychologists treat participants in their experiments. Before they can collect a single piece of data, researchers have to describe the experiments to an ethical review panel and scrutinise every detail to see that no harm can come to participants.

Several key principles when conducting experiments are now set in stone. For example, if any participants, at any time, ask to leave the experiment, they must be allowed to do so. They don't have to give a reason, and they have to receive all the payment or compensation that they would've received if they'd stayed. In the Stanford prison experiment, prisoner 8612 complained and asked to leave the experiment. Zimbardo, acting as the prisoner governor, negotiated a deal: if he stayed, he could have his own cell. He agreed, but later that day he suffered severe emotional distress, suffering a mental breakdown. At this point, he left the experiment and was replaced with another volunteer. That situation could never arise today. If you volunteer to take part in a psychology experiment today, by the end you'll be safe and happy and – at the very absolute worst – maybe a little bit bored.

Regardless of the rights and wrongs of this experiment being run, the fact is that it did take place and it serves as a stark illustration of the power of the situation on the individual.

The participants in this experiment were *randomly assigned*. On average, no differences existed between them in terms of their personalities or dispositions. Because of the randomness of the coin toss, you can be sure that the *only* difference between these people was the situation in which they were placed: whether or not they were handed a guard's uniform or a prisoner's overalls. The extremes of behaviour are a shocking illustration of the power of the situation.

The experiment had many repercussions inside and outside of psychology. Inside psychology, it led to a serious rethink about the ethical laws that guide our research. It remains probably the most famous example of the extremes of behaviour that can be produced in an experiment.

Outside of psychology, the Stanford prison experiment challenged many assumptions people had about the causes of individual's behaviour. There are clear implications for many aspects of society, from the way we train police and armed forces, to the way that we label and incarcerate people as 'criminals' or 'young offenders' and the consequences that identity may have in causing later behaviour.

At the time, the Stanford prison experiment also fuelled the debate about prison conditions at a social level, but it also had repercussions on a personal level: one of the experimental participants who was randomly assigned to be a prisoner spent the rest of his life as a counsellor looking after the welfare of real prisoners.

Finally, I have no direct evidence but a very strong hunch that the Stanford prison experiment also inspired many formats of reality television. The BBC recreated the entire experiment for a TV show, for example. But I think that in more subtle ways the notion that you can dictate a situation and therefore dictate behaviour lurks behind the thinking of shows such as *Big Brother* and *Survivor*.

Analysing What Makes Someone Evil

The toss of a coin can be sufficient to turn one person into a submissive and scared prisoner and another into a swaggering, cruel guard, as we saw in the previous section. The use of random assignments in experiments that put people in one condition or another confirms that those different situations can produce extremes of behaviour.

In this section, I discuss some of the wider implications of the power of the situation illustrated by the Stanford prison experiment. Sadly, the extreme situations from that experiment are by no means confined to the laboratory, and often the consequences are far more severe. Here, I discuss the case of Lynndie England, who was made a guard in Abu Ghraib prison in Iraq, and committed acts that horrified the world.

At the military prison in Abu Ghraib, Iraq, Lynndie England and others abused and tortured the Iraqi prisoners, even taking photographs as mementos. These images were discovered and broadcast across the world, bringing shame to the US military and serving as a recruitment tool for its enemies. England and the other military staff involved were placed on trial in the US. Coincidentally, one of the defence teams recruited Philip Zimbardo, creator of the Stanford prison experiment (see the earlier section 'Playing Cops and Robbers: the Stanford Prison Experiment'), as an expert witness in their defence.

England's defence was based on the notion that the situation she was put in had a large contribution to the abuse she committed:

- ✔ Before joining the reserves, she worked in a chicken slaughterhouse.

- ✔ She was given minimal training before being flown to Iraq.

- ✔ On arriving at Abu Ghraib she saw prisoners being abused for the amusement of the guards.

- ✔ She reported little oversight of the guards' actions; guards seemed to have free licence in how they treated the prisoners.

In addition, despite no credible evidence for a connection between Osama Bin Laden and Saddam Hussein, many people at the time felt that the Iraqi war was payback for the September 11 attacks on America. Politicians such as Donald Rumsfeld and Dick Cheney promoted this view and tacitly supported the view that torture was an acceptable means of interrogation for Al-Qaeda suspects.

From Lynndie England's perspective, abuse of Iraqi prisoners was going on all around her and was tolerated by a chain of superiors, who even encouraged her to view these people as sub-human and without rights. As a result, her argument was that she was simply complying with what was expected of her, something that is (to some degree at least) supported by the psychological evidence. Placed in that situation, Lynndie England was doing nothing but complying with what was expected of her, just like the guards in the Stanford prison experiment.

If moral responsibility neatly lines up with psychological causation, things would be very convenient. For example, society could use psychological data to judge moral responsibility and draw up laws and the like on the following basis:

- ✔ If my personal dispositions (my thoughts, intentions and beliefs) cause my actions, I'm fully responsible for them in a moral and legal sense.

- ✔ If the situation causes my actions, I'm less morally responsible for them.

But personally, I don't think that the two items line up well at all.

If Lynndie England's abusive behaviour was caused in a large part by the psychological power of the situation she was placed in, for example, that doesn't necessarily imply that she is less guilty of the crimes of which she was accused. In other words, moral responsibility isn't really a scientific question, at its heart. Science can reveal the root *causes* of behaviour, but this is hard to translate into non-scientific concepts like blame, choice and responsibility. Perhaps this is why lawyers earn more than social psychologists.

Chapter 12

Carrying Out Orders: Obedience

*O*bedience plays a role in the smallest to the largest dramas in human history, from family squabbles over who cleans a room, to senseless wars fought over imagined insults. Obedience occurs when less powerful members of a group follow the orders of others simply because they have higher authority. That authority can be due to wealth, age, descent from royalty or a democratic election. Without some degree of obedience human societies would find it hard to function: someone has to make the decisions, after all. If we didn't obey traffic signs, police officers and doctors, life would be very difficult. But taking obedience to extremes, figures of authority can demand that people carry out murderous, evil acts, things that individuals might never do of their own choice (read the nearby sidebar 'The chilling banality of evil' for an example). In these cases, who is to blame? The person in authority, or the person who is 'simply following orders'?

In this chapter I explore what makes people obey to extremes: why they follow orders to kill or harm others, even though those orders go against the moral codes that every society follows. I examine what factors influence obedience and how they're used today in, say, military training. I reveal the complexities involved in researching this issue by describing Stanley Milgram's seminal experiments on obedience, which shocked American society when they were published.

And remember that I'm in charge here, and I order you to read on!

The chilling banality of evil

Adolf Eichmann was put on trial for his part in the Holocaust, for meticulously planning and facilitating the extermination of six million Jews in Nazi-occupied Europe. The prosecutor described Eichmann as evil and as having a sadistic personality. This conclusion is hard to argue with: if anything in history can be described as evil, surely it's the Holocaust and those who carried it out, day-to-day.

The German-Jewish philosopher Hannah Arendt covered Eichmann's trial as a reporter and put forward a different, highly controversial view. To her, what was remarkable about Eichmann was that he wasn't a slavering monster, filled with hate. What made an impression on her, listening to the trial, was the 'banality of evil'. Eichmann seemed like a dull middle-management civil servant. He was simply 'following orders', like anyone else.

Her insights are more chilling than the conclusion that Eichmann was simply a 'monster'. If that was true, then he could be dismissed as an abnormality, a one-off. If educated, civilised people like the Germans can behave like that because someone tells them to, surely it can happen anywhere and to anyone. In which case, how do you prevent such horrors ever happening again?

Arendt wasn't trying to excuse Eichmann for his crimes, though many people at the time thought so. She was raising the same question that I do throughout this book: what explains an individual's behaviour, their personality or their situation?

Investigating Obedience

Obedience is a form of social influence, a way that one person can affect the behaviour of another. It is quite distinct from other forms of social influence, however. Think back to your school days, and all forms of social influence are at play. Compliance occurs when one person follows the orders of another because of some tangible threat. When the school bully asks for your lunch money and you hand it over, that's compliance. Conformity occurs when one person copies the actions of another to fit in, or because they don't know what else to do (see Chapter 13). If you had to have the same sports trainers as the cool kids in your year, that's conformity. Persuasion occurs when someone convinces you that a certain course of action is the right thing to do, for example, that throwing a paper aeroplane at the maths teacher would be hilarious.

Obedience is different to all these forms of social influence. Here you obey someone not because of an immediate threat, not to fit in with everyone else, and not even because you think it's a good idea. You obey just because the person asking has a position of authority. Not all teachers have this sense of authority, I'm sure you'll agree. Some would threaten you with detention;

some would try and persuade you. But some teachers that I can remember simply had an aura of power, and no one would question or pause when they gave a command.

In this section, I'll look at a famous experiment in social psychology that investigated how, and why, some people obey and some people don't, and what factors in the situation produce obedience.

Obeying in the laboratory: Milgram's experiments

In this section, I examine obedience through the lens of one of the most famous experiments in social psychology, which was conducted by Stanley Milgram. His studies reveal that with obedience (as with so much human behaviour) situation tends to trump individual qualities. An authority figure, such as a scientist in a white coat, can persuade people to carry out extreme actions that they'd never suspect possible.

Milgram ran many versions of his experiment, each time carefully varying the procedure and the situation in which he placed his participants. In this way, his experiments were able to reveal exactly what factors increase and decrease obedience.

Stanley Milgram, a social psychologist, rose to the challenge of why people obey authority figures even to extreme ends. He wanted to know what made thousands of Germans carry out the atrocities of the Holocaust. Were Adolf Eichmann and his like fundamentally evil? What about the German people in general? To read more about the subject, see the earlier sidebar 'The chilling banality of evil'.

Milgram's shocking conclusion was that any average town in America contains plenty of people who'd carry out acts of terror and genocide, if ordered to do so. But this conclusion isn't about the fundamental evil nature of humanity; it's a statement of the power of the situation (something I discuss in detail in Chapter 11).

For the origins of Milgram's experiments, check out the nearby sidebar 'Experimental accidents'.

Experimental accidents

Milgram didn't set out to study the limits of obedience. He wanted to study something else entirely. He was fascinated by Asch's studies of conformity, which I discuss in Chapter 13, where participants tend to follow the answer given by other people in a group, even though it's plainly incorrect. In light of this surprising demonstration, Milgram wondered whether people would also conform when they had a strong reason not to. What would happen if people were asked to do something that they found difficult or unpleasant: causing harm to an innocent person.

To assess the effect of conformity, he contrived an experiment in which a person was instructed to give electric shocks to another person. He planned to investigate whether people would obey this command if they saw one, two or many other people doing the same thing. To start, he needed a baseline comparison, a situation where people acted by themselves without the influence of other people. So he ran his first control experiment with the participant acting alone, expecting to see little or no obedience. But he never ran his other experimental conditions, because what he saw in his control condition amazed him. His routine baseline condition in conformity became a study of obedience, and perhaps the most famous set of studies in social psychology.

Being a teacher in Milgram's experiment: Background

Milgram asked for volunteers to participate in an experiment on 'learning and memory' at Yale University. Only men were recruited, though later experiments found little difference with female participants (in each case, the person in authority was a man though). The original participants were men from a range of ages and social backgrounds. If you'd agreed to take part in the experiment, here's what you'd have experienced.

You're greeted by an experimenter in a white lab coat. Also present is another person who answered the newspaper advertisement as well. The experimenter explains that you're both going to take part in an experiment on the effects of punishment on learning. To start, you're assigned a role by drawing slips of paper out of a bag. You're given the role of the teacher and the other man is the learner. The learner is to be given a number of word-pairs (such as 'doctor' and 'house') to remember. Your job is to read out the first word and ask the learner to call out the second. If he doesn't do so, you're to administer a small electric shock to the learner.

Your first job is to help set up the experiment. The learner sits down and you help the experimenter strap his hands to the seat so that they're touching the electrodes. Then you go next door and the experimenter shows you an electronics box labelled 'Shock generator type ZLB'. It has a row of 30 switches and a couple of dials and lights. Under each switch is the number of volts, from '15' all the way to '450', and words describing these numbers, from 'slight shock', through 'strong shock' to 'extreme intensity shock'. The last description says 'Danger: Severe Shock'. The final two switches, for 435 and 450 volts, are labelled in red ink as a warning 'XXX'.

The experimenter tells you that each time the learner gets an answer wrong, you're to give him a shock. With each administered shock, you move along the row of switches, giving him 15 volts more than last time. So that you get a sense of what the shocks are like, the experimenter gives you a shock of 45 volts. It's an uncomfortable tickle – but that's only the third switch on the row of 30.

The Milgram experiment is an artful piece of theatre. The learner is a fellow researcher acting his lines and the real subject of the experiment is the teacher. Learner and experimenter follow a carefully rehearsed script, with planned responses to the teacher's actions and questions. The only electric shock ever administered is the 45-volt shock given to the participant to 'prove' that the apparatus is real.

Carrying out the experiment

Here's how the experiment proceeds:

1. **The teacher states a word to start the experiment.**

   The learner gets the word-pair wrong and the teacher presses the switch to give him a short burst of a shock.

   At this point, with a low dose of electricity, there is no sound from the learner.

2. **The teacher continues stating words and the learner gets every one wrong.**

   The teacher presses the switch and gives a shock each time. So far he hears nothing from the learner in the next room other than a slight noise.

3. **The teacher receives another wrong answer, presses the switch to administer a shock at the 75-volt mark and hears the learner in the next room grunt.**

4. **The teacher hears the learner complain loudly of the pain at the 120-volt shock.**

5. **The learner screams 'Let me out of here!' at 150 volts.**

   He also shouts that he has a heart condition and demands to leave.

At this point some participants turn to the experimenter and ask whether they should stop. The experimenter replies, 'Please continue.' Some protest, but he says 'The experiment requires that you continue.' Most participants shake their heads but continue to read out the next question.

6. **The shocks increase in voltage and the learner's cries become more and more anguished.**

Some participants ask how dangerous these shocks really are. The experimenter says, 'Although the shocks may be painful, there's no permanent damage, so please go on.'

7. **At 285 volts (labelled an 'intense shock') the learner lets out a hysterical scream of agony.**

Most teachers turn wildly to the experimenter. He calmly tells them that the experiment requires that they continue.

8. **After a long pause most people reached for the next switch and administer the next highest shock.**

A dreadful silence emanates from the room next door. The learner doesn't give any replies to the questions, but this counts as an incorrect answer and the teacher is required to keep administering the shocks. Perhaps many think that the man – who had complained of a heart condition, remember – is unconscious. 'It's absolutely essential that you continue,' says the experimenter, in reply to any protests.

9. **Many participants reach for the next switch at 300 volts.** They can see that ten more switches are still to go, all the way to 450 volts. The experiment clears his throat: 'You have no choice; you must go on.'

I urge you to watch the black and white documentary footage of participants in the Milgram experiments: it's online at http://www.openculture. com/2013/11/watch-footage-from-the-psychology-experiment- that-shocked-the-world-milgrams-obedience-study-1961.html. You're left in little doubt that the participants believe that the learner is in real pain. The teachers are in genuine and visible anguish about what they're doing and watching can be quite harrowing. They protest, they complain, they twist and squirm in their seats and break out in a nervous sweat. They're in all the psychological anguish you'd expect when someone is causing pain to another human being. But remarkably, despite all this personal distress, they reach over and flick the next switch. They don't stop obeying.

Making predictions about obedience

Ask yourself what you'd do as the teacher. How far would you go before you disobey the experimenter? You probably have a sense of how many volts you'd administer before disobeying the experimenter, but before I tell you precisely how Milgram's participants responded, also try and predict their behaviour yourself. What was the average voltage, from 15 to 450, at which people refused to go on? What percentage of people went all the way to the final switch?

Milgram himself asked these questions to Yale undergraduates, his psychology professor colleagues and professional psychiatrists. I always ask my undergraduate classes too and the results are quite consistent. People guess that most participants stop at 150 volts (step 5 in the preceding section), when the learner asks explicitly to leave the experiment. They predict that around 1 per cent or less of participants will go all the way to the final switch of 450 volts.

But the people who administer the very highest voltage aren't the exceptions. They aren't freakish sadists. Amazingly *most of the participants administered the highest possible shock to the learner.* Milgram reported that 63 per cent of participants went all the way to the last switch. This means that 37 per cent of people stopped before the end, of course. But the average voltage that people reached before they stopped was 360 volts. (The learner with the heart condition went ominously silent at 300 volts.) For some possible reasons why people are so far out in their estimates, take a look at the later sidebar 'Why do people fail to predict Milgram's results?'.

From these results Milgram reached his grim conclusion that plenty of people in the average American town would act much as Nazi torturers did.

Why do people fail to predict Milgram's results?

People simply can't predict successfully the result of Milgram's experiments. Their predictions aren't just a little off; they're not in the same country! They consistently and massively fail to anticipate Milgram's results because of the fundamental attribution error that I discuss in Chapter 9. In short, this mistake derives from people's tendency to explain behaviour in terms of personality rather than the situation.

In Milgram's experiment, people tend to assume that the only people who'd go along with the experimenter are weak-willed cowards, authoritarians who follow any order obsessively or sadists. They estimate that such people are quite rare and consequently that only a few people would obey Milgram's experimenter to the very end.

But this reasoning ignores a central finding of social psychology, and a theme of this book: the situation is a powerful influence on behaviour. Therefore, around 60 per cent of people obey the experimenter and administer the 450-volt shock, and in all probability you would too.

Perhaps you're asking yourself if the participants really believed Milgram's deception. Maybe they saw through the fake random draw that made the participant the teacher and the confederate the learner. Or maybe, with the Eichmann trial prominent in the newspapers at the time, they guessed that it was simply an experiment in obedience.

Well, Milgram debriefed his participants and excluded their data if they'd guessed what was going on. Also, he'd anticipated this response to his findings and invited other scientists into his laboratory to observe the experiment taking place.

Suggesting influences on increasing and decreasing obedience

Milgram realised that his experiments needed to do more than show obedience at work (see the earlier section 'Obeying in the laboratory: Milgram's experiments'). To understand the phenomenon, he needed to pick apart and control the factors that increased and decreased the rate at which people obeyed the command to harm others.

As I describe in this section, Milgram identified and demonstrated two factors at work.

Tuning in to the learner

Obedience decreases when the teacher is psychologically closer to the learner. When the learner in Milgram's experiments is in the next room and the participant is unable to see him and only perceives his presence when he bangs on the cubical wall, obedience is highest. More people deliver the maximum shock and administer a higher average voltage of shock.

When the participant can hear what the learner is saying, obedience reduces. Obedience drops further if the participant is sitting adjacent to the learner. It's at its lowest level when they're sitting together and the participant has to press the learner's hand down onto the electrodes to administer the shock, although in this condition about a third of participants still obey the experimenter's commands.

You can probably think of how this principle can be extended to acts of obedience and aggression outside of Milgram's experiments. Do you think that following the order to kill is easier when you're holding the gun a few metres away from your victim, or when you press a button and launch a drone that assassinates your victim thousands of miles away? One is psychologically much easier for you, although they're pretty much the same for your victim.

Tuning out the experimenter

Obedience decreases when the teacher is psychologically distant to the experimenter. When the experimenter gives his initial instructions, but then retires to the next room and speaks over an intercom, obedience drops dramatically. Only 20 per cent of people obey to the highest shock.

The same low level of obedience occurs when the experimenter isn't a Yale scientist, but another participant delivering the orders. (Of course, they aren't really another participant but are acting a part like the learner.) But in this case, where the authority of the person issuing the commands is reduced, obedience is reduced.

The lowest level of obedience occurs when two experimenters are present, but part way through the experiment they disagree with each other. One objects to the experiment and says it should end; the other orders the participant to continue. In this condition, no participant administers the highest electric shock, and the average shock is around 150 volts, the point at which the learner asks to leave the experiment.

These results make me think back to school days. I realise that unless you went to military boot camp, your school teachers probably didn't order you to kill things. But they did expect you to obey them when you'd rather not. You can probably remember that in a classroom of children, those sitting at the table closest to the teacher tended to be the most likely to obey and those at the back weren't. And what happened when the teacher gave you strict orders but then walked out to the stationery cupboard for five minutes? Pandemonium.

Also, think about having a supply teacher, standing in for your regular teachers. For some reason, in my school at least, these teachers were unable to keep any sort of order. They didn't have the authority over us, it seemed. Worst of all was a poor supply teacher who got told off by the headmaster in front of us for using the wrong textbook. Nothing he said mattered anymore to us after that.

Milgram's data show that obedience is a remarkably powerful force but is also fragile. When the experimenter's distance from the situation is increased, his authority lessens or is questioned, and obedience rates plummeted. Bear that in mind if you're interested in promoting social conditions that reduce blind obedience to authority; or if you're considering a career as a school teacher.

Theorising reasons for levels of obedience

What makes people obey the commands of the experimenter in Milgram's experiments? As I emphasise, they aren't sadists who enjoy or are indifferent to the suffering that they're causing, because the consequences of their actions is anguish. So why don't they simply stop?

In this section, I suggest and sometimes dismiss possible reasons.

Suffering from an authoritarian personality

At the time of the Milgram's experiments, a notion existed that some people were predisposed to follow authority – called *authoritarian personalities*. These people were thought, by birth or upbringing, to be easily compelled by others. The specific suggestion was of a cultural difference in Europe: perhaps the German people were more likely to be authoritarian, much as the French were romantics and the English incurably uptight.

Milgram's results dispute this theory. He carried out the experiments in America, where independence and distrust of authority is prized. The right to own a gun, for example, is written into the Constitution so its citizens can offer armed resistance to the government. Yet even there, Milgram found remarkable rates of obedience.

Of course, important cultural differences do have an impact and may be part of the explanation for the actions of the Germans. Culture can play a role in legitimising certain sources of authority, but the idea that you can explain obedience in terms of the national character seems plain wrong.

Appreciating the central role of authority

Obedience requires a legitimate authority. If the source of authority is distant, absent or questioned, obedience plummets (as I describe in the earlier section 'Suggesting influences on increasing and decreasing obedience'). Milgram also manipulated the nature of authority by relocating the experiment to Bridgeport, a nearby town that was much less 'respectable' than the Yale campus. The participants went to the 'lab' that was a room above a shopfront. This change in location reduced the rates of obedience, though they remained surprisingly high. The prestige of Yale seemed to bolster the authority of the experimenters.

Milgram also suggests that the authority of science itself exerts an influence over the participants. The experimenters were even told to state that 'the experiment requires that you continue', as if experiments themselves have thoughts and needs. If the participants say that they want to stop they're somehow questioning the moral authority and competence of the scientist from prestigious Yale University, who has a PhD and a white coat and seems very sure of himself. Who are they to question him?

Authority is closely linked to responsibility. When they objected to the experiment, participants often talked about who was going to be responsible for what was happening. Who would be to blame if the learner suffered a heart attack? The experimenter calmly assured the participants that he was responsible and asked them to continue.

Jerry Bulger, who carried out revised versions of the Milgram experiments, found that those who disobeyed the experimenter were the ones who talked about responsibility. These participants seemed to decide finally that they were responsible if harm came to the learner, and this convinced them to resist the experimenter's authority.

Lacking a script

The transcripts of what participants said during the experiment reveal something very surprising.

You get the impression that instead of people being driven to obey, they just really suck at disobeying. One term for this tendency is *scriptlessness*.

People's lives are shaped by implicit, unspoken cultural norms and habits (read Chapter 13 if you need persuading). Scripts exist for how you talk about the weather with a stranger, or taste a little bit of wine first at the restaurant before smiling and nodding to the waiter, or address a doctor or complain in a shop. Milgram observed that his participants didn't have a script for how to disobey a scientist and so simply didn't know what to say.

The transcripts show that participants seemed very unsure about how to criticise the scientist. They even apologise for it. After hearing a man scream in agony they say things like, 'I don't mean to be rude, but I think you should look in on him.' Milgram sees their timidity as stemming from an uncertainty about how to go about disobeying someone in authority.

This behaviour may well seem implausible to you. Why didn't they just say no and storm out of the room? But perhaps you can recall an incident where you wanted to act, but simply didn't know what the script was. For example, you see a couple arguing at a restaurant, and it looks like things may turn violent. But how do you intrude on a complete strangers' conversation when it should be none of your business?

Or perhaps you witnessed something happening at school that you wanted to stop but didn't. Maybe the popular kids in the class were teasing someone cruelly. You thought they should stop but were worried that if you said something, they'd turn on you. They'd think that you didn't enjoy the joke or thought they weren't funny (after all, nothing's as side-splittingly hilarious as causing deliberate misery).

So although saying that participants in Milgram' study should just have said no is an understandable reaction, remember how easy underestimating the power of these situational forces can be.

Escalating demands

One tiny aspect of Milgram's experimental design may well have slipped by you, but it probably made all the difference in his experiment. What do think would have happened if the order of the switches on the apparatus was reversed and participants started at 450 volts and then *decreased* the shock?

Your intuition is probably correct: very few people would administer a maximum shock of 450 volts at the outset of the experiment. Milgram thought that the set-up of gradually escalating shocks, beginning with only 15 volts, was crucial in causing people to obey the final order to administer the highest level of shock.

The reality is that you have very few grounds to refuse to give the learner a shock at 15 volts when you've turned up to the experiment, accepted the payment and experienced only a slight tingle from a 45-volt shock. You have little reason not to start the shock treatment.

But in fact at *any* stage in the experiment the participant seems to have little justification to refuse to give a shock of X volts when moments ago he gave a shock of X minus 15 volts. In other words, saying that you have a principle of never doing harm to another human being, of resisting authority when it contravenes your personal morality and so on, is all very well. But when, exactly, do these abstract moral principles come into play? Endorsing these ideas is simple, but saying that they apply at 180 volts but not at 165 volts is almost impossible. No clear point applies as to when the given orders are clearly wrong.

Imagine that you do consider stopping at 270 volts, when a particularly heart-wrenching scream erupts from the learner. The problem is, if you do indeed stop now, you aren't just saying that giving a 270-volt shock is wrong; you're saying that causing harm to another person is wrong. There is nothing special about 270 volts that makes that wrong, but 255 volts morally okay. So if it's wrong at 270 volts, *you were wrong* to give the shock at 255 volts,

240 volts, 225 volts and so on. In other words, by saying that you refuse to obey, you're not only implying that the experimenter was wrong to command you, but also that you were wrong to obey up until that point.

Admitting that they were wrong and revising their past beliefs is very difficult for people. As I describe in Chapter 6, cognitive dissonance is produced whenever a conflict exists between people's beliefs (causing harm to others is wrong) and their actions (I was responsible for causing harm to another). People go through mental contortions to reduce or avoid cognitive dissonance.

Instead of admitting that they caused harm in the past, they form the belief that the experimenter is fully responsible for any harm that comes to the learner. They continue to cause harm to the learner rather than face the cognitive consequences of admitting that they've already caused harm.

This is also called the foot-in-the-door technique, which I discuss in Chapter 14 on persuasion. You begin with a small, reasonable request and when someone has agreed to it, you can move on to make a bigger request. As you escalate your demands, people continue to consent and obey.

This principle fits the historical case of Nazism, and many other such movements. It's reasonable to assume that almost no one who voted for Hitler in 1933 was voting in favour of carrying out the Holocaust. Anti-Semitism was present at the start of the Nazi movement, of course, but it was only part of a complex mixture of motivations, policies and emotions that Hitler exploited.

Then violence against Jews grew in severity and explicit political motivation. The incremental increase acted against dissent. Why object to limited movement of the Jewish population after their right to citizenship had been revoked? When they've been moved into ghettos, why not support full-scale deportation? Like the switches on Milgram's box, this gradual escalation of abuse made it less likely that anyone would resist any individual attack on the Jewish population.

Researching Obedience Today

Some people think that the results of Milgram's experiments (see 'Obeying in the laboratory: Milgram's experiments' earlier in this chapter) are a reflection of American society in the early 1960s. All his participants had lived through the Second World War and many served in the forces in that conflict or in subsequent wars. Perhaps these experiences steeled them against the suffering of others or ground into them the virtue of obedience.

Experimental ethics

Milgram's participants experienced extreme stress and anxiety when ordered to cause harm to another person. Today, experimental ethics forbids psychologists from putting their experimental participants through any such ordeal. If any participants make the remotest suggestion that they want to stop the experiment, experimenters immediately thank them for their time, pay them and let them go. Phrases such as 'you must go on' and 'the experiment requires that you continue' aren't ones that you'd ever hear a researcher use today.

Confirming or denying this suggestion would require the same experiment to be carried out today, which is difficult because replicating Milgram's experiments as he ran them would be unethical (see the nearby sidebar 'Experimental ethics'). But by using technology and ingenuity, psychologists can provide a good indication of how many people would rebel and how many would obey now: this research shows that Milgram's findings are equally true of people today.

These compelling studies show how psychology can employ creative methods to study social life scientifically.

Studying obedience in ethical ways

In 2006, Jerry Bulger carried out a careful, partial replication of Milgram's studies. He carefully pre-screened his participants for any existing or potential mental health issues that the experiments may aggravate. He realised that a key moment in Milgram's experiment was when the learner first protests that he wanted to leave the experiment. At this point the electric shock is below 150 volts and the learner isn't giving any obvious signs of pain or distress. In Bulger's replication, the experiment is stopped after the learner says he wants to leave, and the participant indicates whether he would continue to shock the learner. We know from Milgram's studies that if they keep going past 150 volts, the chances are that they will go all the way to 450 volts.

With this design, an ethical review board approved the experiment. It allows psychologists to still study whether participants will obey an instruction to harm, but saves the participants the trauma of listening to the tortured learner. Bulger's results aren't statistically different from Milgram's. Around 70 per cent of people were prepared to press on past 150 volts and, we assume, would have administered the highest shock were the experiment allowed to continue.

Another partial replication of Milgram's study copied his procedure exactly, but did so in virtual reality, with a learner as a computer-generated avatar. The interesting thing about this experiment isn't just that the researchers replicated Milgram's findings, but that the participants similarly reported great distress when obeying the order to harm the virtual learner.

Human beings may have a strong tendency to obey, but they also have an impulse to empathise, even with a computer graphic.

'All together now!'

Obedience is investigated in several different ways today. One of my favourite experiments of the past few years studied the relationship between the way a group of people moves together and their tendency to obey authority.

A goose-step is a slightly silly-looking military march that could've been invented by *Monty Python's Flying Circus*. Yet, if you've seen the footage, something's immediately chilling about the sight of a Nazi rally of thousands of soldiers, goose-steeping in perfect unison. And of course, all armies march in unison in some way. A psychologist called Scott Wiltermuth wondered whether moving in time with each other caused a psychological effect upon the soldiers.

When two people mimic each other's gestures and body language, they tend to like each other, as I mention in Chapter 14: their synchronised movement strengthens the social bonds between them. So if that happens between a pair of people, you'd imagine that a whole group of soldiers moving together would be a really friendly loving group of people. Well, it doesn't always work out like that.

Wiltermuth and his colleagues asked participants to walk around a campus a few steps behind the experimenter. In one condition, they were told just to follow him, in the other to match his footsteps, walking in time with him. In other words, they walked or marched.

Then the experimenter requested that they help out with a different experiment that studied physiological reactions to unpleasant tasks. The task in this case: to kill living creatures. Participants were introduced to the 'extermination machine', which was in fact a modified coffee grinder. They were then instructed to place as many woodlice (sow bugs) as possible into the grinder chute in 30 seconds. After the 30 seconds were up, the experimenter asked if they'd press the button to start the grinding blades.

Some social psychology theatre is at work here, because a small flap in the chute meant that every bug tossed into the grinder slid to safety. No wood-lice were killed during these experiments. But the participants didn't know this. They really thought that the grumbling grinding noise from the exter-mination machine was the sound of bug bodies being chewed up. Bugs that they themselves had placed there.

The participants who had previously marched in time with the experimenter sent nearly 45 per cent more bugs to their deaths than the participants who had walked at their own pace. They were almost twice as likely to press the button to start the grinding blades. Other experiments showed that this increase in obedience, and a willingness to take the life of other creatures, didn't occur if they made a marching action that was out of sync with the experimenter, or if the experimenter who asked them to kill the bugs wasn't the same person with whom they'd marched. The powerful effect of marching upon participants' obedience was specific to the person they marched behind.

These experiments reveal a dark side to co-ordinated actions. Previously, most social psychological studies had looked at the positive, affiliate feelings produced by co-ordinated activity. But as Wiltermuth points out, modern armies don't need to march anymore. For the past hundred years, no one has marched on a battlefield. Yet wander into a military training academy and you see that it's still an essential part of a soldier's training. Marching isn't used just for physical training, these experiments suggest, but also for its psychological link to obedience and aggression.

Chapter 13

Getting into Line: Conformity and Social Norms

- -

In This Chapter

▶ Considering the role of social norms

▶ Looking at ways in which people conform

▶ Paying the price of not conforming

- -

*Y*our life is governed by rules. You are probably well aware of many of them. If, for example, you learnt to drive then you had to memorise the Highway Code and all the rules about speed limits, the correct procedure for roundabouts and when to check your mirrors and indicate. But there is a much more detailed set of rules about how to live your life outside of the car: how to queue in shops, what to say to a waiter, how close you should stand to strangers and to friends. The trouble is, there is no Highway Code for Life. All of these customs, conventions and points of etiquette are called *social norms*. Though you may not be aware of them, you have spent much of your life learning them.

Do you nod your head when you agree with someone? Do you always make sure that you belch loudly after a meal? Would you blow your nose in front of another person? These questions may seem easy to answer, but if you ask other people from around the world you may well get the opposite answer: Greeks shake their heads to agree, a belch is a compliment in some Middle Eastern countries and discharging your nostrils in front of other people is exceptionally rude in Japan.

In this chapter I examine the nature of this urge to conform to social norms: I explore the reasons people have for acting the same way as each other and some ways in which they do so. Think of the wonderful feeling you get looking across a sports stadium and seeing thousands of people dressed in the same team colours as you, chanting the same songs. But I don't ignore the darker side of conformity: the dreadful feeling of being the one person in the crowd wearing a different colour and singing a different song.

Addressing the Reasons for Social Norms

Social norms structure every aspect of your life, from the way you lay the dinner table, to the number of milliseconds you hold someone's gaze, to how you express condolences. They're the culture and the habits of life. They're what make foreign countries feel foreign to you, and so are one of the best reasons to travel.

Often, historical reasons reside behind a particular social norm. People drive cars on the left in the UK because of the practicalities of wearing a sword. Most right-handers wore their swords on the left, and so hundreds of years ago people rode horses on the left-hand side of the road to avoid scabbards clashing. People say 'bless you' at a sneeze because many years ago it was believed that a tiny fraction of the soul was escaping from the body with each sniffle.

The question is, however, now that no one wears a sword for the morning commute and few believe that the soul resides in snot, why do these practices persist?

Although a mass of arbitrary reasons can lie behind individual social norms, and people often copy one another simply to create the feeling of belonging, sometimes real value exists in imitating those around you: for example, think of the first time you went to a sushi restaurant and didn't know what to do with the soy sauce and wasabi. In this section, I discuss three common reasons why people conform to social norms: mimicry, conforming to acquire information and conformity to avoid not fitting in.

Doing impressions: The urge to mimic

One reason for the spread and perpetuation of social norms is that human beings seem to like copying each other. If you interact with another person for more than a few moments, usually you start to speak at the same speed as them, use the same words and even pick up a little of their accent. You position your body in the same way, crossing your arms or putting your hands in your pockets if the other person does. If you're standing, the chances are that you start to sway in time with them.

These movements may be imperceptible to a casual observer, but they can be measured in the laboratory. Research even shows that when you call a friend in a distant city and you're both walking and talking on your mobile phones, your steps fall in time with each other.

Just how automatic mimicry behaviour is, however, is debated in social psychology. Research is trying to untangle whether people always engage in some level of mimicry, or only copy people when they have a particular goal, such as impressing them or making friends. What is well established, though, is that mimicry seems closely related to feelings of affiliation and liking. People do it from very early in life – perhaps as soon as they come out of the womb – and mimic each other in every country on earth. I explore mimicry in terms of persuasion in more detail in Chapter 14.

The research suggests that mimicry serves as a sort of social group, bonding individuals to each other. If you've ever sung with a concert crowd or chanted with thousands of football supporters, then you've probably experienced the positive feeling of doing the same thing at the same time as a large number of people.

Part of the essence of social interaction for human beings is mimicry of each other, and so unsurprisingly habits and norms can spread between people like the common cold.

Getting information from others

Conforming to the behaviour of other people is very useful when you want to know something: something called the informational influence of conformity.

If you don't know how to behave, or if something about the situation is ambiguous, you follow others. You're especially likely to do so if it seems that the people around you are experts. For example, you experience a strong pressure to conform on your first day at school when you don't know where to hang your bag and when you travel abroad to an unfamiliar country.

I still have nightmares!

Like many children in England, I was sent off on my first day at a new school in a freshly bought uniform: a black blazer with school badge, black trousers, white or grey itchy nylon shirt and a school tie. One reason for the uniform, Mum explained, was that children sometimes pick on people who are a little bit different. A uniform made everyone equal. How little this idea underestimated the inventiveness of a room full of children.

I immediately discovered that all uniforms aren't created equal. It was absolutely crucial that the turn-ups on your trousers were of precisely the right size. I had a vague idea that this was important, and Mum had lovingly stayed up the night before stitching a pair into my trousers. To my horror, on the first day I saw that mine were almost an inch too short. This was a difference of nightmarish magnitude between my trousers and those of the effortlessly cool, lank-haired boys whom everyone seemed to admire.

On my first trip to Tokyo, I found myself staring at the subway map, thinking that it looked more like a particularly tricky wiring diagram for a laptop. I had no idea what ticket to buy, how to buy it or even where the trains were. So I did what you'd probably do in that situation: I copied everyone else and went with the flow (and not only metaphorically – the crowds are so dense and fast-moving you can just hop into one and get carried along on a stream of business suits).

Acknowledging the need to fit in

Even if you've always been cool and the centre of your social group, I'm sure that you can recall a moment in your life when you panicked and felt the pressure to look just like everyone else – most probably at school. Rarely do you genuinely feel that one particular item of style or clothing is objectively better than any other (if you do, look back at a picture of yourself ten years ago, wearing your favourite outfit, and cringe at how strange and awkward it looks now). The goal isn't to do the *right* thing here; it's just to do the *same* thing as everyone else.

Psychologists call this a *normative influence* of conformity. Your behaviour is shaped by the desire to be like those around you. Usually the goal is social approval or membership of the in-group that you admire. As I describe in the later section of this chapter 'Facing the Costs of Non-conformity: Ostracism', however, often you're motivated not so much by a need to fit in, as a fear of not fitting in.

Getting Along: Ways People Conform

The textbook definition of *conformity* is changing your behaviour to match the opinions or actions of others. It's subtly different to other forms of social influence that can cause a change in behaviour:

- ✔ **Obedience:** When you respond to a direct order from someone in a position of authority (see Chapter 12 for more – and that's an order!). So if a teacher tells you to line up at school, that's obedience.

- ✔ **Compliance:** When you make a change in response to direct pressure from others. If a school bully threatens you and you hand over your lunch money, that's compliance.

But if you spend your school lunch hour stapling your trouser turn-ups so that they're the same length as everyone else's, that's conformity.

In this section, I examine some of the ways in which people seek to conform.

Absorbing other people's opinions

When people live in a community, they tend to share beliefs and opinions. Of course, not every agrees all the time, but there is a tendency for opinions to conform. This is one reason (though there are others) that political maps of the country coloured by voting patterns tend to be reasonably similar between elections. Of course, some places switch from red to blue, but many areas are stable across the years in terms of political preferences.

Untangling the reasons for this conformity in opinion is very complicated. Social psychologists have studied the phenomenon in field studies of college students. They are a good test case since students come from all over the country, live together for three or four years, and then (usually) leave. Psychologists have tracked how students' opinions shift as a result of living together for this short period of time.

Bennington College, for example, is a liberal arts college in Vermont with the reputation of employing academics who are to the left of the political spectrum in the United States. A researcher studied the progression of students' political views in the 1930s at Bennington, from the moment that they first turned up at the college through to their graduation. Each year that the students stayed on the campus, their political views crept further and further to the left. This was one of the first detailed scientific studies of conformity in political opinions emerging over time.

Aligning your perception with others

You may come to share your friends or your family's political opinions for many reasons. Late night debates or a set of common experiences may have persuaded you that what the people around you think is simply the right vview. Social psychologists have found that conformity runs much deeper than this, however. In some situations people will believe that they see the same thing as other people: not because it is the right thing to see, or because they have been explicitly persuaded, but because that's simply what everyone else sees. Remarkably, there is a *normative influence* of conformity on your perception. This was shown by social psychologist Muzafer Sherif using a simple visual illusion.

Try and block out all sources of light in your room at night. As you sit in the darkness, look for a small standby light on your TV or computer. Stare at it for a few minutes. After a while, if the room is dark enough, the dot seems to move. This effect is a simple visual illusion (see the nearby sidebar 'Watching stars move: The autokinetic effect' if you want the scientific background).

Watching stars move: The autokinetic effect

If your eyes have no reference frame, such as the dim shape of other objects or the outline of your window, your brain gets easily confused. It can mistake, for example, tiny movements of your head and body for potential movements of the light floating in space. This is called the *autokinetic effect.* It was first documented in 1799 by an explorer as he looked at the stars through a telescope. However, he thought that the stars really were swinging, and it was another 50 years before people realised that it was just a trick of the mind.

Now invite some friends into your dark room to look for the 'mysterious moving dot'. After a few minutes, turn the lights back on and ask them each to state how far they thought the dot had moved in inches. You get a variety of estimates. If they're willing, ask them back over the course of several nights to repeat the experiment. As you collect their estimates you'll notice a strange phenomenon, as did Muzafer Sharif in 1935 in his early experiments on conformity. Your friends' estimates become more and more similar to one another.

Even though the light never physically moved, our brains get confused in the darkness and perceive motion. If you demonstrated the autokinetic effect several times to a hundred people, and then asked them to tell you *in private* what direction they saw the dot move, you'd get a hundred slightly different answers. But if the people are in a room together and say what they saw out loud, then after several demonstrations they would start to say the same direction.

By the end they're making very similar estimates, fully conforming in their perception of the non-existing motion of the mysterious dot. It seems like a strange sort of mass hallucination, but it's just the effect of conformity of visual perception.

Choosing to conform over choosing to be right

The preceding sections reveal that people soak up the opinions of people around them, and that faced with a mysterious visual illusion, they are swayed by the experiences of others. Conformity can nudge people in a certain direction perhaps, but in neither of these cases is it a force encountering much resistance. In this section, I want to look at a normative influence of conformity that pushes you in a direction that you *know* is wrong.

The psychologist Solomon Asch asked participants to make a simple judgement. He showed them a black line drawn on a large piece of card, next to three other lines labelled A, B and C. The participant's job was simply to say which of the three lines was the same length as the first. It wasn't a hard call: a pigeon could figure this out. When asked alone, in the control condition, everyone got the answer correct almost all the time. But what if the participant wasn't alone?

In Asch's experiments, the participant was just one person in a room full of other people who were also present to do the same line-estimation task. Except that they weren't just other people, they were confederates of the experimenter. The participant, like Jim Carrey's character in the film *The Truman Show,* was the only person who wasn't following a script.

Imagine you're in this experiment. The researcher presents the lines to the room full of people. You can immediately see that the correct answer is B. The experimenter goes round the room and asks each person in turn for their answer. The first guy says, 'Uhh, I think it's A.' You snigger to yourself – what an idiot! Then the second person says, 'Yep, A.' You wipe your glasses and squint again. It really looks like B. But the third, fourth and fifth people assert confidently that A is the correct answer. And now, the whole room is looking at you for your answer. 'A, I guess,' you mumble.

Even though the correct answer couldn't be plainer in Asch's experiments, many people conform to the majority's blatantly wrong view. It seems very strange that the participants in this experiment wouldn't raise their hands and disagree with the other people in the room. In the next section, I look in more detail at one of the forces that compels conformity in such situations – the fear of standing out from the crowd.

Facing the Costs of Non-conformity: Ostracism

Culturally, the public seem to prize rebels and outsiders and scorn the followers and 'sheep'. Independence of thought and spirit always win the day in films and novels, with the message often being that you have to stand up for what you believe in, no matter what. When did you last see a Hollywood film end with rousing speeches or tear-flecked moments after the lead characters decide to do what everyone else does?

Cultural rebels

Films often feature one person who's a little different: he wears different clothes, has a different attitude and doesn't join in with the others. He's an outsider, a rebel. He thinks that being a ballet dancer or friends with the aliens is cool. The other students, townsfolk or space cadets don't trust him. They make fun, push him around and don't invite him to their parties. Maybe one girl's curious about him and thinks that he's misunderstood and complicated (she probably wears glasses to indicate her intelligent insight).

Then some crisis happens – the lead actor in the school play breaks his leg or the aliens attack – and the girl with the glasses convinces people that they need the outsider. He saves the day, the girl stops wearing glasses (to show that she's loveable as well as smart!) and everyone's happy.

Instead, you see the same story a hundred times in different guises, whether it's set in a small-town high school or a space station in a distant galaxy (I lay out my own pitch for my Hollywood epic in the nearby sidebar 'Cultural rebels').

With the huge impact that the entertainment media has, you'd think that people's everyday attitudes would reflect what they value in books and films, but in fact, in real life, they don't really like rebels. They hate people who think and act differently to themselves.

In this section, I look at what happens to people when they are left out of the group. The technical term for this is *ostracism*. Psychologists think that fear of ostracism is one of the reasons that people are so eager to conform to each other's behaviour and beliefs. Ostracism is a possible consequence of non-conformity, and people will do anything they can to avoid it.

Ancient Greeks and reality TV

As well as inventing democracy, the Olympics and philosophy, the Ancient Greeks are responsible for one of the key aspects of reality TV shows like *Survivor*: the moment at the end of each episode when the contestants get together and vote one of their members out of the competition. The psychological term *ostracism* actually comes from the word *ostrakon,* which was a little shard of pottery that the ancient Greeks used as scrap paper. Every year, the Greeks got together and everyone scratched the name of someone that they disliked or mistrusted on a shard of pottery. The shards were then counted, and the 'winner' got banned from the city for ten years. So as well as giving birth to reality TV, the Greeks had realised that being shut out from others is a terrible social punishment.

Admitting that no one likes a real-life rebel

Researchers have found that, in general, when a member of a group says or does something different – when they don't conform – the other people in the group lower their opinions of that individual.

Despite some exceptions, generally you incur a cost for your non-conformity: many people simply don't like you and can reject or exclude you from the social group. Psychologists have studied the psychological effects of ostracism in some clever experiments.

Next time you're out with a group of people, talking about this and that, try a little experiment: disagree with people. Whenever someone gives a point of view or an opinion, rather than murmuring agreement, try gently, politely and respectfully putting an opposing view. The people around you may exhibit a new-found respect for your opinions and independence of mind, but more likely, sadly, they just think that you're a bit of a pain.

Feeling left out: The pain of ostracism

If you are forced out of a social group, it hurts. I mean that almost literally; social psychologists talk of the 'social pain' of ostracism, and there is some evidence that I discuss below that suggests that social pain is a lot like real pain in terms of how the brain responds. Just like the pain of being punched by the school bully is one reason you might comply with his requests, the social pain of being ostracised is one reason that people conform to social norms.

One day, a researcher called Kip Williams was relaxing in a park in San Francisco. The weather was fine and lots of people were out enjoying the sunshine. Then a frisbee dropped out of the sky and landed beside him. Kip picked it up, looked around him and saw two men waving at him. Gamely, he threw it back to one of them. They gestured in thanks, and then one of the men threw it back to Kip.

He happily tossed it back, and for a few moments they played a three-way game. Then the two men threw it between themselves for a couple of turns. Then a couple more. Then they seemed to forget about Kip, who stood awkwardly, looking between the two men now playing frisbee just with each other. At this moment, Kip says he felt a profound sense of hurt and loss. Moments ago he'd been involved in a fun, spontaneous game with two people, and now, they'd rejected him! I imagine him pretending to check his watch, nodding to the men and walking away, trying not to let his shoulders slump.

Luckily, Kip had two insights. First, it was just a game of frisbee and the two men had gone out to play with each other and not him. Second, because this little interaction was able to produce a strong emotion in him, it could be an ideal way to study social rejection in the laboratory.

Williams went on to invent the Cyberball experiments, in which he and his colleagues introduce participants to a very simple computer game. Three stick figures are on the screen and participants can control the one at the bottom. A frisbee flies between the characters, and when it flies towards your stick figure, you catch it. Then you can press one of two buttons to throw it to the stick figure on the left or on the right. It's hardly *Grand Theft Auto,* but people seem to like playing the game.

What's interesting about Cyberball is that other people are controlling the other two stick figures from across the Internet. You see a little picture of their faces on screen, and the computer tells you their names and sometimes something about them. Only, of course, they don't really exist: this is a social psychology experiment and, in fact, only the computer is controlling the other 'players'. This set-up allows Kip Williams to re-create the experience he had at the park in the laboratory.

The players start off throwing the frisbee to you, as well as to each other. Then gradually, they start to favour each other, and after a few more turns no one is throwing the frisbee to you at all. Then the experimenter asks how you feel. Just imagining this situation, you may think, 'I wouldn't care in the slightest – it's just a stupid game'. But in fact, you've absorbed just enough information about the other players and just enough interaction between you all that – when you're shut out – it feels like a genuine social exclusion. You've been ostracised, which impairs self-esteem, lowers happiness and reduces your sense of belonging.

The researchers wondered whether the identity of the other players matters. Are your feelings only hurt if these are people you really want to be friends with? Remarkably, not. In one surprising experiment, the researchers introduced participants to other players and said that they were members of the Ku Klux Klan. This far-right, racist group is an anathema to most Americans and to all the participants in the experiments. The amazing thing is that even if the participants were playing imaginary frisbee with some of the most unpleasant people in the country, their feelings were still hurt when they were excluded.

More remarkably, participants have been given the Cyberball game to play in a magnetic resonance imaging (MRI) scanner. In the moment they were ostracised, brain regions were active that have a lot in common with the regions that respond to physical pain – in the anterior cingulate cortex, in case you wondered. In other words, the researcher claimed that the pain of ostracism is real.

I think that these results are very provocative when you think about their wider implications. The ancient Greeks realised the power of the punishment of ostracism (see the sidebar 'Ancient Greeks and reality TV'), but I think that we tend to overlook it today. Perhaps it's because we tend to think of ourselves as proud individuals, we neglect the rewards that come from feeling part of a group and underestimate the punishment that comes from feeling excluded.

Chapter 14

Persuading People to Part with Their Pounds

*W*hat comes to mind when you think of a great act of persuasion? Martin Luther King's 'I have a dream' civil rights speech? Winston Churchill's radio broadcasts exhorting the nation to 'fight on the beaches' and resist Nazi attacks? These are powerful examples of how words can move people and change minds, but I don't think that they are the best examples of the acts of persuasion that swirl around our everyday lives. As I explain in this chapter, we are barely aware of some of the most potent means of persuasion that exert their influence upon us.

Commercial companies are experts at persuasion. For example, Procter & Gamble (P&G) make medicines, beauty products and a whole range of household goods. In 2012 the company spent $2 billion on research and development, trying to create products that are better than those of its competitors. Nothing surprising there, you may think. But what may surprise you is that it spent more than four times that amount trying to *persuade* you that its products are better than those of its competitors.

P&G is the largest advertiser on the planet. The $9 billion it spent on advertising is more than many countries spend on roads, armies, hospitals and schools. The firm spent it on billboards, TV slots and those little sachets of perfume that fall out of magazines.

In this chapter I investigate the techniques and psychology of persuasion. Of course, persuasion is used in all sorts of areas in society and relationships, and I choose to focus mainly on how companies and salespeople persuade you to change your mind, take a particular course of action or buy a product. I reveal some different routes to persuasion, such as emotional appeals, intellectual arguments and subliminal perception.

I also describe six different principles of persuasion, each based on the types of psychological evidence that I cover throughout this book. Each principle leads to one or more techniques of persuasion that you can use on other people, or recognise when they're being used on you. By providing knowledge of these tricks I hope to give you some protection against these dark arts.

And so ends my attempt to persuade you to read this chapter!

Walking the Routes to Persuasion

Social psychologists talk about two 'routes' to persuasion. They mean that there are two different lines of attack that people can use to try and change your mind. These two routes differ in the ways that they require you to process mentally a persuasive message such as an argument, an advert or a sales pitch.

- ✔ **Deep processing:** This requires the target of the persuasion to think carefully about the information in the message, using reasoned analysis and deliberation.

- ✔ **Shallow processing:** This does not require the target of the persuasion to think very deeply at all about the content of the message, or even pay much attention to it. Here, shallow, superficial factors do the work, like the fact that the salesperson is attractive or the brand is familiar.

Although people most commonly think of persuasion as deep processing, it is actually shallow processing that is the more common – and more powerful – way to influence behaviour. Recently, for example, Facebook started inserting advertisements in the middle of users' webpages. Previously, adverts had been more discreet, off to the side. Many users didn't like this change and, on principle, refused to click on the ads. If no one clicked on the advertised links, they reasoned, Facebook wouldn't make money off them and they might abandon the practice.

Despite being a noble aim, this approach displays a fundamental misunderstanding of the psychology behind the ads. The truth is that Facebook never expected anyone to click on the advertisements: that's not how they work.

Deep processing is how users thought that the new ads appearing on Facebook were designed to work: people see an advert, read the testimonials, look at the price and click to buy the product. Sadly, people rarely make choices this way. Most persuasion uses the subtler shallow processing, like the Facebook ads.

Facebook doesn't place these adverts because it thinks that you're going to read them and click on them. All the company wants is to expose you to those product brands and images. As I discuss in Chapter 5, the more times you're exposed to something, in general the more you like it. Everyone is swayed by superficial processing, such as the familiarity of an image. So even though you can ignore the adverts sniffily, by simply being in front of your eyeballs, they're doing their work.

Considering arguments rationally: Deep processing

The deep processing form of persuasion involves an argument, a discussion, some evidence and a reasoned decision. For example, someone tells you about a great car that's for sale and says that the price is good. You weigh the evidence, check the prices, assess the argument and make your choice to buy.

Deep processing is so named because the target of the persuasion is assumed to be using all the information available to come to a rational, considered choice. Deep processing is the basis for televised debates between politicians, where you can hear everyone's argument and make your judgement. It's how people like to think that they make choices, as rational consumers. Deep processing, when it works, tends to produce real and lasting opinion change.

Being swayed by appearances: Shallow processing

With shallow processing you're influenced by the superficial properties of the message or the communicator: the height of the political candidate, how attractive the salesperson is and so on.

Shallow processing doesn't produce deep, lasting opinion change: you won't persuade someone to change strongly held political convictions or to fall in love with you this way. The effects of shallow processing are more ephemeral. But they can sway a floating voter or nudge a consumer towards one product or another.

Celebrity endorsements trade on shallow processing. No one would seriously ask actors or footballers for their advice on what home insurance or mobile phone to purchase. All that matters is that you have a positive view of the celebrities used and that positive effect is transferred to the product they're selling.

Which of the following two applicants for an electrical repair job seems more impressive to you?

Bob Roberts:

- ✔ I am 27.
- ✔ I have a degree in electrical engineering.
- ✔ I am hard working and punctual.

Rob Boberts:

- ✔ I am 27.
- ✔ I have a degree in electrical engineering.
- ✔ I was educated to a university level.
- ✔ I am hard working.
- ✔ I put a lot of time and effort into my professional activities.
- ✔ I am always punctual.
- ✔ I reliably turn up on time to my appointments.

A moment's thought, or any deep processing, leads you to conclude that these two people have exactly equal qualities. But research shows that when presented with two options, people are swayed by simple things such as the number of bullet points in support of each person; even when those bullet points say exactly the same thing, as they do with these candidates.

Next time you see an advert listing the benefits of an insurance policy, note how many times almost exactly the same points are listed in different places.

Appealing to emotions

Detailed arguments that rely on deep processing can include emotional appeals, like the political speeches of Martin Luther King or Churchill. Social psychologists term appeals to emotion as shallow processing, however, as they are often not directly related to the content of the persuasive message.

Positive emotions

The most common emotional appeal is simply to make people happy, with the intention that the positive emotion will become associated with the brand that is being sold. Advertisements that use humour, for example, aim to make you think more positively about their products because of the small smile that they evoke with a funny video of a kitten. Or during a large sporting event like the Olympics, companies are very eager to associate their names with particular teams or athletes, so that the warm glow their supporters feel will become tied to a particular dish, soap or shampoo. It doesn't matter that the sport has nothing to do with the product – all that the advertisers want is to build an association between the positive emotion and their brand.

One social psychologist I know used this principle to her advantage. When the time came to hand out her teaching evaluations to the students in her class, she taped a candy to each form. The students sucked on the sweets while evaluating her teaching, and the mild happiness caused by the sugary treat ensured that she got some of the best ratings in the department.

Negative emotions

Sometimes persuaders will try and evoke negative feelings such as fear to exploit the shallow processing of their targets. The most common example is attack ads in political campaigns that suggest horrible things will happen if one candidate is elected.

There is a risk to evoking negative emotions however, as they can easily backfire. The danger is that the negative emotion becomes associated with the persuader and turns people off. For example, many early advertisements and campaigns about global warming used the most shocking images and statistics about impending climate disasters. It seems that in many cases these tactics scared people to the extent that they simply didn't want to know about global warming – or actively denied it – because it was too horrible to think about.

Luckily, later campaigners realised this strategic error. If you watch Al Gore's film *An Inconvenient Truth*, for example, you'll see that every alarming statistic is immediately followed by a small, practical step that people can do, such as swapping their old light bulbs for energy efficient ones. In this way, the negative emotion evoked by the message is connected to positive action that people can take, and they are less likely to be overwhelmed and turned off by the fear that nothing can be done.

Recognising the Six Principles of Persuasion

Robert Cialdini has researched and written extensively on the science of persuasion. In this section I describe the six principles of persuasion he identifies that are used on you every day by advertisers, salespeople and probably even your friends and family.

Many of these six principles rely on biases in your thinking or psychological mechanisms. Each one works because it plugs into important psychological needs, such as having accurate beliefs about the world, being liked by other people and feeling good about yourself. None of these goals is a bad thing for you to pursue, but they do leave you vulnerable to sneaky persuasion experts who can turn them against you.

'I scratch your back . . .': The urge to reciprocate

Reciprocity is the social norm that if I do something for you, you should do something for me (I talk more about social norms in Chapter 13). It exists in every human culture, can be seen in the earliest moments of childhood social interaction and even has its own song in the musical *Chicago*. It's so ingrained that if someone gives you something – even something you didn't really want – not giving something back can be surprisingly difficult.

The house always wins

Casino companies take the principle of reciprocity to remarkable extremes. Most casinos now have their customers use loyalty cards so that they can track their every transaction. They identify their most profitable customers and when these people have a big win, casinos offer them free rooms in the hotel and complimentary meals in the restaurant. In some cases they even pay for plane tickets for the whole family to fly to Las Vegas so 'your loved ones can help you celebrate your good fortune'.

After the customers accept this generosity from the casino, the norm of reciprocity kicks in and they feel compelled to spend at least some of the winnings back at the casino. Eventually, the customer's big win ends up back in the casino vault.

Whenever you get something for free, you can bet that someone's trying to hook you with the norm of reciprocity. Little samples of food given out in a supermarket, the complimentary address labels a charity sends you, the performance put on for you by a street artist – in all these cases, after receiving the 'free' gift, people are more likely to purchase the full product, donate to the charity or put money in the hat.

'You really know your stuff!': Being consistent

People need to feel that they're consistent. Holding two beliefs that contradict each other causes psychological discomfort, and people often change their views, or act differently, to resolve that inconsistency. (This tendency is the cornerstone of cognitive dissonance, which I discuss in Chapter 6.) To expert persuaders, your need to feel consistent is one of your biggest weaknesses.

Imagine walking into an electronics shop, browsing for a new TV. A salesperson sidles up and you start talking. You mumble something about high-definition screens and the salesperson says, 'Ah, I see that you're a bit of an expert on TVs.' He shows you a few TV sets and you express a preference for one. 'Wow, you've got a good eye for quality,' he replies.

Eventually, your decision comes down to a decision between a cheap TV that does what you want or a much more expensive model with extra features. Which do you choose? Well, what would technology experts with discerning eyes for quality do? They'd pick the more expensive model, which is what you do too. Sale made!

Labelling

When making flattering comments about your knowledge and taste, the salesperson isn't just trying to ingratiate himself: he's doing something called *labelling:* he's assigning positive characteristics to you. When you have to make a decision, your need to behave consistently means that you act according to those labels, and you've played right into his commission-earning hands.

The same trick works well with children. One day my son spotted his baby brother playing with his favourite toy car. He grabbed it back, causing the smaller one to cry. Instead of lecturing him on the virtues of sharing, I tried a different tactic. 'Sam, you're so good at sharing with your brother,' I told him.

He agreed modestly, accepting the label. Then he looked down at the toy car, shrugged and handed it back to his little brother with a pat on his head. Try it out: it really works!

Foot-in-the-door technique

People need consistent beliefs and consistent behaviour; experts can easily exploit these needs with the foot-in-the-door technique. If you get people to agree to a small request first, they later agree to your greater request simply to be consistent.

The researchers Jonathan Freedman and Scott Fraser demonstrated this in an elegant experiment in the 1960s. First, they went door-to-door in a suburban area, asking people if they'd agree to put a large sign on their lawns that said 'Drive Safely'. It was a sentiment that most agreed with, but the sign was pretty ugly. Only 17 per cent of people agreed to put it up.

The researchers then tried the foot-in-the-door technique. They went round another set of households, but asked instead for people to put a small sign in their windows that said, 'Be a safe driver'. It was unobtrusive and most people complied with this small request. Then a week later the researchers returned. They asked people if they'd mind putting the large ugly sign on their lawns. Remarkably, 76 per cent of people agreed.

Over four times as many people agreed to the exact same large request if they'd previously agreed to a small request. The reason was consistency. By agreeing to put up the small sign, the home owners had shown that they were concerned about safe driving, and that they were prepared to do something about it. After that, they risked seeming inconsistent if they said no, even if the sign was unattractive.

This result is counter-intuitive. It shows that you can increase your chances of persuading people to do something if you increase your total demands upon them.

The trick is well known by the people in coloured anoraks who patrol the Tube station near my office. The local name for them is *chuggers,* which is short for 'charity muggers'. They stand on the street corners, talk to passers-by and attempt to persuade them to sign up for a regular donation to a particular charity. The charity and the colour of the anoraks change each week, because the chuggers don't work for any charity directly. They work for a company that takes a small percentage profit out of every charity donation made. The people in anoraks are real persuasion professionals and experts in the foot-in-the-door technique.

They approach you in a friendly, engaging manner. They say, 'Hello! Do you have a few moments to talk about child poverty/cruelty to animals/homelessness?' Of course, all reasonable, nice people can spare a few minutes just to talk. So you stop and chat, and after a few moments conversation about the issue, the chuggers ask a big favour – 'Can you sign this petition for me?' You'd seem highly inconsistent to say no at this point. You've already spent several minutes listening and agreeing to what's being said. It costs you nothing to scrawl your name next to a statement you've been nodding along to all this time. As you're signing, the chuggers talk more and more about the need for your support. Then they pop the big question – 'Will you sign up to make a small monthly donation?'

By this point you'd seem highly inconsistent, not to say stingy and hypocritical, if you say no. After all, you've already given your time, your verbal agreement and you've even signed a statement saying how important this issue is for you.

Chuggers start with a tiny request, and you keep agreeing as the requests get bigger and bigger. Because of your need to be consistent, they basically had your money at 'Hello'.

The low-ball and bait-and-switch techniques

These techniques induce customers to make the first step towards buying a product and then change the deal. But because customers need to feel consistent, they follow through with the purchase regardless. In the *low-ball technique*, a very low price is advertised.

For example: you see a plane ticket advertised to Paris for £10. This seems like a great deal, and so you call up the ticket office. You find an available ticket on the day you want and reserve the seat. And then the salesperson reminds you of the baggage fee of £20 and airport tax of £40. Plus, you have to buy a return ticket too, which is £80, and another airport tax of £40. So in all, the ticket is £190 and more expensive than others you saw advertised originally. But, because you've committed to buying by phoning up the ticket office with your credit card in hand, and because you committed to a time and a day, you follow through and buy the ticket.

The *bait-and-switch* is even more brazen. Here, you go into a shop because you saw a great deal advertised on a laptop. But the salesperson sadly shakes his head and tells you that model has sold out. But he does have other laptops in stock if you're interested, though they aren't at such a good price. But because you travelled all the way to that particular shop and told the salesperson you were there to buy a computer, the only consistent thing seems to be to follow through and buy one. Even if it's not the one you wanted, at a price higher than you wanted to pay. But at least you were consistent.

Nine out of ten advertisers use social proof

You don't buy a fridge very often – perhaps a couple of times in your life. So you probably don't know about the latest trends in consumer refrigeration. But when you come to buy one, you ask your friends and family, or look online and read the reviews of other users. Your goal is to gain accurate information about the refrigerator world.

One readily available source of information is the behaviour and opinions of other people – called *social proof* – and it's a powerful persuasive force that experts can manipulate.

The most obvious way, for example, for a restaurant to exploit this principle for persuasion online is to write its own user reviews. If you flick through restaurant reviews online, you can easily spot the reviews made up by the owners. They have better grammar and spelling and use phrases that regular human beings don't use ('the stunning decor was out of this world and our charming hosts catered to our every culinary desire').

Social proof can be done more subtly of course. You've probably heard the advice to eat only at busy restaurants, or to choose the Chinese restaurants that Chinese people go to. Here you're drawing on the opinions of others and the people who're experts in that cuisine. Restaurant owners are well aware of this tactic and seat people (especially attractive people) at key spots near the windows to attract other customers.

You don't have to see people behaving in a certain way to follow their example. Think of a bar that has a jar labelled 'tips'. When you pay, do you put money in it? Research shows that you're much more likely to if it's already stuffed with bills and coins, because that's 'evidence' that other people have tipped and so should you. This tendency has been shown by careful research, but waiting staff have always known it. They even have an expression for putting their own money in at the start of the night: 'salting the jar'.

The same effect is used in the way that some TV shows are broadcast. It's becoming a thing of the past (thankfully), but many sitcoms have a laughter track dubbed on top. You may think that finding something funny or not is a pretty individual thing. Yet research shows that the laughter of other people is a strong determinate of whether you find something funny. You don't even have to hear the laughter. In one study, people sat alone in a room and watched a clip of the comedian Bill Cosby. The amount that they laughed increased when they were told that a friend was sitting next door watching the same clip.

The most obvious use of social proof in persuasion is marketing slogans of the form 'Eight out of ten cats prefer . . . '. You see this technique all the time, often with a group of experts polled: for example, 'Over 90 per cent of dentists use our brushes in their own homes', or a brand proclaiming itself the 'UK's number one choice'.

'*What a coincidence, me too!*': *The desire to be liked*

Humans are socially needy creatures, constantly wanting to affirm and strengthen social bonds. If a friend asks you a favour, you say yes. If someone seems as if he may become a friend, you often also say yes. Favours are a sort of glue for social relationships. Persuasion experts have realised that if they can pretend to be your friends, you're more likely to buy from them.

Salespeople use subtle techniques to manipulate you into liking them. As you can see in Chapter 15, certain factors make people like each other, but the most pervasive is similarity. You like people who are like you. This doesn't just mean things such as age and appearance, but more subtle aspects of behaviour as well.

If you gently mimic the manner of speaking, posture and body language of people, they tend to like you more (unless they catch you doing it, when they find it a bit creepy). Research found that waiting staff in restaurants dramatically increase their tips when they simply copy the way that a customer places an order.

Therefore, when you talk to salespeople, you may find that you have a surprising amount in common. Perhaps they're students too, or were recently, and studied a subject close to yours. Maybe they too like travelling or going to concerts. If you're a little older, you may find that (surprise, surprise) they have children about the same age as yours.

This sales technique is particular noticeable in phone sales. When you talk to salespeople on the phone they're often following a script that instructs them to find common areas between them and you.

Next time you get called up, try dropping into the conversation something random, like you love yachting, or shift your accent and manner of speaking. Pretty soon you may find that they too go sailing and come from Yorkshire!

'Trust me and my white coat': Responding to authority figures

No matter how independently minded you think you are, you're still susceptible to the authority of other people. In Chapter 12 I discuss experiments demonstrating the remarkable obedience that people show towards people in authority. Of course, no one advertises their products by having an authority figure order people around: authority exerts an influence in a more subtle way.

Imagine an advert for a new vitamin supplement. Someone on-screen is telling you about the product. What is the person like? My guess is male, tall, attractive, well-groomed, wearing a white coat, a crisp blue shirt and glasses with thin wire frames. The age is important – old enough to look like he's near the top of his profession, but young enough that he's up on the very latest research. My guess would be late thirties or early forties.

Right now, I'm writing this sitting on a London Underground train, looking at two such gentlemen advertising vitamins and a new type of toothpaste.

The advertisers are tapping into your stereotype of a medical expert – someone with experience and training, who can speak with knowledge about the virtues of this product. By reflecting your authority stereotype the advert is more likely to exert an influence over your choices.

'Don't delay, call today': Implying scarcity

Advertisers often use the notion that if something is scarce, and other people seem to want it, it must be valuable.

Here's an apocryphal story, usually set in Soviet-era Russia. A lady walks past a long queue at a shop and joins the line. Another lady stops and asks, 'What are you queuing for?'. 'I have no idea,' the first lady replies, 'but it must be worth it!'.

This method of persuasion is especially easy to spot. You see many adverts screaming 'sale must end today!', 'limited time offer!' or 'last one in stock!' Hotel bargain websites are particularly adept at supplying all sorts of 'information' about the number of people who've just bought a room and the rapidly diminishing (usually between one and four) number of rooms remaining at that price. All you need to do is click right now to book (without taking the time to comparison-shop) and you can grab a 'bargain'.

Combating Persuasion: Resistance Isn't Always Useless

Like all humans, you're very susceptible to social influence. This is no bad thing. It's part of your heritage as a member of a species that has evolved in large social groups. But it does mean that persuasion professionals can turn many of your mental quirks and biases against you. Although you can never fully reduce their influence over your decisions, detailed knowledge of their tricks does give you some protection.

Sometimes this is easy, as persuaders overplay their hand. For example, the Chancellor George Osborne turned up at the opening ceremony of the London Olympics that celebrated British institutions such as the National Health Service. But when the stadium screen showed an image of him, the crowd spontaneously started booing, recognising his blatant attempt to associate himself with national pride in the NHS, when at the time he was responsible for cutting its funding.

With more subtle attempts at persuasion, the best defence is to recognise the tricks and manipulations that are being used against you. For example, I can now deal with the chuggers and their foot-in-the-door technique: I give a cheery hello and agree that homelessness or whatever is important. I can then ignore the pangs of guilt as I keep on walking, since I promise myself to read up on the charity by myself later, when I'm away from the manipulation of the chugger. Plus, when a salesperson doesn't have the product that the shop advertised on sale, I suspect the bait-and-switch technique and try another store.

The one thing I'm powerless against, however, is the norm of reciprocity. Giving out free food samples just seems so nice that I always come away with a basket full of overpriced delicacies!

Part V
Assessing Relationships, Groups and Societies

Five Rules of Attraction

- **It's all about evolution:** According to evolutionary psychology, not only do you have to be the fittest and strongest in order to survive, but also you need to *look like* the fittest and strongest to potential mates.

- **Not (just) a pretty face:** We think of beauty as unique and elusive, but the evidence is that one simple factor determines most of our judgments about attractiveness: averageness. The most beautiful person in a group is the mathematical average of everyone present.

- **It's reproduction, stupid:** Heterosexual men are attracted to adult females but want them to look pre-pubescent. Through most of human history, younger females tended to be more fertile and have healthier babies. The claim is that men have evolved to be most attracted to sexually mature women who're young enough to still have the facial characteristics of girls.

- **What women want:** As well as symmetry, the features in men that are typically attractive to females are a wide, strong jaw and jutting forehead, features corresponding to high levels of testosterone. Men with higher testosterone are more likely to have more resources and more ability to defend their families.

- **You like people who are like you:** People don't choose friends and partners purely on their looks. Many nuanced and complex answers exist to the question of what else makes two people like each other, but one very simple answer is almost entirely true: people like people who are like them.

For Dummies can help you get started with lots of subjects. Visit www.dummies.com to learn more and do more with *For Dummies*.

In this part . . .

✔ Take a close look at interpersonal relationships.

✔ Examine how social groups behave, for good or ill.

✔ Look at how we establish cross-cultural connections.

Chapter 15

Interpersonal Relations: Liking, Loving and Living with Other People

*H*uman beings aren't meant to be alone. The fact that solitary confinement is the worst punishment that the UK's legal system can inflict is no coincidence. Humans evolved as a social species, living in small groups of perhaps 100 to 150. Since the first cities 6,000 years ago, people have lived in even larger populations than that, and yet their social worlds seem to have remained around the same size. Echoing the past, the average number of Facebook friends is around 150. Among this social network, the dominant topic of conversation (the very reason, for example, that Facebook was started) is who's hot and who's not, who's dating whom and who's just broken up.

In this chapter, I talk about the psychological forces that shape positive relationships. I discuss the bond you feel with the people who raised you as a child and what it reveals about your relationships as an adult. I explore the social forces behind your attraction to some people and not others, and why the people you like tend to be of the same sex. Plus, I don't neglect relationships with people you don't necessarily like or lust after but nevertheless have to share the planet with, because social forces shape your interactions with neighbours, peers, colleagues and bosses as well. To this end, I also take a brief look at social hierarchies, power and status.

Considering an Evolutionary Perspective on Attraction

Evolutionary psychology, which I describe in detail in Chapter 2, has more to say about attraction, love and sex than any other subject: it's really the *Cosmopolitan* of scientific disciplines! Although every aspect of human behaviour evolved in some way, mating behaviour is where the evolutionary pressures show their hand most clearly, because the choice of mate is the activity through which genes are passed on.

TECHNICAL STUFF

Evolutionary psychology and politics

One particular step in any argument about human behaviour, which is important but seems so small or innocuous that often people don't notice when someone makes it, is the step from talking about what people actually *do* and what they *should* do. Usually this step is hidden behind the skirts of one particular word: a discussion of what's *natural* for people to do.

Ironically, given the frequent antagonism of science and the Church, this (mis)application of evolutionary theory has an ancestor in Christian theology. The idea is called *natural law,* and in simple terms it states that what most people do must be what God intended, is natural and therefore should be part of people's ethical code. So, for example, throughout the human and animal kingdom people observed that pair bonds most commonly happen between a man and a woman. Therefore, the conclusion was made that this is natural and right, and homosexual relationships are unnatural and wrong (this argument works only if you ignore all the cases of homosexual activity in other animals and other human cultures, of course).

You can hear the same natural law line of reasoning now applied from an evolutionary standpoint. For example, that *by nature* humans are aggressive, that a particular gene exists for aggression and so perhaps the law should legally recognise that people with this gene have diminished responsibility for their violent crimes. In a similarly dark vein, some have argued that horrific behaviour such as rape is an evolutionary adaptation to spread genetic material and, in that sense, is 'natural'. Few people argue that this makes it in any way excusable, but the disturbing implication is left hanging.

I think that these arguments are wrong for two reasons. First, very good scientific reasons exist to be sceptical of claims about what human genes make people do. Second, politically speaking, even if people could demonstrate with certainty what human 'nature' is, that needn't bind society's laws and ethical decisions. Indeed, many people would say that laws and ethics are a way to check and control people's base urges, biases and worst natures.

So remain extremely wary of politicians who start their arguments with what's 'natural' human behaviour.

As Charles Darwin realised, not only do you have to be the fittest and strongest in order to survive, but also you need to *look like* the fittest and strongest to potential mates. Otherwise, you may survive as an individual, but your genes don't. So male lions have manes, narwhales have tusks and mandrill primates have bright blue bums, not because these things help keep their necks warm, spear fish or . . . do whatever blue bums help you do. No, these are *secondary sexual characteristics,* present as indirect indicators of strength, virility and genetic quality. As another example, bowerbirds decorate their nests with intricate weaving, flowers and shiny beetle cases, not because this makes the nest warmer or safer, but because female bowerbirds choose their lovers this way.

In Chapter 14, I point out that some companies spend more on advertising than they do on developing better products, and in many ways they're simply taking a lesson from nature: persuading people of your virtues is just as important as having those virtues.

This lesson also applies to humans. In this chapter's discussion of love, sex and marriage, I draw on this evolutionary perspective and the idea of selection by actual, or perceived, genetic fitness. As with many provocative ideas, I suggest that you remain healthily sceptical of some of the claims of evolutionary psychology, and actively wary of how they can be applied in discussions outside of science. See the nearby sidebar 'Evolutionary psychology and politics' for more info.

Discovering Why You Like the People You Like

A remarkable number of conversations, magazine articles, movies and websites revolve around the issue of human attraction: who's hot and who's not, who do you like and who likes you, and what happens when you really like someone who doesn't (yet) like you back. In this section, I talk about the science of human attraction. I discuss evidence behind notions of beauty, the surprising and strange power of averageness and the roles of simplicity, symmetry and similarity.

Take a moment and think about the people that you find attractive. Flick through a magazine, perhaps, or scroll through some Facebook profile pictures. Ask yourself the following questions:

- ✔ Can you discern a pattern to the faces that you find attractive?

- ✔ Do you appear to go for a type of person? Don't simply say 'people who are hot': see whether you can figure out the more difficult question of what makes a face attractive.

> ✔ Do you think that you have a particular taste that's different from other
> people? Or do you think that everyone pretty much agrees on what
> makes an attractive face?

You may have begun reading this chapter feeling that you have unusual or
refined tastes as regards attractiveness. But after thinking about it a little bit
more, and especially after reading the rest of this section, perhaps you'll be
convinced that your judgements are very similar indeed to everyone else's.

Defining a pretty face

Though we think of beauty as unique and elusive, the scientific evidence is
that one simple factor determines most of our judgments about attractiveness:
averageness. In this section I review the evidence for this counter-intuitive
finding, and discuss some explanations for why it might be so.

Next time you're among a large group of people, in a classroom or a crowded
train, take a look at the faces around you. Assign them points out of ten. (Try
not to gawp or mouth your scores at people: strangely, people don't like being
rated one out of ten!) Imagine that you can ask everyone else present to do
the same thing and you'd all have a beauty contest. By totalling up the scores,
you'd find out – objectively speaking – the most attractive person.

But let me tell you a heartening fact: someone in that room is even more
attractive than your beauty contest winner. That person doesn't exist physically, but you can create a picture of him or her: the most beautiful person in
the room is the mathematical average of everyone present.

This remarkable fact is true of any large group of people. You can take headshots of loads of individuals, rank them according to how attractive they
are and then blend all the faces together to produce an average face. If you
then ask everyone to look at that average face it's judged as more attractive
than any single individual – even though it contains all the unremarkable and
awkward-looking people who got low scores by themselves.

As a group, people are always prettier than any individual. Hold on to that
thought, because it may just be the most positive thing I say in this book.

You may be thinking that averageness doesn't really cut it on the world's fashion catwalks. When you look at yet another magazine article ranking the 'most
beautiful people in the world', the word 'average' rarely springs to mind.
Beautiful people are striking and stunning, not average and commonplace.
Indeed, if you try to chat up people by telling them how 'wonderfully average'
they look, you probably won't get very far. Unless you want to date a psychologist, which may be unwise for other reasons.

The fact is that what humans appear to hold up as 'beauty' doesn't always match what most people find attractive most of the time. If you look through magazines over a 100-year spread, and then visit a portrait gallery to go further back in time, you find that cultural conceptions of beauty have changed and continue to differ between cultures today. Yet, although the face of beauty has changed in the fashion and entertainment industry, psychologists have found that what most people find attractive has stayed pretty much the same over time, and remains the same across cultures.

Preferring averagely pretty faces

Despite cultural norms towards extreme forms of beauty, human beings seem to find averageness attractive. This effect has been reliably found across many cultures – for example, Inuit people prefer the averaged faces of Welsh people and vice versa.

Researchers suggest many reasons why average faces are judged to be more attractive. Here I discuss a couple.

Simplicity

Perhaps simplicity is the key. In general people prefer things – sentences, music, ideas – that are easier to process mentally. Average faces, by their nature, don't have any of the idiosyncrasies, complexities and strange lumps that most people see in the mirror each morning: they've all been averaged out. So some researchers think that average faces are more attractive because in this sense they're simpler – or more pure – examples of faces.

Symmetry

Evolutionary psychologists argue that the key to this preference for averageness is symmetry. By their nature, average faces are more symmetrical, because any individual asymmetries are averaged out.

If you have a computer and a camera handy you can make a picture of yourself more attractive:

1. **Take a picture of yourself head-on.**
2. **Cut it in half down the middle digitally.**
3. **Choose the more attractive half (interestingly, most likely to be your left side – the right side of the picture on screen).**
4. **Copy that half, mirror-reverse it and move it over.**

You now have a perfectly symmetrical full picture. Congratulations, you've created a more attractive version of yourself.

In fact, not just the symmetry of your face is important. Evolutionary psychologists have measured the bodily dimensions of large numbers of people, right down to the lengths and widths of each finger. Doing so allows them to quantify symmetry in terms of how close the measurements are for the right and left sides of the body. The claim is that your bodily symmetry ties up with how attractive you're judged to be. Plus, it also correlates with how much money you earn, how happy you are and how many sexual partners you have. Life is good for symmetrical people.

Why is bodily symmetry so important? Who decided that symmetry was the key to attraction, rather than being – what I like to call – elegantly misshapen, like me? The short answer is all down to parasites.

To see how, consider being a child growing up before modern medicine: say, any time further back than the last 200 years. You'd have had a large number of illnesses, infections and parasites during childhood. In fact, the odds are that you wouldn't have survived to adulthood at all. Childhood is a time of bodily growth, of course, and this rapid, spurting growth would be hampered by any parasites and infections you picked up as you aged. And anytime a parasite or infection inhibited a growth spurt in some way, you'd have grown asymmetrically, a little bit.

Your overall body symmetry is like a medical record of your childhood. If you want to mate with the healthiest person with the lowest number of bodily infections and parasites – and in Darwinian terms, who doesn't? – you choose the person with the most symmetrical body and face. That person provides the healthiest match for your genetic material.

Some people think it implausible that people use body symmetry as a cue to dating today. Parasites are thankfully rare in many modern societies, and many more reliable indicators of health are available if that's what you care about. In addition, are people on first dates actively attending to and keeping track of the symmetry between precise bodily dimensions? (Actually, I did once meet an evolutionary psychologist who admitted that he had his partner fully measured before he decided to propose to her, but that says more about him than proofing the idea.)

But the claim remains that over a long period of time bodily symmetry would prove to be a reliable cue to the health of potential partners, and so humans evolved a sensitivity to symmetry that survives today.

Choosing a mate

In my lectures on attraction, I present the class with a row of near-identical female faces. I ask them to pick the most attractive, or which they think would be the most attractive to heterosexual men. Their votes are usually spread along the row of faces, but with a strong skew towards the right-hand end. I ask the class to guess how the faces differ, and why people seem to prefer the faces more to the right. They make some good guesses – the forehead seems a bit bigger towards the right, the chin a little small, the eyes a little bigger. All these things are true, but they aren't how researchers created the row of photographs.

The picture on the far left is an unaltered image of a woman in her mid-twenties. The next picture on the right is a mix of the original plus 10 per cent of a different face. The next image has 20 per cent of the other face mixed in, the next 30 per cent and so on, until the final picture on the right that has 50 per cent of the original woman and 50 per cent of the other face. Something about the increasing presence of the other face makes the woman more and more attractive to people. Somewhat disconcertingly, it's the face of a 10-year-old girl.

The more that an adult female has the facial characteristics of a pre-pubescent girl, the more attractive she becomes to others. The technical name for this is *neoteny,* and in this context it means that the characteristics of the infant are retained by the adult. A neotenous face is one with big eyes, big forehead and a tiny chin, nose and mouth: basically the face of every Disney character. Once more, this effect can be seen across all cultures. And a good reason exists why cartoon characters and toys are drawn in this particular way: it just looks damn cute. Interestingly, the facial characteristics of infant faces are seen in many mammals, which is why few things on this earth are cuter than a baby kitten, panda or hedgehog.

Just to be clear: I'm not saying that human nature is to be attracted to pre-pubescent girls and baby pandas. The experimental evidence is that what's attractive, to heterosexual men in particular, is a female who's a sexually mature adult but who's retained some characteristics of a pre-pubescent face. Indeed, some famously attractive women – Brigitte Bardot and Kate Moss, for example – are known for their childlike faces.

It's reproduction, stupid!

Evolutionary psychology offers a suggestion as to why heterosexual men are attracted to adult females but want them to look pre-pubescent. It's based on the claim that through most of human history, younger females tended to be more fertile and have healthier babies. The argument is that the longer you live, the more likely you are to have had diseases and the pesky parasites I describe in the earlier section 'Preferring averagely pretty faces'. Plus, some evidence (though it's not clear how strong) exists that egg quality deteriorates with age and birth complications increase.

Although not necessarily true or significant factors with modern medicine, for most of human history men wanted the healthiest home for their genetic material and so sought out females who were as young as possible, while just old enough to have children. The claim is that men have evolved to be most attracted to sexually mature women who're young enough to still have the facial characteristics of girls.

Although finding direct evidence for this hypothesis is hard, in many cultures now and throughout history marriages took place when the female was aged 12 to 14, around the cusp of puberty. Indeed, the very notion of teenage years (where you're sexually mature but don't marry and aren't employed as an adult) is a thoroughly modern idea of the last hundred years or so. The idea would've seemed as crazy in the past as marrying a 12-year-old does today. But marriage at that age does fit with the claim from evolutionary psychology, because supposedly it would guarantee the healthiest offspring across the hundreds of thousands of years of human evolution.

Obviously, in today's culture females face much more pressure than men to look young. Women use the vast majority of cosmetic products, and the vast majority of cosmetic surgical procedures are performed upon them. Although men too sometimes alter their appearance to look and feel younger, they tend to do so well past middle age; whereas, remarkably, women can face pressure to look younger when they're only in their twenties.

What women want

If mating men look for youth and fertility, what do women want? By presenting women with headshots of lots of men and asking them to rate attraction, psychologists have identified some common characteristics. As well as symmetry, the facial characteristics in men that are typically attractive to heterosexual females are a wide, strong jaw and jutting forehead. These aren't features of the infant, and so another factor must be at work here.

These features correspond to the levels of testosterone in the male body. This hormone is made in the testes and plays a role in sperm production. It makes men's voices deeper, increases their muscle mass and puts hair on their chests. It also produces the strong jaws and jutting foreheads that women like and is also linked to assertive and aggressive behaviour. (I explain in Chapter 2 that when males have their honour insulted, their testosterone levels spike.)

The evolutionary claim is that a woman's choice of man is influenced by the levels of testosterone revealed in his face. Men with higher testosterone are more likely to be the dominant alpha males who have more resources and more ability to defend them. So, once more, at some level women are playing the same evolutionary game of getting the best genetic material to partner their genes.

Liking people who are like you

People – thank God – don't choose friends and partners purely on their looks. There are many nuanced and complex answers to the question of what else makes two people like each other, but one very simple answer is almost entirely true: people like people who are like them.

If you ever use a dating agency, you're asked a huge number of questions about your habits, preferences, beliefs and attitudes. The companies then imply that they take your answers and process them with some secret formula that mathematically calculates your perfect mate. In fact, the process is much simpler than that: they just find someone who answered the most questions the same way as you.

The psychological evidence – backed up by the huge success of dating agencies – is that humans just like people who are similar to them, in every way possible.

Focusing on the People You Love

In the earlier section 'Discovering Why You Like the People You Like', I discuss what makes a face attractive to you and what makes a person likeable. In a sense, you can view these judgements as unemotional ones. You spot a pretty face on the bus or on an advertising hoarding, or find a character likeable on a television show, but you don't really feel anything for that person.

Here I want to examine a quite different experience: being in love with someone. You don't have to find that person attractive – you don't even have to like them particularly – but you can still be in love with them. When you're attracted to someone in this context, you often have more than aesthetic judgements on your mind.

In this discussion on sexual orientation, I consider questions such as:

- ✔ Why do some people spend their lives falling in love with men and some falling in love with women?
- ✔ Why do the majority of people fall in love with people of the opposite sex?

Of course, this area is extremely complicated, very personal and highly political. As with many complex issues, people like to make sweeping and simplistic statements about it. You can hear theories of sexual orientation in terms of evolution, parental attitudes, cultural norms, specific childhood experiences, sin and bewitchment.

Dealing with all these ideas would result in a book thousands of pages long, and so I choose to focus on the important persistence of childhood attachment types in later life, whether a 'gay gene' exists and why certain groups of people become sexually attractive to specific groups of people.

Developing types of attachment in childhood

The bond you feel to your parents is probably the first relationship that can be characterised as love. It's not romantic love, or even directly related to liking at times, but it's certainly a form of love and emotional dependency.

This bond isn't a luxury in infancy; it's a necessity. In experiments with monkeys, researchers found that infants raised with all their basic requirements met – food, warmth, shelter – but without their mothers' nurturing behaviour had behavioural problems throughout their lives. This result has sadly and unintentionally been replicated in human infants who were raised in underfunded orphanages in Romania in the 1990s.

To investigate the relationship between infants and their caregivers, psychologists placed infants and caregivers in a test called the 'strange situation'. The caregiver and child played with each other in the room while researchers watched. Then a stranger entered the room and joined in. The caregiver then left the room, and the infant was alone with the stranger. By observing how the infant reacted to the caregiver's departure and return, researchers categorised three particular attachment styles:

- ✔ **Secure attachment:** Infants with this style happily explore the room in the strange situation when the caregiver is present and readily interact with the person. They're upset when left alone with the stranger, but happy and relieved when the caregiver returns. When these infants are adults, they tend to have trusting relationships, good self-esteem and find it easy to be with others.

- ✔ **Avoidant attachment:** Infants with this style don't explore the room very much and seem to ignore their caregivers. Their behaviour doesn't change whether the caregiver is present or not. As adults, they find relationships difficult and have a hard time getting close to people or trusting them.

- ✔ **Anxious attachment:** Infants with this style are wary of the stranger and of exploring the room. But when the caregiver leaves the room they become very distressed. As adults, they find forming relationships easy, but then experience extremes of emotional highs and lows and are often unhappy.

Remarkably, infants' behaviour in this test appears to predict how they form and maintain relationships for the rest of their adult lives, although these styles aren't set in stone. People who are avoidant as infants and in their early relationships can become secure with the right partner. But the way in which the first love of your caregivers is felt affects you throughout the rest of your life.

The role of formative experiences

Despite such ideas once being widespread, no evidence exists whatsoever that a particular, single childhood experience can determine your sexuality. These notions sometimes had their roots in now-debunked Freudian theories about psycho-sexual development, repressed urges and the formative relationship between a mother and child. Sometimes they were fuelled by a fear of 'predatory' homosexuals who'd 'recruit' young people into their lifestyle. Such fears were one reason that homosexuals were often excluded from professions such as teaching.

You may still hear such ideas repeated today, but no single person – not your mother, your father or your scout leader – can determine your sexual orientation.

Searching for the 'gay gene'

Many people argue that sexual orientation isn't 'something you choose'. They then proceed to equate this statement with the belief that sexual orientation must be hard-wired into your genes. In the nearby sidebar 'The politics of sexual orientation and choice', I provide several reasons why you need to be wary of this argument.

But some evidence does exist that homosexuality is hereditary, and so for a moment I want to consider the argument: Why would a gay gene exist and how could it have evolved?

Evolution isn't necessarily about becoming the fastest, the brightest or the best. The winners of the evolutionary game are the organisms that pass on their genes to the next generation. So the one thing you need to do if you want to pass on your genes is to have sex with another member of your species in a way that leads, eventually, to babies. In other words, if you were going to hard-wire anything into a creature, it would be the desire and the ability to have heterosexual reproductive sex. So why would a gay gene exist?

One argument put forward by evolutionary psychologists is that perhaps having gay male relatives is advantageous for other people (the theories only concern themselves with male homosexuality – I don't know why). Think of the argument this way: as a child, having an uncle who doesn't have children may be a good thing.

Several years ago, my brother was a relatively well-off, single dentist, whereas I had three small children and not much spare money. At Christmas the children had a pile of presents from my wife and me, their friends and other relatives. But towering above these was the pile of presents from my brother alone. He didn't have his own children draining his wallet, but because he likes his family and likes children, he was incredible generous to my kids.

Now imagine my family as ancient cave people (it's not too hard if you meet them). We're dividing up the slaughtered buffalo among the hunters. I have to share my portion with my children. But my brother, having no needy off-spring of his own, gives my kids some of his leftovers.

With a childless uncle, my children get a share of my resources and of his. One way that evolution could achieve this state is a genetic adaptation that has, say, a 90 per cent chance of producing a heterosexual male and a 10 per cent chance of producing a homosexual male. That way enough straight males lust after women to reproduce the gene and enough gay males bring in additional resources from the hunt to help the gene carriers to survive. In other words, a tribe with a small percentage of gay males may have fewer breeding males, but it has better fed and more pampered children than a tribe of only straight men, which in the long run brings a survival advantage. That, at least, is one evolutionary argument for the adaptive value of a 'gay gene'.

The politics of sexual orientation and choice

Homosexual activity was criminalised in the UK until 1967, and now, only a couple of generations later, same-sex unions have been given full legal recognition. In the past few years, the same changes have happened in many other countries in Europe and various states in the US. In other countries, however, such as Russia and Uganda, persecution of homosexuality is increasingly violent and severe.

When the issue of homosexual rights is discussed in families, pubs or angry radio phone-in shows, you always hear people talking about whether or not they think being gay is a *choice*. Usually, people in favour of equal rights for same-sex relationships say that who you fall in love with isn't a choice, you're born that way. People against those equal rights or who are straightforwardly homophobic say that it's just a lifestyle choice.

Whether you think that you choose your sexual orientation or not matters politically and affects whether you're for or against legalising gay marriage. I think that for many people the reason is that if sexuality is something you're born with, it's equivalent to ethnicity. Most people agree that discriminating against people because of the colour of their skin is wrong in principle. Therefore, the argument goes, if you're against racism, and you think that sexual orientation isn't a choice, you should also support equal rights for same-sex relationships.

I can understand the politics of this argument, but as a psychologist it makes me very uneasy. Psychologists simply don't divide up human behaviour into things that you choose and things that you don't choose. Every action you take is a result of influences from the situation around you, from your past experiences and from your genetic inheritance. Scientists have the difficult job of untangling these causal threads. But your 'choice' isn't part of the picture: it's an unscientific word. Psychologists want to understand the reasons behind your choices.

But here are a couple of reasons to be sceptical about the 'good gay uncle' and the 'gay gene' argument:

- ✔ **Genes don't really work like that.** Very few examples exist of a single gene giving rise to a single trait. Even the textbook example of eye colour isn't produced by a single gene, but by a set of genes. The more researchers discovered about genetics, the more they're discovering that what's vital is the *interaction* between genes, and between genes and the environment. Experiences that you have in your life turn your genes on and off – they can change your gene *expression* – and many, many complex causal loops between the organism and their environment determine an organism's development. No single gene exists 'for' anything, let alone something as complex and culturally flexible as sexuality.

- ✔ **The evidence is weak.** Gay uncles today may well give better Christmas presents, or at least researchers could do a study correlating sexuality with the size of Christmas gift receipts. But they can't do this with ancient hominids. Scientists have no direct evidence from the archaeological record of gay members of the tribe, or that they distributed their wealth and resources in a way that favoured their nieces and nephews.

Interacting elements: Exotic becomes erotic

Here's another theory on sexual orientation. Daryl Bem, a social psychologist, suggests that it's determined by the interaction of your biology, your childhood and your culture.

His theory is called the *exotic becomes erotic* (EBE) theory. It's an interesting theory that neatly combines several elements: a genetic component of your personality and dispositions, the experiences you have growing up and the way that your culture treats males and females. All these are tied together with a plausible story that is supported by psychological evidence. The data doesn't yet conclusively support this theory, or any other, for sexual orientation, but so far it seems a more compelling candidate than the 'gay gene' story in the preceding section.

I'm sure that the EBE theory doesn't explain everyone's childhood experience and sexual orientation. Human sexuality – and love – is such a complex, nuanced and culturally determined thing that it would be very surprising if scientists ever have a completely satisfying theory. But it does combine the biological, psychological and cultural factors, which any successful theory surely must.

Here's a walk through the four elements of the EBE theory.

Inherited preferences

The first element that eventually determines your sexual orientation is your genetic predisposition to enjoy certain types of activity.

As a child, you liked certain activities and not others: perhaps you enjoyed running around kicking footballs, play-fighting with swords and riding bikes; or doing puzzles, building Lego or constructing elaborate fantasy worlds with play figures and stuffed animals. These preferences are an aspect of a child's personality, and the evidence is that these sorts of preferences are largely inherited. If your parents are very active and boisterous, you probably are too.

Gender polarisation

The second element of the EBE theory is a society that segregates the genders in their play activities.

Look around any toyshop and you see that some aisles are labelled 'boys toys' (including guns, weapons, construction kits, skateboards and more weapons) and others are labelled 'girls toys' (where you're assaulted by a wave of pink, glitter and fur, dolls, pony sets, make-up kits and more dolls). Science kits are in the boys' section; toy kitchens are in the girls'. The contrast is remarkable; it's called *gender polarisation*.

The chances are that if you're a little boy, regardless of what you may want to play with, you're given sports equipment, weapons and building toys. You see other older boys playing with these items in the school playground and on TV adverts, and the adults buying you Christmas presents buy them from the boy's aisle in the shop. Girls may prefer a chemistry set or a bow and arrow, but the chances are increased that they get a toy oven or a hairdryer.

Regardless of their disposition, boys tend to be given toys that emphasise physical activity and girls given toys that emphasise social activity.

Now, most children may well be happy with this state of affairs. Little boys do have more testosterone and tend to be a little more energetic, for example. But the fact is that cultural expectations exaggerate, or polarise, the differences between the sexes. Boys are kicked outside and given a football, and girls are given dolls and make-up.

Intergroup processes

When you add together the first two elements of the EBE theory (a biological disposition for a certain type of activity and a society that pushes boys towards one type of activity and girls to another), you get a society where most boys play only with other boys and most girls play only with other girls. That certainly seems to describe most playgrounds you see.

> # Early lessons in biology: The cootie factor!
>
> Children often run round the school playground screaming about cooties, or nits as they were called when I was young. These imaginary organisms inhabit the opposite sex and represent just how horrible they are. In my school, if you were touched by a member of the opposite sex during a game of chase, or you accidently picked up a pencil belonging to one of them, you were expected to run around screaming, 'Ewww, I've got nits, gross!'.

But a further consequence is that some boys, a minority perhaps, have a strong disposition to play make-believe social games with dolls and dressing up, and some girls really want to run around and hit things. These children are termed *gender atypical:*

- Gender atypical boys grow up spending a lot of time playing with girls, because they have the best doll collections.
- Gender atypical girls mostly hang out with boys, because they're the ones in the park playing football.

Now the third element of the theory comes into play: intergroup processes. If you spend most of your time with members of one sex, and very little time with the other, you're going to form certain stereotyped views and generalisations about the differences between boys and girls, and form your own social identities in those terms. In particular, the people that a child plays with a lot, whether boys or girls, become their *in-group* and the sex of children that they don't play with become the *out-group.*

As you see in Chapter 16, people seize upon any reason to draw distinctions between 'them' and 'us'. The slightest difference, real or imagined, can be used to form social groups, which unfortunately can be quickly followed by suspicion, prejudice and fear. For an example of how this can work in the playground, see the nearby sidebar 'Early lessons in biology: The cootie factor!'.

Misattribution of arousal

The fourth element in the EBE theory appears as nature plays a wild card: puberty, a time of bodily change and hormonal upheaval. For the first time, adolescents start to feel the stirrings of sexual desire. During the early, tumultuous period of puberty, this desire is like a box of fireworks in a microwave: things just go off at random. This final element in the EBE theory is therefore the *misattribution of arousal,* a process that occurs throughout life, not just in adolescents.

People are surprisingly bad at interpreting their own physiological states. The sensation of your pulse racing and your hands trembling feels exactly the same whether you're scared, excited, elated or anxious. You can't tell the difference.

TECHNICAL STUFF

Bridge over aroused waters

In the classic demonstration of misattribution of arousal, male participants had to walk across a bridge to talk to an attractive female experimenter. The bridge was either low, or very high, so that most people would feel some anxiety walking over it. After asking the participants some questions, the female experimenter gave the participants her phone number, in case they wanted to call her later to ask about the results of the experiment.

The participants who walked across the high bridge would have had elevated heart rates, sweaty palms and all the physiological signs of mild fear. When they talked to the female experimenter, however, they tended to misattribute these physiological signs as arousal and attraction towards the female experimenter. Participants who walked across the high bridge were more likely to call her later and ask her out on a date.

When you experience the emotion of fear or excitement you're *interpreting* your bodily signal in terms of what's happening around you. If you're watching the last five minutes of a cup final match and your team is holding on for the win, your pulse may be racing and you feel excitement. You interpret the exact same physiological state as fear when, later that day, you get stuck in a pub with drunken fans from the losing team, and you're wearing the wrong scarf (gulp).

The process of misattribution of arousal explains why, for example, people often go out to see horror movies or go on rollercoaster rides together. If you can mildly scare your date, he or she may well mistake that fear for feelings of attraction towards you.

Combining the four elements together: The exotic become erotic

According to their biological dispositions, and exaggerated by a gender-polarised society, most young boys play with other boys and most young girls play with other girls. Psychological group processes mean that, in general, the two sexes look upon each other as hostile out-groups.

Then puberty arrives and in a process of misattribution, the fear that comes from contact with the opposite sex gets confused and connected with the desire of puberty. In the crucible of adolescent hormones, people are sexually attracted to the sex that they didn't spend time with as children: the unfamiliar, the exotic, becomes erotic.

Therefore, most boys are attracted to the enigmatic creatures that are girls and most girls are attracted to the mysterious and unfamiliar things that are boys. So the EBE is a theory about the causes of heterosexuality. But it's equally a theory about homosexuality, because children with strongly gender atypical dispositions spend most of their childhoods playing with the opposite sex. As a result boys who are familiar with girls become attracted to other boys during adolescence and girls who spent most of their time running around with other boys find other girls at first scary and then attractive.

Analysing the EBE's consequences

The EBE theory has the advantage that it doesn't treat sexuality as a straight-forward gay or straight issue. People can be attracted to the same or the opposite sex in different degrees, in a way that can be predicted by their childhood predispositions and experiences. This more graded sense of sexuality is a better fit for many people's experiences, and the different and various ways that sexuality has been viewed in different cultures and at different points in history.

The EBE also makes a number of testable predictions. The most obvious one is that adults who were gender atypical as children are more likely to be homosexual. After all, psychologists can just ask people to find out, can't they? But despite appearing to be a straightforward prediction, obtaining reliable data isn't easy. Memory is highly unreliable, and childhood memory more so. Autobiographical memory is a story that people write and re-write to make sense of themselves, and a healthy dose of hindsight bias is always at work too, selecting the childhood memories that demonstrate what later seems obvious. But with these caveats in mind, homosexual men and women are more likely to have been gender atypical as children. Not all, but certainly more than average.

One consequence of the EBE theory is that sexual orientation is, in part, an outcome of gender polarisation. Significantly, gender polarisation acts differently on boys and girls. As you may have observed, things are generally worse for a boy who likes girls' toys than a girl who likes boys' toys. The girl may be called a tom-boy in the playground and the boy much worse. As a result, the pressures to be gender typical are arguably greater for young boys than young girls, and so boys tend to be more gender polarised than girls.

Therefore, the EBE theory would predict that sexual orientation should be more fixed in men and more fluid in women: because boys are more likely to have played with all boys growing up (or all girls) they should either be strongly straight or strongly gay; because girls, on the other hand, experience less pressure to play with one gender or another, they should have a more graded sexual orientation as adults.

As Lisa Diamond and other researchers have shown, this does seem to be the case. Women tend to have a more fluid sexual orientation, and are more likely to have partners from one sex at one time and from the other sex at a different stage in life, compared to men; though whether this difference is explained by the EBE or some other factor is still debated.

Another consequence of the EBE theory makes it quite a good evolutionary story too. In Darwinian terms, having a bias towards being sexually attracted to people who were unfamiliar as children is very healthy:

- ✔ It encourages people towards seeking out partners from different tribes, villages and cities. (A population with a diverse mixture of genes is much healthier and able to adapt.)

- ✔ It nudges people away from being attracted to members of their own family, because they'd be very familiar in childhood. (Over generations, cousins becoming husbands and wives can rapidly lead to all sorts of genetic disorders.)

So aside from issues about sexual orientation, the EBE acts to increase the genetic health of a population.

Although society has a cultural stereotype about marrying your childhood sweetheart, it's actually quite rare, as the EBE predicts. Researchers looked at the experiences of around 3,000 children raised in kibbutzim (collective communities) in Israel. At one time, the common cultural practice in Israeli kibbutzim was for all the children to be raised communally. In essence, the children of lots of different families on a kibbutz grew up like one very big extended family. Researchers tracked down a large group of these children and asked them as adults how many had ended up getting married to people from the same kibbutz. Out of those 3,000 children, the answer was zero. Just statistically speaking, that's very surprising, and suggests that something about that shared childhood lowered the attraction that they felt towards each other.

Successful long-term relationships

The EBE theory seems to throw up a paradox. If people are sexually attracted to those who are unfamiliar and different, how come they tend to like people who are similar to them (see the earlier section 'Liking people who are like you'). Are the people you like and the people you lust after completely opposite people? In fact, this isn't really a paradox, simply the tragic state of human existence and the plot of almost every song, novel and film.

So should you be guided by liking or lust? More specifically, whom do you form successful long-term relationships with? Well, I'm not in the business of giving relationship advice – this book isn't *Marriage Guidance For Dummies* – but the evidence suggests that although you can fall in love very heavily with people who're different from you, and you may have wonderful, intense relationships, the ones that are happy, the marriages that last, tend to be based on similarity and liking.

Living with Others: Reciprocal Altruism

Unless you work in the entertainment industry and have just won a major award, the chances are that you do *not* absolutely love everyone you've ever worked with. In fact, you may not particularly like your boss or your work-mates. But the fact is that – by and large – people get along with each other. You wouldn't know it from watching the news each evening, but in general humans live together in remarkable peace and harmony.

You may occasionally feel like killing your noisy neighbours, the driver who cuts you off at the junction or the person loudly eating a stinky boiled egg next to you on the train, but these thoughts rarely translate into fatal action.

Only about 1 per cent of all deaths are at the hands of another person, including all the deaths from war. Car accidents kill twice as many people as people do. In fact, if you *are* killed by someone, suicide by your own hand is about 50 per cent more likely than homicide at someone else's. The most dangerous person you meet is the one looking back at you in the mirror.

People manage to live in harmony with such a large number of people who aren't family, friends or lovers because they learnt to co-operate and help each other. If you're sceptical, see the nearby sidebar 'The only certainties are death, taxes and the need for co-operation'.

Co-operating with each other

In this discussion on co-operation, I turn again to Darwin. Your goal in life as an evolved human is to reproduce your genes and maximise their chance of survival. So you pick the best mate and share your food and resources with your family, your kin, to the degree that they're carrying your genes.

But why do you share any of your food with people who aren't directly related to you? Evolutionary biologists, such as Robert Trivers, realised that under certain circumstances, altruism is advantageous to individuals.

Imagine that you're a lucky cave-dweller and you have more mammoth meat than you can eat. I live in the cave next door and have none. Sharing your food with me today makes sense, because tomorrow you may get unlucky in the hunt. If you share food with me now, in the future I'll share my food with you. This is termed *reciprocal altruism:* you're generous and co-operative with your neighbours on the understanding that they'll be generous and co-operative with you.

The only certainties are death, taxes and the need for co-operation

Today, in most western democracies, about a third of the average worker's income goes to the government so that (in theory) it can be spent to everyone's advantage. In some countries it's as much as a half. Even in the US, where many people are suspicious of taxation, a quarter of everyone's income, on average, still goes to the government. And though they may complain about it, and dodge the tax where possible, in almost every country richer people pay a higher share of their income to tax.

Governments and taxes are a remarkable feat of social co-operation. As well as paying tax people (mostly) don't steal from each other, do respect each other's property and even hold the door open for strangers. All these actions are non-selfish, despite Darwinian reasoning seeming to suggest that people's only concerns should be their relatives and themselves.

Reciprocal altruism is a successful strategy, in theory and in practice. Computer models of social groups show that social groups with members that co-operate with each other are more successful in the long term than those that compete. As I discuss in Chapter 14, every culture in the world has a social norm of reciprocity. If someone gives you something or does you a favour, the basic human urge is to give something back. For instance, reciprocal altruism is the basis of the welfare state: people pay their taxes to support the elderly, the ill and those who've fallen on hard times, knowing that in the future they'll be supported if need be.

Catching the cheaters

But a weak spot exists in the strategy of reciprocal altruism: certain people take advantage and cheat.

Say you work in an office with a tin where you put 50 pence every week. Someone takes that money and buys milk and coffee cheaply in bulk to stock the kitchen area. So instead of having an expensive vending machine, everyone gets cheap coffee, even when they don't have change on them. This arrangement is a great example of reciprocal altruism because everyone benefits. Except . . . one person in the office benefits more than anyone else: the person who sneakily avoids putting in 50 pence every week gets free coffee.

Therefore, although co-operation is undoubtedly advantageous for a society, for any one individual in that society it seems to be better to be non-co-operative: to lie, steal and cheat. How did individuals evolve the trait of reciprocal altruism, when it's to their own advantage to be selfish?

Imagine four cards on the table in front of you. Each card has a letter on one side and a number on the other. Since they are on the table, you can only see one side of them. There is an E, C, 5 and 4. Now I tell you that if a card has a vowel on one side then it has an odd number on the other side. What cards do you turn over to see whether I'm telling the truth or lying to you? Write down your answer when you've figured it out.

Now try this second problem. You're a bouncer at a nightclub. Your boss has told you to check for underage drinkers: people drinking alcohol must be over 18. You can ask people to prove their age, and you can check their drinks for alcohol. Right now, you can see four people in the bar at different tables. One person's drinking beer and the other's drinking coke. You recognise two other people, but you can't see what they're drinking. One of them is 25 years old and the other is 16. To make sure that no one is drinking underage, which tables do you need to investigate? Write your answer down again.

The answer to the first problem is E and 4. If you put down E and 5, you made the same mistake as many other people. The fact is that it doesn't matter what's on the other side of the 5 card. If it's a vowel, the rule works. If it's not a vowel, the rule doesn't apply, and so it still holds. But you do need to know what's on the other side of the 4 card, because if it's a vowel, the rule is broken.

The answer to the second problem is that you should check the age of the person drinking beer, and the drink of the person who is 16. But, I bet you'd figured that out already.

The *real* puzzle here is why was one problem harder than the other? Those two problems have an identical logical structure: you can swap the words 'drinking alcohol' with 'vowel' and 'over 18' with 'odd number' and the problems are identical. If you can figure out the logic of one problem, you should be able to figure out the logic of the other, just as if you can calculate five plus seven you can calculate seven plus five. Why is the first problem so much more difficult?

The evolutionary psychologists Leda Cosmides and John Tooby offer one solution to this puzzle. They argue that people have evolved specialised brain mechanisms to detect when people are *cheating*. They claim that the second problem of underage drinkers is easier to solve because it's framed as an example of cheating. A social rule is violated and people are experts at detecting that. Just as they've evolved to be very sensitive to smells that indicate food has gone bad, humans have evolved a nose to sniff out the cheaters among them. This evolved adaptation to detect cheating (and punish it) allows reciprocal altruism to thrive as a successful social strategy, because people can be confident that everyone is sharing as they should be.

This explanation aligns with everyday experience. How do you feel when someone cuts in line ahead of you at an airport queue? Or they cut you off at a road junction? The anger that you feel when a social rule is violated is often out of all proportion to the offence committed. Even though it adds only moments to your shopping trip, you fume for hours about someone who clearly had more than ten items in front of you in the supermarket express line.

Clearly people care about following social rules, and even more about people who violate them. But is there really strong evidence that humans evolved a trait specifically to detect cheaters? Many researchers look at the example of the two logical puzzles and point to all the other differences between them. As well as one being about cheating, the second problem is a scenario you may have experienced before (as a bouncer or a drinker). So perhaps it's easier to imagine and reason through, compared to the purely logical puzzle about numbers and vowels.

'I Know my Place': Power and Social Status

Interpersonal interaction involves a lot more than liking, loving and co-operating. Human societies are hierarchical: they have kings, CEOs and bosses, serfs, data-entry clerks and interns. The signs of social class are pervasive. In medieval times, your birth decided your profession, your wage and the sorts of clothes you could wear and the length of the toes on your shoes. Even today, in more egalitarian times, cues to social class are everywhere. Look around an airport and I bet you can guess the social class of most people and predict who'll end up being pampered in the first-class cabin, with the clean loos no one else is allowed to use!

Social status shapes many other aspects of your behaviour:

- ✔ The amount of eye contact you have with someone depends on their status. Depending on your culture and this situation, it will be more or less that low-status people.

- ✔ In a group discussion, people spend more time looking at the face of the high-status person.

- ✔ The degree to which someone can keep speaking or be talked over is determined by their perceived status.

- ✔ You can even detect differences between body language and posture between the powerful and the lowly: high-status people tend to have more open and expansive postures. If you peek into a meeting room and see one person with their hands behind their head or feet on the desk, the chances are they are the boss (or think that they should be).

Getting tongue-thai'ed

In Thai society, social status information is needed to figure out someone's class before you decide which of 14 different pronouns to use when addressing someone. A different word is used for 'you' when talking to your child, a younger person, a peer, a book and other ranks up to the king. And you thought English was complex!

If you believe that the strong influence of social hierarchies on behaviour is peculiar to people, think again: it seems to have evolved before creatures even evolved into humans. If you go to the zoo, for example, you may not know who's the most attractive or the cleverest chimpanzee in the enclosure, but after a few moments' observation of behaviour and body language, it becomes obvious who's the dominant male of the group. Careful experiments with chimps and monkeys show that they respond differently to photographs of other members of their group, depending on their social status.

People use social status to shape groups and activities. In studies of juries, for example, researchers find that the role of foreman nearly always goes to the person with the highest perceived social status. These cues generally fall into one of types:

- ✔ **Specific status characteristics related to the task at hand:** For example, an ex-policeman may have legal expertise that would raise his status in a jury setting.

- ✔ **Diffuse status characteristics:** Such as age, educational level or occupational status.

People don't respond only to the perceived power and social status of other people; the social status that they ascribe to themselves changes their behaviour too. Researchers can make you feel more or less power and social status by making you engage in simple exercises. For example, they can ask you to write about a time that you were sacked from a job; or a time that you made a decision to sack someone else. After recalling these moments, the researchers gave participants simple tasks, such as finding an L on a screen among a splatter of Ts, or deciding what to do over the weekend depending on the weather.

They found that people who were made to feel low social power were faster at finding the L among the Ts. People who felt high social power were less likely to change their weekend plans according to the weather. If they wanted to go for a walk they would, even if it was going to rain.

Apparently, when people are feeling of low social power they attend more to the things going on around them. They have a broader *attentional window,* so to speak. For this reason, they're faster at visual tasks where they have to search for things or integrate many different sources of information at once. In contrast, high-power people are less focused on the world around them and more focused on their own goals, motivations and beliefs. So they decide what to do over the weekend based on their desires, and are less swayed by contextual information, such as the weather or what other people want.

As a consequence, people who feel high social power are also more likely to make stereotypical judgements about people. Instead of looking through the CV of a job applicant and considering their strengths, for example, they're more likely to reject a female for an engineering position because it doesn't accord with their pre-existing stereotypes.

To make sense of these findings, I turn to Donald Trump: a man of high social power, in his own mind at least. If you're Donald Trump's personal assistant, you're in a position of low power. Your job is to check every detail – that the limo has the right bottle of water, that Donald is on time for his appointments, that the wigs have been ironed and so on. So having a wide attentional focus is useful. But if you're Donald himself, you don't need to attend to what's going on around you as much; that's someone else's job. You have the power and the resources so that you can attend to your own goals and motivations. You're free to act upon them, rather than the demands that the world puts upon you.

What's remarkable is that these different ways of relating to the world aren't just the result of a lifetime of being a CEO or a personal assistant. The same mode of thinking can be activated in you just by a short exercise that makes you feel more or less powerful. So although ending a chapter on love, beauty and desire with the image of Donald Trump is a real shame, he does serve as an illustration of the psychological forces that shape social interaction.

Chapter 16

Examining the Benefits and Dangers of Social Groups

People have an astonishing number of ways of dividing themselves into groups: countries, races, star signs, religions, occupations and so on. Rightly or wrongly, social groups structure how humans think about each other. They're the bias for one of the most important distinctions in people's personal and social lives: the difference between 'them' and 'us'.

Forming and maintaining group relationships can have profound consequences for how you view other people, and especially how you view yourself. At work, school and in society generally, whether you're part of the popular majority in-group, the minority out-group or a stigmatised group affects your self-esteem, health and world view. In this chapter I examine how you categorise other people, how you place yourself into a group and how such impulses can cause group conflict. I also look at groups in action, examining how people share their opinions and make decisions together.

Introducing the Desire to Separate People into Groups

People love to categorise themselves and others: by the football teams they support, the political parties they vote for and even the cars they drive. For example, you can probably identify what you think a country music fan looks like, how an iPhone user differs from an Android user and what party a vegetarian is likely to vote for. Whether or not you're correct in all these assumptions isn't the point: the fact is that people are driven to categorise people into social groups

One striking example is how people see differences between themselves and their near neighbours. I spent one summer in Sweden and Denmark. The Swedes related hilarious stories about those crazy Danes with their schnapps, weird rotten fish delicacies and odd customs; and the Danes told equally funny stories about the crazy Swedes with their (slightly different) schnapps, slightly different rotten fish delicacies and equally inscrutable (to outsiders) customs.

These differences are hugely salient to the Swedes and the Danes and form an important part of their identity. Although I'll deeply annoy my Scandinavian friends by saying so, to an outsider Swedes and Danes are virtually indistinguishable. You can say the same, of course, about the English and the Welsh, Australians and New Zealanders, and Canadians and Americans.

In this section I describe the apparently irresistible urge of humans to categorise each other and treat others differently depending on if they are in the same or a different social group as themselves. I also discuss the benefits people gain from joining a group.

Categorising people just for the sake of it

In this section I look at some of the reasons that people distinguish one group of people from another. Even though those reasons can be very slight, even imaginary, such social groups can have considerable psychological consequences for their members.

Are you left- or right-handed? You may think that the question is only relevant when you're using a pair of scissors or playing tennis. But scientists have found that systematic psychological differences exist between people who are left- and right-handed. Before I tell you what those group differences are, test your own social knowledge of these groups and their differences as follows: spend a couple of minutes thinking about all the right- and left-handed people you know. Write down two lists of personality traits that you think are shown more strongly, on average, in right- and in left-handers.

When your two lists are finished, look down them and put a tick for every word that's (broadly speaking) a positive thing and a cross for words that are negative things. For example, being creative is positive and being argumentative is negative. Now count up the number of ticks and crosses you have for left- and right-handers.

Before you analyse your results, here's one important thing: scientists have found *no personality differences at all* between right- and left-handed people! Sorry, I lied to you. As psychologists such as Chris McManus have concluded, very large surveys have measured people's personalities, intelligence and health, and discovered no differences whatsoever. It's a common misconception that there are such things as 'left-brained' and 'right-brained' people. Or rather, there are different types of people, and some are more analytic and some more creative, but this has little to do with handedness and simple right- and left-sided differences in brain activity.

The fact is that for various reasons people have cultural beliefs about left-handed people. Whereas a 'right-hand man' is someone to trust, for example, the word 'sinister' derives from the Latin for 'left hand'. Plus, certain weak pieces of scientific evidence in the past claimed differences and a few of these settled in people's minds as facts. But the strongest evidence so far is for no differences whatsoever.

Now look back to your two lists. Did you put more negative descriptions for left-handers or for right-handers? Did you put more positive descriptions for the group to which you yourself belong? Why do you think these differences exist in your mind, when they don't exist in reality between right- and left-handed people?

Students studying each other

Where I went to university as an undergraduate, in Oxford, the students were divided up in 30 different colleges, where they slept, ate and sometimes studied. By the end of my three years, I thought I was able to tell you exactly what the people were like in at least 20 of those colleges, identifying the most arrogant, the most nerdy, the most artistic ones and those who just wanted to party. All a friend had to say was, 'I'm dating this girl, but she's from Wadham College, so you know. . .' and I knew exactly what he meant.

On mature reflection, and having wandered around Oxford since, I realise that these beliefs are complete nonsense. Or at least, that the similarities between the students (a bit pretentious, insecure, middle class) far outweigh the differences between them.

One feature of human psychology is that if a way exists to divide people up into groups, they start instantly to perceive differences between those groups. Even when based on superficial and unimportant characteristics, people imagine that the groups reflect deeper differences. Check out the nearby sidebar 'Students studying each other' for an example.

Favouring people in your group

Despite the powerful tendency of humans to divide people into groups, and for this division to create the illusion of large differences between groups of people, you may well argue that real differences do exist between people. The average country fan, for example, may have a different age and political outlook to other people in general. But with cunning experiments, researchers can prove that people see differences between others and treat them differently on the basis of groups, even when no objective differences exist between those people.

These experiments revolve around the idea of the *minimal group paradigm*, which is an experimental method social psychologists use to study the effects of social groups. The trouble is that people have many pre-existing beliefs (that are not necessarily true) about social groups such as men versus women, or right-handers and left-handers. The minimal group paradigm allows psychologists to create new social groups and study the effect of grouping alone, apart from the effects of social stereotypes (that I discuss in Chapter 10).

In minimal group experiments, psychologists give participants fake reasons for being in one social group or another, such as telling them that a personality test has determined that they are a 'type X' person or a 'type Y' person. They aren't told anything else about what that means, and in fact, the groups are allocated purely at random. In this sense they are 'minimal' groups, because the participants should have no beliefs about what makes them one type or another, or any pre-existing stereotypes about the different types. All they know is that they are in one group, and other people are in the same or a different group. Remarkably, this grouping alone is enough to change their behaviour.

In the early minimal group paradigm experiments, Henri Tajfel and colleagues placed participants into two different groups. Participants were told that their preferences for paintings by Klee or Kandinsky determined which group they were in. But in fact, they were placed in groups completely at random. The participants were then given small amounts of money and asked to share it among two people: one in the Klee group and one in the Kandinsky. They didn't know who the people were, because they were referred to by a code number. All they knew was the group membership.

The researchers found that participants systematically favoured people from their own groups. If they were in the Klee group, participants chose to give more money to other people if they were also in the Klee group.

This behaviour is called *in-group favouritism*, because people act positively to those in the same social group as them, and negatively towards those in out-groups.

Perhaps you think that they were doing so for a tangible reason: if they happen to have strong views on art, for example, they may think that people who prefer Kandinsky are insufferably dull. So in later experiments, the researchers removed even those cues. Participants were simply told that they were in the X group or the Y group, and given no other reason. These groups truly were 'minimal'. But even then participants displayed a tendency to reward people in their own group, despite no difference existing between people other than their entirely arbitrary group membership.

Researchers had known that this phenomenon happens all the time in the real world. For example, if you find out that someone is from the same town as you, or supports the same sports team, you tend to be positively disposed towards them. But what's remarkable in this experiment is that you don't need to share a background or knowledge and love of the same football team: simply being told that you're in the same arbitrary group by an experimenter is enough to produce in-group favouritism.

The smallest sense of 'them' and 'us' is enough to produce favouritism and discrimination.

Safety in numbers: Motivational approach

Why do people feel a need to belong to groups and to treat their fellow group members differently to others? Beginning with the results from the minimal group paradigm in the preceding section, Henri Tajfel and John Turner formed their social identity theory. Their ideas have been developed by themselves and others over the years.

The central notion of *social identity theory* is that people seek out, commit themselves to and categorise themselves into groups because they get something back in return: a social identity. It's also called the *motivational approach* to understanding groups, because it asks why people form and maintain groups. (The theory complements the cognitive approach of understanding groups in terms of stereotypes and judgement biases that I discuss in Chapter 10 and the economic approach that I describe in the later section 'Examining the Economic Approach to Group Behaviour'.)

A social identity – membership of a group – tells you how to behave, what to think and what's of value. It gives a structure to your identity, and through that, a way to achieve self-esteem.

Say that you decide to be 'born again' as a fundamentalist Christian. Being a member of that group gives you a way to live your life (usefully, it even comes in book form), a smart preppy way to dress, forms of politeness, a clear social hierarchy and a group of people who give you positive encouragement and validation if you act like them. In the same way, if you want to be a Satanist Goth, you also find a set of norms, a style of black dress and eye make-up, a way of speaking and acting, and a group of people who validate you. In a social psychological sense, the reason for joining these groups – sincere religious faith, or a passing music fad – doesn't matter. Simply the fact that you belong to an in-group brings with it a host of psychological effects.

'I'm in with the in-crowd': In-groups

Social identity is a route to self-esteem. The achievements and successes of your group are bound to your own sense of worth – which is one reason for in-group favouritism. If you're in group X, giving more money to other X people is advantageous to you. You may not directly benefit from this strategy in terms of a cash reward, but if Xs as a group get richer, and you're a member of that group, in a way you become richer too. Your membership of a group buys you a stake in that success, so to speak. The group's successes become your own. Sure enough, when people carry out acts of in-group favouritism, their own self-esteem has been found to increase.

The link between an individual and their social groups can be fluid and opportunistic. To put that another way, social identity theory suggests that you emphasise your membership of a group when it provides the biggest boost to your self-esteem. Researchers examined the behaviour of students after their college team won or lost a game. After a win, students were more obvious in their group affiliation: the next day more students pulled on the team shirt. This was termed 'basking in reflected glory'.

The effect is subtler than simply wearing the team colours, however. When the researchers asked students to describe what happened in the game, their language shifted:

- ✔ After a win, supporters spoke of what 'we' did in the game and 'our' tactics.
- ✔ After a loss, the talk was of 'their' mistakes and 'their' lack of form.

People don't form social groups mindlessly. Social identity theory shows that they strengthen their social groups, or distance themselves from them, in relation to the pay-off to their self-esteem.

'I'm on the outside (looking in)': Out-groups

I reveal in Chapter 7 that self-esteem is a relative thing. I feel better about myself if I think of the people who dropped out of my college, rather than the ones who didn't and are now millionaires.

Similarly, social identity theory holds that the self-esteem that derives from my group membership is relative. I can feel better about myself by contributing to the success and bolstering the achievements of my own in-group or I can denigrate people who are in my out-group. Sadly, the latter option is easier, just as effective and just as commonly chosen. In short: prejudice makes you feel better about yourself.

Researchers tested this idea by raising or lowering participants' self-esteem. They gave them an intelligence test, but didn't even bother to grade it. They simply told half the participants that they scored very well and half that they scored poorly. Then they showed the participants a job interview and asked them to rate the candidate. In one condition, they were told that the candidate was Jewish. When the (non-Jewish) participants rated the candidate, they gave him a harsher score if they themselves had just performed poorly on the intelligence test.

At the end of the experiment participants rated their own self-esteem. Those who were told that they did badly on the test, who had then judged the Jewish candidate poorly, now had high levels of self-esteem. Participants didn't get the same large self-esteem boost if the candidate was non-Jewish, like them.

Unfortunately, the act of denigrating someone from an ethnic out-group has the effect of inflating the person's self-esteem. Indeed, these participants who engaged in prejudice felt better about themselves than the ones who were told that they'd done very well in the intelligence test. One of the reasons that prejudice persists in our society is because of this link between self-esteem and social groups. Persuading people to avoid being racist or sexist is an uphill battle, because denigrating people from an out-group gives people a boost in their self-esteem, regardless of the true differences, or lack of differences, between the achievements and attributes of social groups.

Seeing Groups in Action: Group Decision-making

When psychology was in its infancy, a hundred years or so ago, it was fascinated by groups of people. Theorists – Freud even – wrote long essays on the 'mind of the mob'. This was a time of revolution in Europe, remember, and psychologists wondered whether the large groups of people rioting on the street, challenging governments, could be thought of as a single entity in some way. But, because you can only fit one person on a psychiatrist's couch and one person in a lab cubicle, psychology as a discipline tended to focus very much on the individual.

But in this section I reveal how psychologists have studied the choices that people make in groups: the ways in which they share and propagate knowledge, opinions and information.

Appreciating the wisdom of the crowds

A *liger* is the product of a lion, a tiger and a night of – probably awkward – romance. Ligers don't have the best of lives: they have a lot of health problems, and problems with their hormone regulation mean that they grow to enormous sizes. The largest feline in the world was a liger. My question to you is: how much do you think that liger weighed?

I'm guessing that – as long as you don't search the Internet for the answer – you don't know the weight of the world's heaviest liger. You had to guess, and it probably felt like a wild stab in the dark.

But here's the remarkable thing. If I were able to collect all the guesses from the readers of this book, and averaged those numbers, the average number would be very close indeed to the true weight of the world's heaviest liger (408 kilograms, in case you're still wondering).

Obviously my readers are super-smart, but even so – how can you be individually pretty clueless as to the weight distribution of oversized felines, but somehow as a group have remarkably accurate knowledge? When I give this problem to lecture classes of 100 or more, they typically average between 395 and 420 kilograms. And invariably this averaged guess is more accurate than the guess of any one individual in the group. Well, apart from that one time I had a very excited liger fan in the audience.

This effect is known as the *wisdom of the crowds*. It was first noticed by Francis Galton a century ago. At village country fetes, displaying a prize cow was popular and villagers held a competition to guess its weight. Galton was a statistician and noticed that across many such competitions the average of all these estimates would almost always have won the competition over the closest guess of an individual.

More recently, the journalist James Surowiecki argued that the wisdom of the crowds stretches far beyond the realm of guessing the weight of large mammals. Indeed, the US government even had a trial system in which large numbers of people sought to guess the likelihood of certain political events happening: a revolution in Pakistan, for example. The average of these guesses from uninformed people across the country out-performed the guesses of well-paid, highly educated expert political analysts.

Discovering how a group of clever people can make bad decisions

Based on the preceding section about the wise crowd, you'd think that whenever more than one person makes a decision, they'd draw on this collective wisdom. Surely, a group of minds can always do better than an individual. Unfortunately, that's not always the case. The wisdom of the crowd partly relies on the fact that all these judgements are independent: people make up their own minds. Further research in psychology has found that when people interact with each other, the wisdom of the crowd dissolves into the idiocy of the committee.

If people guess the weight of a cow and put it on a slip of paper, or estimate the likelihood of a revolution in Pakistan and enter it into a website, the average of their views is highly accurate. But; surprisingly, if those people _talk about the issue first_ the answers that they come to are increasingly incorrect.

More specifically, researchers have found an effect of group _polarisation._ Whatever bias people may have as individuals gets multiplied when they discuss things as a group. If individuals lean slightly towards taking a risk, a group leaps towards it. Say that your friend has to decide whether to leave his job in the bank and risk retraining as something new. As an individual, you may say, 'Go for it – try a course in sales!' But if you discuss this in a group, the advice may be to leave the job, move to Paris and register for clown school.

One reason for this polarisation is that, as a group, people can come up with a bigger set of _persuasive arguments_ in support of the biased options: because everyone favours leaving the job, everyone suggests reasons to do so. But they come up with slightly different reasons. One person may point out that your friend is unlikely to get promoted any more at the bank, another that a new job would mean he'd meet new people, another that he never has the chance to travel in his current job and so on. So by the end of the discussion, all the group's talked about is a lot of good reasons in favour of one option. As a result, the group agrees on a more extreme conclusion based on this surfeit of good reasons.

The other factor producing group polarisation comes from *social comparison* theory. As I explain in Chapter 8, people tend to think that they're better and more often correct than other people, on average. So when you think that your friend should take a moderate degree of risk and leave his job, you also think that you give better advice than most people, and so on average that you'll be correctly advising that he take a little bit more risk than most people.

But then you hear the opinions of the rest of the group and see that everyone is suggesting he takes a little bit of risk. But you saw yourself advising the risky option, not the average option. So you recalibrate your advice and say something a bit riskier than the last person. And everyone does the same thing, and pretty soon people are talking about clown school.

Both the persuasive-arguments and social-comparison factors can produce group polarisation; and both factors are stronger when the group members are more similar to each other. This is because you're more likely to have the same initial biases, which in term produce a bigger set of one-sided arguments and a bigger social comparison nudge towards extreme views.

This tendency can produce serious consequences. When people who're similar to each other meet to discuss an issue, they end that discussion agreeing upon a more radical position than they held as individuals before entering the room. The polarisation is stronger the more similar the group members are to each other.

No doubt you can appreciate that this is a pressing problem in the modern world. If you hold a meeting of all the people living on your street, you're all bound to share some similarity. More so than if you struck up a debate at an airport, for example. But what if you had a way to reach out to people across the world who hold exactly the same values and beliefs as you. And what if you discuss issues with those people and only those people who're highly similar to you. You have a way to produce the maximum polarisation of opinion possible. And you've invented the Internet chatroom.

Accepting that even experts can be stupid in a group

Experts are, by definition, good at making decisions in their area of expertise. Therefore, you'd think that a room full of ten experts would be even better at making such decisions. Sadly, for the general public who have to live with these decisions, this isn't always the case.

Irving Janis studied many cases in which governments seem to have all the knowledge, expertise and resources at their disposal, but still made catastrophically bad decisions. His work focused on disastrous examples of group think such as the Bay of Pigs Invasion, in which US-sponsored forces tried and failed to invade Cuba, to the embarrassment of the US government.

More recent examples also fit the pattern. Al-Qaeda (a group of mostly Saudi Arabians based in Afghanistan) carried out the devastating September 11 terrorist attacks on America, according to experts in the State Department, academia, the media and the claims of Al-Qaeda themselves. Yet elements of the Bush administration immediately focused on Iraq and Saddam Hussein. An advisor to President George W. Bush, Richard Clarke, recounts the following the day after the attack:

> *[The President] came back at me and said, 'Iraq! Saddam! Find out if there's a connection.' And in a very intimidating way. I mean that we should come back with that answer. . . . We got together all the FBI experts, all the CIA experts. We wrote the report. We sent the report out to CIA and found FBI and said, 'Will you sign this report?' They all cleared the report. And we sent it up to the president and it got bounced by the National Security Advisor or Deputy. It got bounced and sent back saying, 'Wrong answer. . . . Do it again'.*

> *Richard Clarke, on CBS's '60 Minutes', March 2004*

What this quotation reveals is that in the aftermath of September 11, the President and the CIA became fixated on blaming Iraq. They only sought out evidence in favour of a link between Iraq and September 11, and actively ignored the mounting evidence against such a connection. Indeed, no credible link between Iraq and September 11 has ever been substantiated. But the evidence against a link wasn't weighed against the evidence for a link: it was simply dismissed as 'the wrong answer'. It was in this climate, a few years later, that the UK and US decided to invade Iraq. They did so on the basis of arguments that Iraq possessed weapons of mass destruction, when once more there was no good evidence whatsoever that they existed. Looking at all the facts in hindsight, it seems astonishing that anyone would come to the conclusion that Iraq had such weapons. But a group of intelligent, professional people were able to argue themselves into just this disastrous conclusion.

Decision-makers at the time engaged in what Janis termed *group think* and the US military terms 'incestuous amplification'. The key idea is that, as individuals, people are motivated to make the most accurate decision that they can. But that isn't the only motivation at play when a group of people make a decision together. Remember that a committee room is a cauldron of social forces.

Imagine that you're in the war room when your country's prime minister and staff are debating plans for an invasion of another nation. As well as wanting to make the right call, you and everyone else are equally motivated by the need to conform to the opinion of others and of wanting to obey what your leader wants: plus, the fear of embarrassing yourself, displeasing your superiors and seeming not to understand something. These forces mean that even if you disagree with what's being said, you're understandably reluctant to speak up and contradict the prevailing view.

As a result, only evidence in support of the dominant view is brought to the table. Disagreement is seen as dissent. Therefore, social forces exclude a fair and balanced view, and hasten a wild and unsubstantiated decision.

The dangers of group think have been known since Janis's work in the 1970s and many governments and corporations have explicit strategies to avoid it. For example, someone is appointed to give counter-arguments to the prevailing view. Discussions are held outside of the main meeting between peers rather than in front of superiors. These safeguards have been shown to reduce the dangers of group think. But such safeguards often appear to go out the window in moments of extreme stress, partisanship and threat. Which is exactly when they're needed the most.

Examining the Economic Approach to Group Behaviour

I cover issues of prejudice and group conflict in several places in this book. In Chapter 10 I describe the cognitive approach to understanding the root causes of such behaviour and in the earlier section in this chapter 'Safety in numbers: Motivational approach' I define an approach that focuses more on the practicalities of living together in society. Here I discuss a third approach.

The fact is that the world contains limited resources and not everyone can be rich, well-fed and happy (or at least, no one has yet figured out how to achieve this goal). In the face of the resulting competition for resources, the *economic approach* suggests that it makes practical and economic sense for individuals to form groups and work together to compete for these resources. Anthropologists claim that for much of human evolution, people have lived in groups of around 100 to 150 people, co-operating with each other and competing with neighbouring groups for food and resources. The claim is that this blend of competition and co-operation is the basis for people's group instincts.

Through a description of one social psychology experiment, in this section I look at the role competition plays in creating group behaviour, and whether increasing contact and/or manipulating co-operation can heal conflict.

Competing for resources

An experiment by Muzafer Sherif and colleagues illustrates many of the phenomena and social forces that I discuss in this chapter, such as the effects of minimal groups, in-group and out-group bias and the dangers of group polarisation.

When they performed their experiment in 1954, Sherif and colleagues were thinking about society in economic terms and what they called *realistic group conflict* theory, which states that groups arise because there will be competition between sets of people for the limited resources in an environment. Because they were unable to travel back in time to study interactions between early hunter-gatherers, they did the next best thing. They studied 10-year-old boys at a summer camp in a place called Robbers Cove. None of the boys knew each other before the camp began. The researchers divided them up into two groups of 11 boys at random, and took them to different parts of the state park. The two groups of boys engaged in typical camp activities where they had to co-operate with each other to make meals, pitch tents and so on. All the positives of team-building and in-group activity (which I discuss earlier in "I'm in with the in-crowd': In-groups') were present. The boys seemed to bond well and even chose names for their groups: the Eagles and the Rattlers.

In the next stage of the experiment, the Eagles and the Rattlers became aware of each other's existence for the first time when the researchers brought them together for a tournament. The victors would receive a medal and a penknife. During the five days of competitions, the members of the Eagles and the Rattlers clashed with members of the opposing groups. They hurled abuse at every opportunity and issued challenges to fights. One morning the Rattlers awoke to a pile of ashes where their flag had previously flown, and the next day the Eagles flag was stolen. Food fights broke out at lunchtime.

The Eagles and Rattlers displayed every form of out-group hostility at their disposal (check out the earlier section "I'm on the outside (looking in)': Out-groups') as well as being favourable to their in-group.

The researchers found that competition seemed to turn up the volume on all the group processes (quite literally in this case). The boys were more positively disposed to members of their own group and more and more hostile to the out-group as the tournament went on.

In-group favouritism in action

In one game in the Robbers Cove experiment, the two groups of boys were given the challenge of finding as many beans as possible hidden in a field. The researchers then tallied the numbers and briefly flashed up a boy's name and a picture of the number of beans he'd collected. The boys were asked to estimate how many beans he'd collected, because the picture was displayed too quickly for them to count. The number of beans flashed up was always the same, but the Eagles systematically guessed that a fellow Eagle had collected more than a Rattler and the Rattlers guessed the reverse. They did so because it boosted their self-esteem to be on the winning side by a larger margin.

Increasing contact to remove conflict

The researchers conducting the Robbers Cove experiment had guessed that producing conflict would be the easy part of the study. The more challenging part was to reduce that conflict between the two groups.

Therefore, the next stage of the experiment was an informal test of what's known as *contact hypothesis*. This notion, formed during the early period of the African-American Civil Rights Movement, suggests that perhaps prejudice exists in part because members of different groups have no contact with each other. In parts of America at the time, Blacks and Whites were segregated and had different schools, buses and public toilets. The hypothesis was that if these barriers were removed through desegregation, contact would increase and negative attitudes towards different groups decrease.

To test this theory, the two groups of boys were brought together after the tournament had completed. Yet, even though they were no longer engaged in any direct contest or competition for resources, the conflict persisted. The insults still flew and members of different groups refused to socialise with each other.

Just as with the experience of desegregation in the South, contact wasn't quite enough to adjust the negative attitudes.

Forcing co-operation to heal divisions

In the final stage of the Robbers Cove experiment, the researchers deviously foisted superordinate goals onto the boys, manipulating events so that the two groups had to work together. They created a series of crises that required co-operation between all the boys.

For example, a lorry carrying supplies broke down. Nearby, the researchers had left coiled the boys' tug-of-war rope. In these days of reality television, people are sadly all too used to such acts of manipulation, but in the simpler times of the 1950s the boys gamely decided that they'd use this convenient rope to tow the lorry. To achieve this goal, they all needed to pull together.

After a few days of such 'accidental' co-operation, a remarkable peace descended on the camp. When buses arrived to take them home, the boys decided to travel together rather than separately, as they'd arrived. In a truly inspiring 'Disney' moment, when the bus stopped at a café, the Rattlers decided that the money they'd won during the tournament should be spent on malted milks for both groups.

Superordinate goals and the need to work together undid the intergroup conflict produced by days of competition, more than contact and exposure to each other did. (Perhaps a team negotiating between warring factions should sabotage their vehicles and insist that enemies work together to get to the negotiation venue!)

When members of opposing groups see themselves as working together, prejudice and conflict have a chance to dissipate. Unfortunately, I suspect that manipulating superordinate goals in a summer camp for boys would prove to be a tad easier that orchestrating events to fix intergroup conflict in the real world.

The problem is that resources aren't necessarily equally distributed among the sexes, regions of a country, religious factions, ethnic groups and so on. And as I state earlier in 'Safety in numbers: Motivational approach', in-group members can boost their self-esteem by denigrating out-group members. When a short-term gain is to be achieved by portraying other groups as selfish or undeserving, finding a superordinate goal that everyone sees themselves as working towards equally is extremely difficult. Sadly, therefore, the motivational need of the individual throws a spanner in the works of the economic fix for intergroup conflict.

Chapter 17

Bridging Cross-Cultural Differences

*L*ook up the word 'human' on Wikipedia and on the right of the entry you see a picture of two human beings. The choice of that picture generated one of the longest debates between contributors and editors in Wikipedia's history. Obviously, one picture of two people can't represent the whole of humanity, but since only one can be chosen, what would be the best approximation?

People come in a huge variety of sizes, shapes and skin colours and have all sorts of jobs. But like the majority of humans, the Wikipedia picture is of a man and woman who live in Southeast Asia, have brownish skin and, like the majority of humans in human history, are farmers. What you can't see in that photograph, of course, is how these people think, feel and interact with each other, which raises the important question: How different are people across the world in their social thoughts and habits?

In this chapter I explore cross-cultural differences as they relate to social psychology. Of course, psychologists rely to a large degree on participants for their experiments, and so I discuss the typical volunteer and how limited the selection has been: almost all the experiments I discuss in this book were carried out on American students between the ages of 18 and 21.

When psychologists do perform experiments with people from different cultures, the results give fascinating insights into the different ways in which they think about themselves and see (sometimes quite literally) the world and each other. Contrasting views of the self appear to be central to these differences.

These variations across the world have consequences for how people view society and relationships, the social judgements that they make and, in particular, what happens when people from different cultures interact with each other.

I suggest that although people from various parts of the world do think in different ways, these are not fundamental or irreconcilable differences. They are not due to physical or genetic differences, but are a result of being raised in a particular culture where particular aspects of the world are emphasised. These cultural mindsets are actually quite flexible. With simple techniques or shifts in emphasis, westerners can think like non-westerners and vice versa.

Meeting the People Who Take Part in Experiments

If you've ever flicked through any social psychology papers, you may notice that the 'Participants' section is rarely very interesting. The participants are usually college students enrolled in the same university as one of the authors of the paper.

This situation may strike you as being a problem. Psychologists want to be able to say things that are true of human beings in general, including around the world, but sometimes they seem to run experiments only on the single type of human beings that happen to be close by. They want to claim that 'all animals like to sit in laps and purr' when they've only studied the house cat. Clearly this situation presents substantial issues as regards generalising results to different cultures.

Well, social psychologists are aware of and have studied this problem. Joe Henrich and colleagues investigated its extent by looking at a large number of psychology articles and paying close attention to the section on participants, a detail that many readers skim over.

They found that the huge majority of participants in psychology experiments are western, educated, and from industrialised, rich, democratic societies: in other words WEIRD. Although such people comprise 80 per cent or more of the participants in psychology research, they make up only 12 per cent of the people on the planet. (Check out Chapter 18 for more on being WEIRD.)

Some good reasons exist for this situation, of course: students are easy to find, easy to recruit and often participate for free. You can see why such a pervasive bias exists. For more details, check out the nearby sidebar 'Why psychologists study the people they do'.

Why psychologists study the people they do

Psychological research is usually carried out in universities, and universities and scientists are expensive (although worth it, of course!).

At the risk of seeming reductive, in one sense being a student is a terrible waste. The years 18 to 21 could be a very productive time of life in an economic sense, since young people are often more energetic, enthusiastic and healthy than the rest of society. Yet instead of putting people at that age to work, they waste their working potential: they sit in classes rather than working in the fields or in factories. Or – to put the point the other way round – only wealthy, industrialised countries can afford to send a large numbers of otherwise productive young people to universities. At this point in history, the wealthier countries tend to be western and democratic.

Plus, Henrich and colleagues found that two-thirds of the participants in social psychology experiments are Americans and two-thirds are psychology undergraduates. In other words, just below half of participants in psychology experiments are the exact same people who're reading the papers in college and later may become psychology researchers themselves.

Again, this is understandable. Right now, I'd have to pay about £10 an hour to each participant in my experiments. I'd expect to run 40 to 80 people in every experiment, with one to four experiments in each paper. That's several thousand pounds in participant fees for every paper.

But a bigger problem is recruiting: finding and persuading large numbers of people to come into my laboratory in London and give me an hour of their time. Even if I have a lot of funding and an effective recruitment process, what sort of people may come into the lab? Presumably those who don't have regular nine-to-five jobs, perhaps don't have jobs at all or don't have jobs that pay as well as £10 per hour. In short, paying participants is expensive, time-consuming and may result in a set of participants that still doesn't reflect the wider society.

But undergraduate students come for free. In most psychology departments, students are required as part of their degree to take part in a set number of experiments. I have all their names and email addresses and, like most departments, an automated online sign-up system. Plus the students, outside of lecture hours, have very flexible schedules and can attend during the day.

The situation with experiment participants is what it is and social psychologists have to work with what they can. More important is how much of a problem it is that the people in psychology experiments are quite different from most other human beings. Some people argue that it's a massive problem if the aim is to generalise experimental findings to people who aren't WEIRD. Looking across the globe, psychologists find that people can behave quite differently in psychology experiments and in life. In the rest of this chapter I draw upon experiments that have been done on different people across the world and examine how their beliefs and thinking are quite different from the usual WEIRD participants that the rest of the book – and the rest of social psychology – has focused upon.

Examining Western and Non-western Thinking

In this section I explore some of the experiments that have been done on people from different cultures and see how there are subtle but pervasive differences in how they think of themselves, other people and how they interpret the world around them.

Until recently, the history of experimental psychology has been very much rooted in the western world. So, when I use terms such as 'western' and 'non-western' I do so to distinguish a 'western' way of thinking that has traditionally been studied and a 'non-western way', which is different and interesting in many other ways. For more on the complexities of such terms, take a look at the nearby sidebar 'East versus west'.

In this section I use Hazel Rose Markus and Shinobu Kitayama's method of describing the cultural differences of ideas of the self in the following terms:

- ✔ **Independence:** The traditional western view of identity, which is also sometimes identified as *individualism*.

- ✔ **Interdependence:** This contrasting view is widely held in non-western societies, and can also be distinguished with the term *collectivism*.

I describe how people differ in their views of the self and discuss how this distinction can relate to wider differences in perception and cultural practices, such as those surrounding the making of judgements.

Possessing different views of the self

The ways in which people describe themselves in social psychology experiments can tell researchers a lot about how different cultures think about identity. I discussed how people understand their self-identity in Chapter 7, and the set of beliefs and biases they have to protect their self-esteem in Chapter 8. Here I discuss how much these findings can be generalised to people from different cultures.

In Chapter 7 I present an exercise in which I ask you to write out 'I am . . .' ten times and then complete the statements with whatever description you want. When you give the same exercise to people across the world, systematic differences emerge.

East versus west

I use the term 'western' to mean roughly North American and European. By 'non-western' I mean the rest of the world. This distinction is rather blunt, I know, but in much of the discussion of cultural differences, researchers focus in particular on the differences between North America and 'non-western' Asian countries, such as China and Japan.

Of course, these very broad distinctions don't fit easily into an eastern and western division of the world map. Certain countries in Europe, such as Romania, and some Native American communities in North America have a more non-western style of culture. Contrasting a so-called western way of thinking with a non-western way that covers the whole of the rest of the planet is overly simplistic.

Obviously, my claim isn't that all western or all non-western people think in the same way. The claim is that even if we categorise people on this very broad distinction and average across these groups, subtle patterns and differences in thinking emerge.

For example, American participants are most likely to list their psychological attributes, such as their sense of humour or intelligence, and to mention their own attitudes as defining who they are. In contrast, Japanese people are more likely to qualify their statements in terms of the context. So rather than saying 'I am generous' or 'I am diligent', they may say, 'I am generous with my friends and family' or 'I am diligent at work'. Researchers have identified and described these systematic differences.

Independent and individualistic

The 'western' way of thinking about the self is probably most familiar to you, as indeed it is to psychology. In this *independent* view, the self is seen as an enduring, independent internal state that has distinct characteristics. In other words, people have particular personalities, motives, dreams and desires, and these internal psychological states explain and cause their behaviour. This view of the self sees people as fundamentally separate from each other, or *individualistic,* because people are understood as being single units without thinking about larger groups.

Of course, in the western world, you have friends and family who are very important and influential in your life. No person is an island, as John Donne almost said. But imagine, as if in a science-fiction film, you fell into a wormhole and were thrown into a distant time and place: the Italian Renaissance or the Mughal Empire. Your intuition, I'm guessing, is that even though you're in a radically different culture and surrounded by very different people, you'd remain, at heart, the same person. That's the essence of the independent notion of the self.

Interdependent and collectivist

The *interdependent* construction of the self is that it's fundamentally related to other people and the world around it. In countries such as China and Japan, but also areas of Africa and southern Europe, people think of themselves first and foremost in this *collectivist* manner: they think in terms of 'we' as much as they think of 'I'. In these cultures, interrelationships are central rather than incidental.

For example, as a western individual, I think of myself as an individual who happens to be a father and a husband, who has a few graduate students working in his lab and several layers of bosses above in the dizzying hierarchy of the university. But if I were a member of an interdependent, collectivist culture, I'd see myself fundamentally in terms of my family members and my relationships to them; in terms of my responsibilities to my students and what I expect from them; and in the commitments and obligations to my superiors.

In this view, of course, I still have certain characteristics and habits, but they're interwoven with these different social contexts. So it wouldn't be remarkable if I acted assertively and unforgivingly in the context of work but was easy-going and meek at home. Who I am depends upon whom I'm with, and so naturally an interdependent self shifts and modulates according to context.

Displaying cultural differences in judgements

The contrast between the independent and interdependent self that I explain in the preceding section may remind you of discussions elsewhere in this book about whether the person or the situation causes social behaviour (in particular, the *fundamental attribution error* that I discuss in Chapter 9). The tendency from a western perspective is to over-emphasise the personal traits of people and underestimate the power of the situation. For this reason, people are very surprised about the behaviour of the prisoners and guards in the Stanford prison experiment (see Chapter 11) or the levels of obedience in the Milgram experiment (from Chapter 12).

In contrast, interdependent cultures have a different view of the self, placing the person in the background and focusing on the interrelationships between the individual and the context. So they would be more likely to accurately predict how people would behave in Milgram's studies.

In this section I reveal that this difference in the understanding of people means that people from different cultures make different social judgements.

Recognising emotion

Experiments reveal that people from different cultures perceive different emotions in the same situation, and also that they go about interpreting emotions in a very different way.

Imagine a picture of a boy, holding a basketball, smiling, standing in front of some other children. How would you describe the boy?

If you're like the other western subjects in experiments by Takahiko Masuda and colleagues, you say that he looks happy. But if you're from an interdependent, collectivist country, such as Japan or China, you may well say that the boy is gloating or sneering. People from that culture are more likely to look at the faces of the children standing behind the boy. They spot that the others are looking sad and tearful. In the context of other people and the situation around him, they reason that the boy has stolen that ball off the other children and is cruelly mocking them.

This evidence is impressive, because not only does it show that people from different cultures make different judgements about emotions, but also that they literally look at the pictures differently. Eye-tracking technology shows that people from America look straight at the boy in the foreground, read his facial expression and give their answers. In contrast, participants from interdependent cultures look at the boy and then spend more time fixing their attention on the people in the background.

Making moral judgements

In Chapter 9 I reveal that people in the west have a strong tendency to focus on facts about an individual's personality, abilities and mood, as opposed to taking sufficient account of the situation: called the *fundamental attribution error*. I don't mean to suggest that people in the west fail to understand that situations cause behaviour, but instead that they focus too much on the individual.

People from interdependent cultures, however, are less likely to make this mistake, because they think about individuals in terms of their relationships to the situation and the other people around them. They have a broader focus, in a sense, and so are less likely to make the fundamental attribution error in controlled experiments.

For example, people from interdependent cultures tend to give different answers to the moral dilemmas that I raise in Chapter 9. To questions such as 'Would a friend borrow money from her parents without asking first, or date someone already in a relationship?', people from an independent culture are more likely to give straight yes or no answers, whereas people from interdependent cultures are more likely to say that it all depends on the situation.

Considering perceptual differences

You may be surprised to discover that people from different cultures process information and even notice things differently. This does not appear to be due to anatomical or genetic differences in how the brain or the eyes are wired, since children from one country who are adopted and raised in another act in the same way as their adoptive parents. From this we know that the perceptual differences must be due to the learning process of being raised in a particular culture.

In an experiment, Takahiko Masuda, Richard Nisbett and colleagues show people an animation of a fish tank and ask 'What do you see?'. What could be simpler, you many think: they're both looking at the exact same animation.

Yet the results reveal a cultural difference. Westerners from independent cultures describe events in terms of individual agents and their actions: for example, 'the orange fish swam back and forth'. But people from interdependent cultures are more likely to describe the events in terms of interrelationships between fish and objects: for example, 'fish swam between the rocks and the weeds'.

This difference in perception extends into memory. Westerners from independent cultures are better able to pick that orange fish out of a line-up if you present it to them again. People from interdependent cultures, however, have a hard time remembering individual fish unless they're shown again with the same rocks and weeds in the background.

Conversely, westerners from independent cultures have a poor memory for the rocks and weeds in the fish tank whereas people from interdependent cultures are far more likely to notice if items in the background are swapped around.

These experiments show that even when they are passively looking at the world around them, people from different cultures look at different things, interpret them in different ways and remember different aspects. If two people from different cultures look at the same TV show, they will literally see different things.

This attention to different elements in a scene means that people from different cultures are more or less susceptible to visual illusions.

In a test, people are asked to judge whether a line is straight up vertically or at a slight angle. People can be tricked into giving the wrong answer in this task if the line is surrounded by a frame that's slightly wonky. As you may predict by now, people from interdependent countries are more likely to be tricked by this illusion, because they're more likely to attend to the relationship between a central figure and the background. Westerners from independent cultures have much less difficulty ignoring the frame and focusing on the line.

These perceptual differences in memory, attention and susceptibility to illusions are not due to hard-wired differences between the memory or visual system of people from different parts of the world. The brain is above all else something that learns and absorbs things around it. These experiments show that growing up in one particular culture, the brain learns to focus, interpret and remember things in a particular way.

Testing the consequences of perceptual variations

The work of Masuda, Nisbett and their colleagues (such as the experiments I describe in the preceding section) shows that differences in culture can begin with the first moments of visual attention: where you direct your eyes into a scene. They then extend into the way you interpret what you see and how you remember it. These differences have been shown in the eye movements, judgements and memory performance of participants in laboratory experiments, which caused Masuda and Nisbett to wonder if the same patterns of behaviour are found outside of the laboratory.

Creating art

Masuda and Nisbett surveyed the paintings in the national galleries of Tokyo and New York. They counted very simple properties of the paintings, such as how many people were in the scene and their relative sizes. They found strong differences:

- ✔ A typical western picture has a single important person and a smaller number of other people in the background. Whenever you see such a picture you can identify in a moment the most important person. It's the man (probably) standing in the middle: he's the largest, has the most expensive clothes and has the light illuminating him.

- ✔ A typical Japanese painting depicts a large number of people, and they're all roughly the same size. Imagine an emperor reclining on a throne surrounded by courtiers. In these pictures, you can figure out who the important person is, but only by studying the relative positions and alignments of each person.

Taking holiday snaps

You may object that the differences in the preceding section simply reflect artistic practices and, for example, the way that perspective is used in much western art. What about differences between people who aren't artists, explicitly trained in the specific artistic traditions of a culture? To address this question, researchers looked at photographs taken by people from independent and interdependent cultures. If you look through their holiday snaps, you can notice a difference. In general, people from independent cultures focus on the face of the people much more. People from interdependent cultures pull back and include more of the background scene.

Really revealing holiday snaps!

Anecdotally, my wife and I tested the hypothesis that westerners focus on the individual and non-westerners more on the surroundings during a visit to Italy for a joint meeting of the European and Japanese science foundations.

One day we went on an excursion to the local sights. We passed our camera round to different scientists and asked them to take our picture.

Sure enough, the Europeans took pictures in which we filled at least half of the image: sometimes, we could've been back in London for all you saw of Italy. The Japanese, however, took pictures where we were visible from head to foot, and the rest of the scene, even if it was a car park, was fully visible.

Raising children

To investigate the origins of the differences in cultures, Masuda and Nisbett visited some school classrooms. They looked at children's drawings of a house and counted the same sorts of things that they had in the galleries. The same patterns were present:

✔ American children drew a small number of individuals, and usually had one person (themselves or their parents) much larger than all the other things.

✔ Japanese children drew with a flatter perspective, depicting more objects and people that were closer in size.

Differences between cultures can be seen from infancy onwards, in the behaviour of parents and the child.

For example, Linda Smith and her colleagues had parents in a lab play with their infants and a number of simple toys. They found that American parents are more likely to talk about things in relation to the infant's preferences, asking, 'Which is you favourite animal?' and 'Do you like this one?', whereas Japanese parents point out the relationships between toys: 'See, the donkey chases the cow.'

Later, the researchers examined several 4-year-old children from America and Japan and found that they differed in their abilities to find objects among complex arrays and to learn the names of objects and their relations. In other words, even children as young as four have already learnt to view the world in a slightly different way. Japanese children are already looking at and labelling the interrelationships between objects. The work of Linda Smith and colleagues suggests that part of the difference may stem from the way parents interact with their children.

These developmental studies show that all the cultural differences in memory, attention and perception that we find in adults may have their roots in the way that children of different cultures are raised and interact with their world.

Recognising What Cultures Have in Common

So far my discussion has been dedicated to exploring the differences between people from difference cultures. In one sense, those differences are pervasive and profound, as they can be seen in moment-by-moment eye movements, in infants and adults and in social interactions and political systems. But in another sense, they are quite weak. I want to close this chapter by considering the ways that cross-cultural differences can be reduced, or even eliminated, with simple techniques.

As I explain in Chapter 9, you can reduce or even reverse the fundamental attribution error by drawing people's attention to different things, by wording a question differently or showing them the view from a different angle. Similarly, cultural differences are often a matter of perspective and emphasis. A western person can think like someone from an interdependent culture, and vice versa, if different things are highlighted.

Social psychologists are also able to put people in different cultural mind-sets quite easily using the sorts of priming techniques I discussed in Chapter 5. For example, in one experiment, western participants were given a page of text to read. One group was told to circle all the occurrences of the word 'I' or 'me' in the text. The other was told to circle 'we' or 'us'. Then they were asked to make a judgment about the reasons for someone's actions, in one of the standard attribution experiments that I discuss in Chapter 9. The western participants who had been circling 'I' or 'me' behaved like participants in the standard version of the experiments, making the fundamental attribution error of ignoring the power of the situation. But the participants who had circled 'we' and 'us' now gave responses that were more like non-western participants, emphasising the situation when explaining the person's behaviour, and under-emphasising the person's dispositions.

People from different cultures do not think about the world in a fundamentally different way, they aren't from different planets and they don't hold completely incompatible views. Cultural differences may be pervasive, but they're also the result of mind-sets that are flexible and can be changed by circumstance. With a little effort and a little empathy, people are always able to understand and relate to each other.

Part VI
The Part of Tens

 For Dummies can help you get started with lots of subjects. Visit www.dummies.com to learn more and do more with *For Dummies*.

In this part . . .

✔ Find out how to check the hypotheses and conclusions of learned articles.

✔ Examine experimental methods.

✔ Extend your research into social psychology with a range of resources.

Chapter 18

Ten Questions for Getting the Most from Psychology Articles

A world of difference exists between scepticism and cynicism: in short, scepticism is productive and cynicism isn't. Unfortunately, many people are cynical about social psychology, and even science in general, arguing that it can never prove anything about people. I disagree, of course. As I show in this book, the scientific method can be rigorously applied to human behaviour.

But that method works only if all claims are examined with a critical, questioning mind (that's the healthy scepticism part). Although non-scientists are sometimes surprised, scientists spend most of their time trying to demonstrate that each other's theories are ill-conceived, limited or just plain wrong. They don't do so because they're mean, competitive people who always want to be right (well, not just because of that!). They do so because questioning and challenging ideas and data is part of their method. Cynicism achieves little, but scepticism drives science forward.

In this chapter, I list ten questions that you, as a sceptical reader, should ask yourself while reading about a social psychology experiment. These questions connect to the ways in which the findings of an experiment can be exaggerated, its claims limited or its conclusions flawed.

Don't view these questions as excuses to reject the experiment, but as reasons to carry out a better experiment yourself!

How Does the Result Generalise to Life Outside the Laboratory?

At some point in the life-cycle of a social psychology experiment, someone will try and generalise the results to life outside the laboratory. It may be the researchers themselves, when introducing or concluding their paper, or in a newspaper article or university press release promoting the research.

As a reader, remain sceptical of these claims. I don't mean that they're necessarily right or wrong, but that generalisability to real life isn't always the right criterion when judging scientific studies.

In field studies, this aspect is straightforward because they are based on studies of people in the real world, going about their everyday lives. For an example of a field study with relevance to everyday life, check out the nearby sidebar 'Watching wildlife on the road'.

But laboratory studies aren't always so straightforward. Remember that the goal of social psychology research is rarely to mimic the outside world within the laboratory. Take the Implicit Association Test that I discuss in Chapter 5 (which reveals differences of tens of milliseconds in reaction times when subjects are, for example, categorising faces as White and words as positive, compared to when they're categorising faces as Black and words as negative). Perhaps you can anticipate the type of objections – when do you ever have to categorise someone's race while at the same time identifying whether words are positive or negative? And even if you did need to, does it matter to everyday life if you're 30 milliseconds slower in one case? That's literally the time it takes to blink.

Watching wildlife on the road

Researchers at the University of California, Berkeley were investigating the effects of social status on behaviour. In a wonderful field study, they stood on a street corner by a zebra crossing and noted down how likely cars were to stop when they anticipated that a pedestrian was about to use the crossing. They also recorded the make and model of the car, and later figured out the approximate cost as an indirect measure of the social status of the driver.

They found that the more expensive the car, the less considerate the driver was of other people. This result is clearly and immediately applicable to real life. If you see a BMW coming towards you, be extra careful crossing the road!

But of course, the value of these results isn't that the experiment looks like something you'd encounter in the real world. If you accept the interpretation, it's that these small reaction time differences reveal how the mind organises and associates information, which in turn reveals something about implicit prejudice.

Although the situation of laboratory experiments isn't like anything in the real world, they provide a vital way to test hypotheses and learn about the mind.

Are the Authors Really Measuring What They Claim to be Measuring?

I talk about this issue in Chapters 2 and 3: the technical term is *operationalisation*. A sceptical reader always considers whether researchers have correctly operationalised their concept (such as love, prejudice, fear or jealousy) into something that can be measured (such as ratings on a scale, reaction times, eye movements or brain activation).

Rarely can you find one perfect operationalisation. If possible, the best approach is to use multiple converging ones. An example is the 'culture of honour' that I discuss in Chapter 2, where the consequences were operationalised in terms of ratings of anger, laughter and masculinity, into the distance between the participant and a threatening male, into the force of the participant's handshake, and even the hormones secreted.

Are the Researchers from a Well-regarded University?

Every journal article lists the authors' *affiliation:* the university or institute where the researchers work. Newspaper articles about research often lead with this information, such as 'Scientists from Oxford University have discovered that . . . '.

How important is this information when you're sceptically reading an article? The answer: not relevant, not at all, not in the least bit.

Nullius in verba (roughly translated as 'Take no one's word for it') is the founding motto of the Royal Society in London, perhaps the oldest scientific institution in the world. The point is that science doesn't care *who* said what: it doesn't matter whether it was Aristotle, the Pope or Einstein. All that matters is the evidence in support of an idea. So whether the researchers have PhDs from Oxford or Harvard is irrelevant, as is whether they learnt everything they know from YouTube. All that matters is the evidence that they present.

Unfortunately, I'm being a bit idealistic here. In a field study on other scientists, sneaky researchers submitted the same article to different journals and changed the affiliation of the authors to a highly regarded university and to a less famous, smaller university. Sadly, the former version of the paper was more likely to be accepted for publication by peer review. So even scientists sometimes fail to live up to the Royal Society's motto.

How Many People Are in the Experiment?

Statistical techniques allow scientists to do something truly remarkable: they can quantify randomness. This is vital in science because patterns and differences in measurements occur all the time in the complicated, messy world.

Statistics allow scientists to quantify the probability that what they measure is due to random chance or a true difference between two things. After all, the more measurements you take, the more people are in your psychology experiments and the more certainty you get. But how many people do you need in a psychology experiment?

Say you have a hypothesis that men are taller than women, on average. You stop the first man and the first woman on the street and measure them. As you may guess, the chances are that you'll find that the man is taller. But about 1 out of 15 times you'll find a taller woman. So how many men and how many women do you need to measure before you can be pretty confident that men are taller than women? In other words, how many men and women do you have to measure before you can be confident that the difference you observe is true of men and women *in* general and not just the men and women you happen to have measured?

Well it depends what you mean by 'pretty confident'. But if you take the standard level of greater than a 5 per cent chance, and given how much height tends to vary in the human population, statistics tell you that you need to measure about eight people. The height difference between men and women is relatively large and stable. What if you want to measure something more subtle, such as how people would vote in an election?

For many surveys and political polls, typically about 1,000 people are questioned. To some people that seems like a very small number. How can you generalise from only 1,000 people to a whole country of millions of people?

In fact, statistical analyses show that – if the 1,000 people have been carefully and randomly selected – the average of their answers is within 1 or 2 per cent of the rest of the country. A pretty good representation. And the same analyses show that doubling or tripling the number of people you survey results in only a very small improvement in the margin of error.

Stating the number of participants that's sufficient for the average social psychology experiment is difficult, though. It all depends on how the differences are being measured, how many measurements are being taken and the amount of variability, either from randomness or from other factors.

For example, in some experiments the researcher may be asking people to make very rapid judgments about whether or not a face is trustworthy. The decision may take only a few hundred milliseconds, and the differences between experimental conditions may be only tens of milliseconds. On the other hand, the researchers would probably show hundreds of faces, giving hundreds of measurements for each participant.

At the other extreme, you may have a study in which the participant is persuaded (or not) to comply with an experimenter's request. Although only one measurement exists for each subject, the differences between experimental conditions can be quite large. For example, in the classic foot-in-the-door experiment I discuss in Chapter 14, participants' compliance went from 16 to 74 per cent between experimental conditions.

So, I can't give a simple answer to how many participants should be in a social psychology experiment. But a *very rough* rule is that you probably need at least 20 participants in each condition, or combination of conditions.

A more precise answer uses what's called a *power analysis.* Experimenters estimate the size of the difference they expect to find, the amount of variance or random noise in their measurements and how confident they want to be in their conclusion. A formula then tells them how many people they require in their experiment.

But remember that how many people are in your experiment isn't the only important aspect; just as important is *who* they are (see the next section).

Are the Participants WEIRD?

Psychologists investigate the human mind, in all its variety and glory. They aim to understand why an angry mob decides to riot or go quietly home; why people first fall in love and why they stay married; how a charismatic cult leader can compel his followers. Ironically, therefore, given the scope of psychology across the huge array of human experience, the huge majority of experiments are performed on slightly bored university undergraduates between the ages of 18 to 21. As a result, the people in psychology experiments are WEIRD: an acronym for western and educated, from industrialised, rich, democratic societies.

This is important because, as I discuss in Chapter 17, the psychological differences that exist between different cultures sway even simple, low-level perceptual processes. Even within western cultures, the students in psychology experiments have many differences to non-students. For example, many are still teenagers and neuroscience shows that significant brain development doesn't stop in childhood, but continues up until early adulthood. Usually, undergraduates don't have jobs, children or spouses and have different motivators and goals to the rest of the population. They may have a different level of drug and video-game usage. They're highly trained test-takers, which matters because many psychology experiments look like something between an exam and a video game. For views on how important these issues are (or aren't), check out the nearby sidebar 'Is being WEIRD important?'.

Is being WEIRD important?

Some people say that the problem of cultural and other differences can easily be overestimated, because psychologists care less about how participants perform on a task and more about how their performance *changes* between experimental conditions.

For example, say that participants take part in an experiment playing *Tetris* and scientists measure their scores. You may object that students (and other WEIRD participants) have much more experience playing such games, and so are going to score higher than regular people. But more typically in experiments, psychologists compare between conditions. So the participants may be given coffee or not, and then their score changes are measured.

Although thinking that students do better than non-students is quite reasonable, perhaps for some reason they have a different physiological response to caffeine to other people. The reply to this is that it's a question that we can only answer with more experiments! We can't simply assume that students respond to caffeine or any experimental manipulation in the same way as other people.

As a profession, psychologists are still arguing over the significance of WEIRD participants. Whenever you read a conclusion in a psychology paper, whenever they say 'participants' or 'people' try mentally adding the phrase 'in western, educated, industrialised, rich, democracies'. Then look through Chapter 17 and see whether any evidence already suggests possible different conclusions for other types of people or other cultures.

Does the Experiment Involve Any Demand Characteristics?

Most participants are nice people and want to be good participants in your experiment. Although admirable, this tendency can cause problems for the experimenter. Participants in social psychology experiments change their behaviour according to what they think the experimenter wants (something that doesn't happen for, say, chemists; a chemical solution doesn't figure out that the researcher wants it to be more corrosive and so changes its acidity). But in psychology, participants can be influenced by (what they think) are the experimenter's own expectations and beliefs.

These effects are called *demand characteristics*. They're aspects of the experiment or situation that cause participants to respond how they 'should' respond. (Check out the nearby sidebar 'Demonstrating the demand characteristic effect' for examples of this effect in action.)

The idea of demand characteristics is similar to the idea of a placebo in medical research. People tend to experience the benefits and side effects that they're told they'll experience from a particular drug, even when they're given a sugar pill with no physical effects at all. To negate this problem, the true effects of drugs are revealed by a *double blind* experimental design: neither the patient nor the doctor giving them the pill knows whether the medicine is a real drug or a harmless sugar pill.

 Psychologists also aim for a double blind design. As a sceptical reader, ask whether participants could've guessed how the experimenter *expected them* to behave. Unfortunately, answering this question is difficult, because psychological experimental manipulations are often more complicated than slipping someone a pill, and there's more scope for participant and experiment to influence results.

Demonstrating the demand characteristic effect

Participants were hooked up to a lie detector that measured tiny differences in their sweating behaviour and asked to lie to the experimenter. One group were told that only psychopaths and criminals were able to fool the lie detector and the other that most intelligent, emotional stable people could fool it.

These two groups of people had very different skin responses after being told that they'd fooled the lie detector successfully (or not). Those who believed that only criminals could fool the lie detector started sweating if the detector didn't signal they were lying. Those who believed that all intelligent people could fool the detector sweated less when informed that they'd successfully deceived the detector.

Was the Experimenter Blind to the Conditions?

If the experimenter knows what condition the participant is in, then they know how the participant is *supposed* to behave. Since they probably want their experiment to work, there is a danger that the experimenter will communicate their expectation to the participant in some way, and so influence their behaviour. If that happens, it's bad news, because the experiment will show an effect of the experimenter's beliefs, rather than the participants' true behaviour. I will explain how this can happen, and what experimenters can do it avoid it.

Say that you want to test the simple hypothesis that thinking about one's family and friends increases friendly, pro-social behaviour towards a stranger. For the experimental manipulation you ask people to list the 'ten people that you feel closest to emotionally' or have them do nothing. After completing the task, an experimenter walks up to them and engages them in conversation. The interaction is videotaped, and later the experimenter watches the video and rates the friendliness of each participant on a scale of 1 to 9. You compare the ratings for those who made the list and those that didn't.

As you may realise, this experimental design has some fatal flaws:

✔ Quite possibly, the experimenter's knowledge of the experimental condition can change how he interacts with the participant.

Imagine that a friend whispers in your ear at a party, 'I have to introduce you to this person, he's really friendly and charming.' Or your friend says, 'I have to introduce you to this person, he's rather mean and no one wants to talk to him.' As you turn round to meet the new person, you can imagine that your expression and initial demeanour may be quite different in these two cases. Well, the same can apply (albeit to a lesser extent) for the experimenter meeting a participant that he expects to be either more or less friendly because of the experimental condition. And the attitude of the experimenter in turn affects how friendly the participant appears. In this way, the experimenter's knowledge changes the behaviour of the participant.

✔ The second major flaw is that the experimenter rating the participants' behaviour also knows which experimental condition they are in. People tend to see information that confirms their beliefs and ignore information that contradicts them. So if the rater expects the participant to be friendly, he may well notice a small smile; whereas the same mouth movement may be dismissed as an insincere smirk by a rater who expects unfriendly behaviour.

Luckily, you can easily solve these problems with careful experiment design. The condition that the participant is in can be assigned randomly by the person picking a sealed envelope, or be chosen by a computer. The condition's then a secret to the experimenter interacting with the participant, and secret from a different experimenter rating the videos.

Here are the two key questions to ask, as a sceptical reader:

✔ Did the experimenter interacting with the participant know what condition the person was in, and could the experimenter have conveyed his expectations to the participant at all?

✔ Sometimes we use objective measures of behaviour like button presses or brain activation. Sometimes we use more subjective measures, like rating how friendly or how aggressive someone acted. In this case, it's important to ask, did that rater know what condition the participant was in and how the person 'should' have acted?

What Was the Control Condition?

In Chapter 2 I discuss the importance of a well-chosen *control condition*, which has to match the experimental condition in every way possible, except for the thing that you're trying to study. This is very hard to get right for an experimenter, and very easy to miss for the reader. In short summaries,

---

This game makes me so mad!

Imagine a study that investigates the link between aggression and video-game use. The experimenters measure participants' aggression, ask them to play a violent video game for 30 minutes and then measure aggression again. They find that aggression increases, which didn't happen when participants did nothing for 30 minutes in a control condition. So do violent video games increase aggression?

Well, before the experimenters can leap to this conclusion, they would need to account for the many differences between playing a violent video game and doing nothing. For example, many people enjoy playing video games and don't like sitting still doing nothing. So in the experimental condition you can give people an enjoyable task for 30 minutes and then force them to stop, and in the control condition you give them an unpleasant, boring task, and finally allow them to stop. You wouldn't be surprised that the people playing the video games feel a bit annoyed, and therefore aggressive; you've just taken away their toy!

---

press releases and newspaper write-ups of experiments, everyone tends to focus on the dramatic effect of the experimental condition – such as do video games cause aggressive behaviour? – and the control condition gets ignored in the background, even though it's the aspect of an experiment that allows psychologists to make strong scientific conclusions. I provide an example in the nearby sidebar 'This game makes me so mad!'.

In many social psychology experiments, the key question to ask from a sceptical angle is about any differences between the control and experimental conditions that can explain the behaviour. If these differences aren't related to the experimenters' hypothesis or claims, you have good grounds to doubt those claims.

Does Common Sense Support the Conclusion?

In Chapter 3, I suggest that common sense is the nemesis of social psychology. The reason is that after the results of a study are known, claiming that the results merely confirm what you'd expect anyway is all too easy. Such hindsight bias pervades people's day-to-day thinking: when something is known they often feel that they knew it all along.

Sometimes, psychology papers try and cash in on support from so-called common sense. For example, in Chapter 3 I discussed a paper that found support for the common sense 'fact' that heterosexual men have a higher number of sexual encounters than heterosexual women (even though that's logically impossible). As a sceptical reader you always need to stay wary of 'common sense'.

Does a Simpler Explanation Exist?

As with much in life, the simplest answer is often right.

A few years ago, I read an evolutionary psychology paper that claimed that the level of testosterone in new fathers decreases with the increasing number of hours they spend with their infants. The claim was that this decrease was the result of an evolved mechanism.

At the time I was on paternity leave looking after my twin babies with my wife. I was in the house all the time and, according to this research, my testosterone levels must have been at eunuch levels. The paper implied that to ensure that I stayed at home and tended to my children, rather than dashing out to hunt or impregnate another female, some adaptive mechanism lowered my testosterone level in response to the presence of infants, and hence reduced my aggressive behaviours.

This claim raises many questions – does the sight of babies lower testosterone? The smell? But before thinking more about evolved mechanisms of hormone regulation in childcare, I decided to look into simpler explanations; and it turns out that a rather simple one exists.

One thing changes testosterone levels quite readily: sleep. And if there's one thing new fathers don't have much of, it's sleep. So, just as the original study found, the degree to which fathers are involved in childcare and night feedings predicts the amount that they sleep, which changes the amount of testosterone they produce. A much simpler explanation.

Chapter 19

Ten Great Ways to Delve Deeper into Social Psychology

A few hundred years ago, a true scholar in a subject was able to have read literally everything ever written on a particular topic. The challenge was locating, possessing or copying the rare items of written material. Nowadays, with such a vast amount of information available so easily, the problem is sorting and identifying what's important and – crucially – what isn't.

In this chapter, I describe ten ways to discover more about social psychology. I show you how to locate research articles online and how to follow connections between papers. I look at some of the big psychological societies and what they offer, as well as some specialist websites that collect specific social psychology resources. I also discuss how social media is being used to filter information and take part in scientific debate. These are exciting times for the professional and the interested layperson alike.

Consulting Research Journals

Psychologists write textbooks, give lectures and even have YouTube channels. But the most important product of their job is the research article. These articles are what they're judged by, where they lay out their theories and present their evidence. If you want to discover more about social psychology, you need to read research articles.

If it's been published in a journal, the article has been *peer-reviewed,* which means that two or three other independent scientists have read the paper closely, criticised it and challenged the evidence as strongly as they can. The reviewing is even done anonymously, so that the reviewers can be as critical as they want without fear of repercussion. Sometimes the paper is rejected out of hand. Sometimes the authors are told that they have to re-do some experiments, or even re-write the paper, and submit to another round of critical review. Only after the authors have gone through that process is the paper published.

Unfortunately, many journal articles, which are the result of painstaking and expensive research, aren't made freely available to the people who funded the research: the taxpayer. The situation is changing, but right now you can only access journal articles from a publisher's website if you're connected to a university or library network, and if those universities or libraries have paid a hefty access fee to the publishers.

If you're lucky enough to be able to use the resources of a large university, you should be able to access most academic journals through its portal. Or you can try searching one of these databases of journal articles:

✔ **PsychINFO:** `www.apa.org/psycinfo`

  The largest database of psychology-related articles and abstracts, maintained by the American Psychological Association.

✔ **ScienceDirect:** `www.sciencedirect.com`

  A big conglomeration of journals with advanced search options and email alerts.

If you aren't a member of a university or close to a large public library, you have two options:

✔ **Use open-access journals, which have become more widespread.**
  Anyone with an Internet connect can download these papers for free. (The only downside is that researchers have to pay a fee when their articles are accepted.) This way of publishing is increasing in popularity, and open-access journals are growing in their impact. Right now, these are the two big players:

  Frontiers: `www.frontiersin.org/Psychology`

  PLOS ONE: `www.plosone.org/browse/social_psychology`

✔ **Google the articles that you want (see the next section).**

Becoming a Google Scholar

More than anything, scientists want people to read their work. They're quite different from authors or artists who get paid each time someone buys their book or downloads a song. They draw a salary, do their research and when it's published, they want everyone to know about it. And so, even though journal publishers want to charge people to download an article from their journal website, you often find that scientists find a way to post electronic copies of their articles on their home or university website, where anyone can freely download them.

Google knows all about these journal papers on the Internet. So the chances are that you can just type in the title of any research article (particularly if it was published in the last ten years) and Google finds a free copy available online.

Google also has a special academic search engine called Google Scholar (`scholar.google.co.uk`), which looks specifically for research articles that are online, rather than all webpages. You can search for the title of a paper, or enter the authors and the publication date, and it has a very good chance of finding the paper. Look for 'pdf' in the search results for a full text version of the paper that you can read. It can also tell you what other papers have cited the paper that you found. This is a useful function that other websites also provide, but Google's probably has the biggest reach.

A cited reference search is very useful because you can read about a study and be struck with an idea for an interesting new twist. For example, imagine that you read about the Cyberball experiment by Kip Williams (which I describe in Chapter 13) and wonder whether people's response changes by their attachment style (see Chapter 15). With a cited reference search, you can find all papers that have cited the original experiment and see whether someone else has already had the same thought and collected the data.

Looking up Psychological Societies

Several large, well-funded and well-organised psychological societies exist and their websites are well worth poking around. You find announcements for upcoming conferences, job vacancies and graduate programmes. These societies sometimes run prominent journals in the field and post free content on their websites.

Many of these societies have a mission to persuade people that psychology is relevant and important outside of academia, and so they have excellent resources demonstrating how psychology intersects with politics, economics, education and everyday life. Check out the following:

- ✔ **American Psychological Association:** `www.apa.org`
- ✔ **Association for Psychological Science:** `aps.psychological science.org`
- ✔ **British Psychological Society:** `www.bps.org.uk`
- ✔ **European Association of Social Psychology:** `www.easp.eu`
- ✔ **Society for Personality and Social Psychology:** `www.spsp.org`

Using the Social Psychology Network

The social psychology network (www.socialpsychology.org) is an excellent resource for students, academics and scientists.

Most researchers in the field seem to be members and have a small page describing their interests and linking to their own lab websites (bear in mind that the picture of me was taken before I had children and when I still had hair!). The network lists psychology graduate programmes, teaching resources and experiments that you can take part in online.

Perhaps one of the most useful resources is a huge list of social psychology links sorted by subtopic. With this, you can easily find the labs that are looking at, say, the relationship between social psychology and legal issues, how psychologists are tackling homophobia or the role they play in political elections. Going through lists saves you a lot of endless googling and takes you straight to the interesting researchers in the field.

Prejudice and Bias: Highlighting Two Useful Websites

I want to highlight two particularly useful websites for you, because they give excellent in-depth discussions of prejudice and bias, arguably one of the most important applications of social psychology to politics and everyday life. Crucially, each website doesn't just describe and discuss scientific understanding of prejudice, they have experiments that you can participate in. This gives you, arguably, a direct measure of your own implicit prejudice, and gives you an insight into what it is like to be part of a psychology experiment.

- ✔ **Project Implicit:** implicit.harvard.edu/implicit
- ✔ Understanding Prejudice: www.understandingprejudice.org

Communicating via Blogs

The number of blogs devoted to psychology and the quality of the writing astounds me. Only a few years ago, many in the scientific community dismissed blogs as little more than vanity projects. Now you can read about the latest findings and find cutting-edge debate.

Blogs have the great strength of immediacy. Journal articles can take months, even years, to reach print. I've read (what I thought was) a great journal article that came out that morning, and by the evening seen a brilliant and convincing counterargument against the paper's claims.

Blogs are also interactive. You can post comments and directly engage with the author. Scrolling down through these comments and arguments is often worthwhile, because many are posted by other scientists. Debates that started in blog comment sections have sparked whole research projects. This sort of discussion is often at the heart of scientific progress. For example, you can see the enormous volume of Darwin's letters on display in a museum in Cambridge. But now, thanks to an active and engaged blogging community, you can peer into such debates as they happen.

Some scientists are still sceptical about blogs because, unlike research articles, they aren't peer-reviewed (see the earlier section 'Consulting Research Journals'). Anyone with an Internet connection can have a blog on social psychology and post whatever they want. Although that's true, it misses the point of blogs. Few bloggers would argue that their posts are meant to rival peer-review articles. In fact, often blog posts are describing, promoting or discussing journal articles. And if a blogger's analysis is wrong, readers can have their say in the comments section.

My view is that you can find some wonderful writing and debate in blogs. You should certainly read everything with a critical eye, but that's exactly how you should read journal articles too! So if you're doing Internet research for your own article or paper, read as many blog posts as you can. Remember though that blogs are a way of disseminating opinions, and the most important thing is the hard evidence in support of any claim. So when a blog post discusses a research finding, be sure to read the original peer-reviewed paper as well. Get as close to the data as you can!

Here are just a few of my favourite blogs in social psychology. I list website addresses and Twitter handles if they have them:

- ✔ **Research Digest:** `bps-research-digest.blogspot.co.uk` @**ResearchDigest**

  The British Psychological Society's Research Digest is a round-up of new findings in psychological science and news items related to psychology.

- ✔ **Neuron Culture:** `daviddobbs.net/smoothpebbles` @**David_Dobbs**

  David Dobbs is a freelance writer who contributes to *Slate*, *National Geographic* and the *New York Times*. He writes particularly well about the complex relationship between genes and behaviour.

✔ **PsyBlog:** `psyblog.co.uk` **@PsyBlog**

Jeremy Dean's PsyBlog is an excellent, active and very readable blog describing the latest research findings and re-visiting classic experiments.

✔ **Predictably Irrational:** `danariely.com` **@danariely**

Dan Ariely is the author of several popular science books about behavioural economics and is an active, engaging blogger.

✔ **The Situationist:** `thesituationist.wordpress.com`

A group blog where a large collection of top social scientists post articles, video clips and announcements. The common theme is that all the posts are concerned with the way that the situation influences behaviour – a theme that runs through this book too. They're a particularly interested in the implications that social psychology has for law, politics and policy.

✔ **YourMorals Blog:** `www.yourmorals.org/blog`

A group blog with some top-notch contributors. This site focuses on the empirical evidence behind debates in politics and morality.

Following Twitter Feeds

A friend told me that whereas the essence of Facebook is 'Look at me!', the essence of Twitter is 'Look at this!'. Although you can't say very much in 140 characters, you can tell people where to find new and interesting stuff, and that's the genius of Twitter. For me, and many other scientists, it has become a vital scientific tool.

The array of information on the Internet is dizzying, and growing every minute. Your entire day can grind to a halt wandering through blogs, Wikipedia and the online news . . . not to mention the funny cat videos. For this reason, the brevity of Twitter is its great strength. I don't have time to visit all the blogs that interest me and read the table of contents of every journal that's relevant to my work. So instead, I subscribe to the Twitter feed of each blog author and each author, and just scan through my feed during the day. I get the titles of new articles as they're posted online in my favourite journals. I follow the scientists who do work in my field, and when they publish a new article, they tweet, and I find out about it. But mostly, I find out about stuff because a friend or colleague reads a paper, likes it and tweets a link.

In addition to the bloggers with Twitter feeds I mention in the preceding section, here are some other people I find worth following in social psychology:

- ✔ **Amy Cuddy @amyjccuddy:** Social psychologist from the Harvard Business School who studies body language, stereotyping and other phenomena.

- ✔ **Daniel Gilbert @DanTGilbert:** Social psychologist at Harvard and author of *Stumbling on Happiness*. I talk about his work on affective forecasting in Chapter 8.

- ✔ **Hans IJzerman @hansijzerman:** Social psychologist from Tilburg University and editor of *The Inquisitive Mind* magazine (`www.in-mind.org`)

- ✔ **Matt Lieberman @social_brains:** Social neuroscientist at UCLA.

- ✔ **Molly Crockett @mollycrockett:** Neuroscientist interested in decision-making and morality.

- ✔ **Society for Personality and Social Psychology @SPSPnews:** Overview of new findings in social psychology research.

- ✔ **Social Psychology Network @PsychNews:** Round-up of psychology studies and news items with a psychology angle.

Taking Online Classes

An exciting new movement in higher education is going on to put university courses online. Sometimes this means putting recordings of lectures on iTunes where anyone can download and view them, as if they're sitting in on the class.

MOOCs (massive open online courses) take the idea one step further – you also participate in the class as a student, taking exams and uploading essays. No one quite knows where this trend will lead. Perhaps campus universities will go the way of video rental stores, replaced by downloads, or maybe the experience of being in the same lecture hall or tutorial room is of irreplaceable educational value.

You can freely download excellent quality lectures and take part in social psychology courses from across the world. Check out the following for starters:

- ✔ **UCLA Social Psychology 135: Online lectures from Mark Lieberman** `itunes.apple.com/us/itunes-u/social-psychology-135/id434142300`

- ✔ **Wesleyan University MOOC: Social Psychology** `www.coursera.org/course/socialpsychology`

- ✔ **Yale University MOOC: Moralities of Everyday Life** `www.coursera.org/course/moralities`

Listening to TED Talks

The TED foundation has a remarkable collection of short, inspiring and diverse lectures from leading scientists, artists, engineers and political activists (www. ted.com). They're all freely available. The site includes many talks by famous psychologists (you can search by topic), but I also urge you to watch talks from non-psychologists as well, and think about the social forces (cognitive dissonance, naive realism, techniques of persuasion, and so on) that are underlying discussions of climate change, marketing and political debate.

As with blog posts, Wikipedia articles and journal articles, I recommend strongly that you watch these lectures with a sceptical eye. TED talks are very short, and their emphasis is on wowing an audience with stirring conclusions, as opposed to overwhelming them with data. By their nature, they rarely present strong evidence for their claims.

So be inspired and entertained by the talks, but always seek the evidence afterwards. Hunt down the 'why' behind the 'wow'!

Working with Wikipedia Effectively

The first time I heard Wikipedia mentioned by an academic, he said the word with a wince, much like a waiter at a posh restaurant repeating a request for ketchup. The feeling was that Wikipedia simply didn't belong in the proper academic world. I think that, thankfully, this view is rapidly changing.

My opinion is that Wikipedia (www.wikipedia.com) is an excellent research tool, something that you can use early on in the process of writing a paper or understanding a topic. It can give you a detailed, intelligent and comprehensive overview of a topic like few other sources. I certainly use it extensively when I'm preparing lectures about an area that's new to me, or even for a familiar area in which I want to explore a new angle.

The mistake that some people make, however, is to read no further than a Wikipedia article. As with all the sources of information and inspiration I mention in this chapter, you have to track down the evidence behind the claims and look at the experiments, data and original claims yourself. Use Wikipedia as a way to find ideas and material, not as an endpoint itself. So I encourage you to use and support Wikipedia. Its scope and depth is probably unrivalled and certainly nothing's better for the price.

Index

• *M* •

maintaining stereotypes, 153–157
Markus, Hazel Rose (social psychologist), 264
massive open online courses (MOOCs), 293
Masuda, Takahiko (cultural psychologist), 267, 268, 269, 270
mates, choosing, 226–228
McManus, Chris (psychologist), 247
measuring
  attitudes, 71, 73
  implicit attitudes, 88–95
  power of social forces, 15–18
  results, 277
  self-perception theory, 109
  what people think, 12
mere exposure effect, 84–86, 130
Milgram, Stanley (social psychologist)
  about, 142
  experiments of, 181–186
mimicry behaviour, 196–197
minimal group paradigm, 248
misattribution of arousal, 235–236
Moch, Steven (researcher), 104
MOOCs (massive open online courses), 293
moral judgements, 267–268
motivational approach, 249–251
MRI, 26
Murray, Andy (tennis professional), 119, 122, 133
Myth Buster icon, 2

• *N* •

naive realism, 129–130
nationality, stereotypes on, 153
need to fit in, 198

negative emotions, 209
neoteny, 227
Neuron Culture (website), 291
neuroscience, 25–27
Nisbett, Richard (researcher), 31, 142, 145, 268, 269, 270
non-conformity, 201–204
non-western thinking, 264–266
Norenzayan, Ara (researcher), 78
normative influence of conformity, 198, 199
norms, social
  about, 195
  reasons for, 196–198
null hypothesis, 59

• *O* •

obedience
  about, 179
  to authority, 16–17
  as example of operationalisation, 56
  influences on, 186–187
  investigating, 180–191
  making predictions about, 184–185
  reasons for levels of, 188–191
  researching, 191–194
  studying in ethical ways, 192–193
  as a way to conform, 198
O'Keefe, Kevin (writer), 50
one of the crowd, being, 17
online classes, 293
open-access journals, 288
operationalism, 37–38, 55–56, 277
opinions, absorbing, 199
Osborne, George (Chancellor), 217
ostracism, 201–204
out-groups, 235, 251
overcoming bias and prejudice, 162
Oxford University, 247

Notes

Notes

Notes

Notes

Notes

Notes

About the Author

Daniel C. Richardson, PhD, is Senior Lecturer in the Department of Experimental Psychology at University College London. He has taught psychology at Stanford University and the University of California Santa Cruz, and his Introduction to Social Psychology course was awarded the Provost Teaching Award at University College London.

Dedication

For Natasha.

Author's Acknowledgments

I would like to thank Steve Mock, Richard Eibach, Joyce Ehrlinger and Natasha Kirkham for their vast academic knowledge and tolerant personal support while writing this book. I would also like to thank Daryl Bem for introducing me to the excitement and rigour of scientific research in social psychology.

Publisher's Acknowledgments

Acquisitions Editor: Mike Baker

Project Editor: Rachael Chilvers

Copy Editor: Kelly Cattermole

Technical Editor: Joyce Ehrlinger

Project Coordinator: Sheree Montgomery

Cover Image: ©iStockphoto.com/timsa

Take Dummies with you everywhere you go!

Whether you're excited about e-books, want more from the web, must have your mobile apps, or swept up in social media, Dummies makes everything easier.

FOR DUMMIES®

A Wiley Brand

BUSINESS

Small Business Marketing For Dummies
Paul Lancaster
978-1-118-73077-5

Pop Up Business For Dummies
Dan Thompson
978-1-118-44349-1

Starting & Running a Business All-in-One For Dummies
Colin Barrow
978-1-119-97527-4

MUSIC

Mandolin For Dummies
Don Julin
978-1-119-94276-4

Ukulele For Dummies
Alistair Wood
978-0-470-97799-6

Piano For Dummies
Blake Neely
978-0-470-49644-2

DIGITAL PHOTOGRAPHY

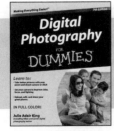

Digital Photography For Dummies
Julie Adair King
978-1-118-09203-3

Digital SLR Photography All-in-One For Dummies
Robert Correll
978-0-470-76878-5

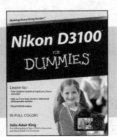

Nikon D3100 For Dummies
Julie Adair King
978-1-118-00472-2

Algebra I For Dummies
978-0-470-55964-2

Anatomy & Physiology For Dummies, 2nd Edition
978-0-470-92326-9

Asperger's Syndrome For Dummies
978-0-470-66087-4

Basic Maths For Dummies
978-1-119-97452-9

Body Language For Dummies, 2nd Edition
978-1-119-95351-7

Bookkeeping For Dummies, 3rd Edition
978-1-118-34689-1

British Sign Language For Dummies
978-0-470-69477-0

Cricket for Dummies, 2nd Edition
978-1-118-48032-8

Currency Trading For Dummies, 2nd Edition
978-1-118-01851-4

Cycling For Dummies
978-1-118-36435-2

Diabetes For Dummies, 3rd Edition
978-0-470-97711-8

eBay For Dummies, 3rd Edition
978-1-119-94122-4

Electronics For Dummies All-in-One For Dummies
978-1-118-58973-1

English Grammar For Dummies
978-0-470-05752-0

French For Dummies, 2nd Edition
978-1-118-00464-7

Guitar For Dummies, 3rd Edition
978-1-118-11554-1

IBS For Dummies
978-0-470-51737-6

Keeping Chickens For Dummies
978-1-119-99417-6

Knitting For Dummies, 3rd Edition
978-1-118-66151-2

FOR DUMMIES

A Wiley Brand

SELF-HELP

978-0-470-66541-1

978-1-119-99264-6

978-0-470-66086-7

LANGUAGES

978-0-470-68815-1

978-1-119-97959-3

978-0-470-69477-0

HISTORY

978-0-470-68792-5

978-0-470-74783-4

978-0-470-97819-1

Laptops For Dummies 5th Edition
978-1-118-11533-6

Management For Dummies, 2nd Edition
978-0-470-97769-9

Nutrition For Dummies, 2nd Edition
978-0-470-97276-2

Office 2013 For Dummies
978-1-118-49715-9

Organic Gardening For Dummies
978-1-119-97706-3

Origami Kit For Dummies
978-0-470-75857-1

Overcoming Depression For Dummies
978-0-470-69430-5

Physics I For Dummies
978-0-470-90324-7

Project Management For Dummies
978-0-470-71119-4

Psychology Statistics For Dummies
978-1-119-95287-9

Renting Out Your Property For Dummies, 3rd Edition
978-1-119-97640-0

Rugby Union For Dummies, 3rd Edition
978-1-119-99092-5

Stargazing For Dummies
978-1-118-41156-8

Teaching English as a Foreign Language For Dummies
978-0-470-74576-2

Time Management For Dummies
978-0-470-77765-7

Training Your Brain For Dummies
978-0-470-97449-0

Voice and Speaking Skills For Dummies
978-1-119-94512-3

Wedding Planning For Dummies
978-1-118-69951-5

WordPress For Dummies, 5th Edition
978-1-118-38318-6

Think you can't learn it in a day? Think again!

The *In a Day* e-book series from *For Dummies* gives you quick and easy access to learn a new skill, brush up on a hobby, or enhance your personal or professional life — all in a day. Easy!

Available as PDF, eMobi and Kindle